THE CINEMA
OF
EDWARD G. ROBINSON

THE CINEMA
OF
EDWARD G. ROBINSON

by
James Robert Parish
and
Alvin H. Marill

research associates
JOHN ROBERT COCCHI,
FLORENCE SOLOMON,
T. ALLAN TAYLOR

South Brunswick and New York: A. S. Barnes and Company
London: Thomas Yoseloff Ltd

A. S. Barnes and Co., Inc.
Cranbury, New Jersey 08512

Thomas Yoseloff Ltd
108 New Bond Street
London W1Y OQX, England

Library of Congress Cataloging in Publication Data

Parish, James Robert.
  The cinema of Edward G. Robinson.

  1. Robinson, Edward G., 1893–   I. Marill, Alvin
H., joint author. II. Title.
PN2287.R67P3   791.43′028′0924   75–146781
ISBN 0–498–07875–2

Printed in the United States of America

to DeWitt Bodeen
A Cinema Scholar

CONTENTS

ACKNOWLEDGMENTS

ABC Television Program Information
Alan G. Barbour
DeWitt Bodeen
Richard Bojarski
Bruco Enterprises
Mrs. Loraine Burdick
CBS Television Program Information
Cinemabilia (Ernest Burns)
Jane Danziger
Guy Giampapa
Pierre Guinle
Mrs. R. F. Hastings
Kenneth G. Lawrence
Ken D. Jones
Albert B. Manski
Peter Miglierini

Movie Poster Service (Bob Smith)
NBC Television Program Information
Norman Miller
Lyle W. Nash
Jack Edmund Nolan
Michael Pitt
Dr. Marvin Robinson
Fred Romary
Charles Smith
Mrs. Peter Smith
Chris Steinbrunner
Lou Valentino
David Williams
Paul Myers and the staff of the Theatre Collection Lincoln Center Library for The Performing Arts, New York City

INTRODUCTION

I have been asked to write the introduction to this wonderful book about one of the dearest men I know, Edward G. Robinson. To write an introduction about him is very simple, as he is a very simple man and a very great man. He is a great humanitarian and a great actor, having made *Little Caesar* as well as *Five Star Final* with him. There is nothing that I could say about this great artist that would really praise him enough. I wish there were more actors in the world like him and more who had his heart.

Mervyn LeRoy

THE CINEMA
OF
EDWARD G. ROBINSON

INTRODUCTORY ESSAY

"If I were just a bit taller and I was a little more handsome or something like that," Edward G. Robinson admitted a few years ago, "I could have played all the roles that I have played, and played many more. There *is* such a thing as a handicap, but you've got to be that much better as an actor. It kept me from certain roles that I might have had, but then, it kept others from playing *my* roles, so I don't know that it's not altogether balanced."

Edward G. Robinson is probably the foremost example of an actor making the most of his disadvantages. Lacking both looks and height, and working against type by making the "little man" the dominating character, he managed to carve out a career which made him the most successful leading man in films (as opposed to the starring "love interest") during the 1930s and early 1940s. "I remember just before going onto the soundstage," he said, "I'd look in my dressingroom mirror and I'd stretch myself to my full 5′5″ or 5′6″—whatever it was—to make me appear taller and to make me able to dominate all the others and to mow them down to my size."

Robinson's versatility is indeed far greater than the type-casting as the arch-gangster character with which most have identified him for the four decades that span the entire history of sound films. True, his Rico Bandello in *Little Caesar* created a sensation—a landmark on which he built an illustrious screen career, as well as the definitive style that became the model on which virtually all other actors would pattern their own gangster characterizations. To this day, a Robinson "gangster" imitation is standard repertoire for nearly every impressionist in show business, although Robinson maintains that it is they who have created this legend and the image of this gangster.

Nevertheless, *Little Caesar* was the prototype. There was never a picture like it before and there was never an Edward G. Robinson before. And the Brothers Warner were quick to realize this and turned a tidy profit by almost completely cornering the market on this fast moving, genuinely exciting, totally unsubtle genre of social film.

As a motion picture, *Little Caesar* was far from the best of its type; in fact, it has always been considered only slightly better than average, and is viewed today primarily as a curio. However, Robinson's portrayal of the title character as an analytical study of a merciless killer still holds up (taken in the proper context) nearly forty years later as a superb conception by exactly the right performer whose acting abilities and physical traits melded perfectly to the universal—or, if you please, Warner—image of such a character. And when Robinson goes down under a fusillade of police bullets in the final scene, gasping "Mother of Mercy! Is this the end of Rico?", one knows for certain that he will be back and back and back—as Joe Krozac, as Remy Marco, as Little John Sarto, as Johnny Rocco, as Vincent Canello, as Leo Smooth. . . .

But Robinson's film career neither began nor ended with *Little Caesar*. Of the more than eighty films he made subsequently, only a quarter of his roles called for gangster portrayals. In about an equal number, he was the unswerving, if occasionally unappreciated, upholder of law and order. He also limned five "real" people, appearing in two of the finest biographical films ever made; he won and lost the girl an equal number of times (nine); and he confronted Humphrey Bogart five times (usually preceding a shootout), four as the good guy.

And before *Little Caesar,* Robinson spent sixteen years on the New York stage, perfecting his craft in more than thirty plays, eleven with the Theatre Guild and "about ten with Arthur Hopkins, who was perhaps the most literate producer we had on Broadway."

He was born Emanuel Goldenberg in Bucharest, Rumania, on December 12, 1893, the fifth of six sons of Morris and Sarah (Guttman) Goldenberg. His father, a builder by trade, decided—partly because of religious persecution—to take the family to America. He took his three older sons with him, and young Manny followed shortly thereafter with his two other brothers, their mother and her mother. He was nine when he arrived in Manhattan, but he later said, "I was born when I came to America." As a minor, he automatically acquired United States citizenship when his father obtained final papers.

The family lived in an East Side tenement before moving uptown to the Bronx, where Morris Goldenberg ran a candy store, and later became an antiques dealer. One of young Manny's brothers, who had been seriously injured in a street fight back in Bucharest, died not long after the family moved to America, and the other three older ones eventually drifted into the jewelry business. The youngest was to become a dentist. Said Robinson: "I was number five. I became the black sheep of the family, since nobody in it had ever had anything to do with the theater."

According to a series of in-depth articles by Georald Nachman in *The New York Sunday Post,* young Manny gave the longest Bar Mitzvah speech in the history of the Rumanian Synagogue on Rivington Street; it was such a success that he gave more than a passing thought to becoming a rabbi. "For about six weeks, I became a fanatic, and I drove momma and poppa crazy, and I wanted them to take me down to the seminary and enroll me there. But then I realized that I would probably have to be a moron or a charlatan to pose as a sancrosanct gent, you know, twenty-four hours a day—and I gave up that idea. The reason I wanted to be a rabbi, though, is the same that motivated me to want to be a lawyer after that—a defense lawyer, but never a prosecutor. I wanted to instill the right sort of ideas into children."

He attended Public School 20 (whose alumni ranged from George Gershwin to Paul Muni to Senator Jacob Javits) and he was editor of the school paper. An exceptional student record provided him with the opportunity to enroll in Townsend Harris Hall, a preparatory school, where he became interested in acting. "I was trying to find my way," he told an interviewer. "I read Shaw's dramatic criticisms and I saw that acting was not all strutting and fretting. The thing got hold of me in my junior year at high school. Now, everyone has dramatic instincts, but I began to realize the scope of it. To be entrusted with a character was always a big responsibility to me."

In 1910, he entered City College of New York, and after reading Antony's soliloquy in *Julius Caesar* he was elected to the Elizabethan Society. Oddly, he was never to play Shakespeare professionally. On scholarship, he joined the American Academy of Dramatic Arts (AADA) in October 1911, where his closest friend was Joseph Schildkraut. The late actor once noted: "Manny stuck to his work, and I looked at the girls."

It was while with AADA that Emanuel Goldenberg became Edward G. Robinson. "Franklin Sargent told me that I had to get an Anglo-Saxon name, whatever that is," Robinson told UPI in 1963. "I kept the initials E.G. but I don't know to this day why I chose Robinson as a last name. If I had to do it again, I'd take a shorter name. You have no idea how long it takes to write Edward G. Robinson for a flock of autograph hunters."

Robinson's first exposure before a non-classroom audience was in 1913 when at Loew's Plaza's amateur night he tried out a monologue he had written. Calling his reading "The Bells of Conscience," he had put it together from generous portions of Henry James's "The Bells"—a murderer's confession under hypnosis. It helped him get his first professional job with a stock company in Binghamton, New York, and he made his stage debut as Sato in Eugene Walter's *Paid in Full* in April 1913.

Noted Robinson: "I was aware early in my career that the acting profession had to be created and carved out by oneself, so that I decided that I wanted to do a certain amount of stock to develop myself in a variety of roles and build my sense of projection bit by bit to be solidly founded. I wanted to start at the very beginning to ring the curtain up and down, and I played little bits in stock after I got out of the Academy. I wanted to spend a year with Shakespeare, but I revised those ideas when I found out that no individuality was permitted as far as interpretation was concerned—you had to read it a certain way, stand in a certain spot—and I realized that there was little chance for development. I also wanted to be with a circus, with a burlesque company, in vaudeville, to touch every branch of the entertainment world."

Using the Binghamton troupe as a springboard, Robinson moved in 1914 to a role in Edward Knoblock's *Kismet* in a company touring Canada. "We were booked in the provinces," he recalled, "when the war came on and that absolutely killed the theater, and we had to shut down prematurely after about five or six weeks. I went to New York and started making the rounds looking for a job, and I found that nobody knew me and I thought, at the time, it was a very undignified business to be in. In those days, I would go for an interview and find myself competing with this other chap who would always be younger and taller and much handsomer than I. I would recognize immediately that the producer wasn't particularly sympathetic and I learned to say, out of intuition, 'I know I'm not much on face value, but when it comes to stage value, I'll deliver for you.'"

Robinson continued: "I was about to give up acting for teaching—again, to mold kids—but I was saved because I happened to know something about languages." He found that a play, *Under Fire,* by Roi Cooper Megrue, was being cast with German- and French-speaking parts needed to be filled. "Because I doubt whether my looks could have gotten me by, the sheer fact that languages had always been a hobby of mine and that I could play various ethnic types, gave me my first chance on Broadway. I was a French soldier, a Belgian patriot, a German. In the last act, I came in as an Englishman, a Cockney. They used to call me the League of Nations. After that I never left Broadway." The play opened on August 12, 1915, and he was billed as E. G. Robinson. He was not overlooked by the critic for *The New York Times,* who wrote: "In minor roles, exceedingly good work is done by Robert Fischer, Norman Thorp, E. G. Robinson and Henry Stephenson."

In October 1916, he was cast as Fagan in *Under Sentence,* a play Roi Megrue co-authored with Irvin S. Cobb, and he was again billed simply as E. G. Robinson.

Later in the season he turned up as a Japanese named Hushmaru in *The Pawn,* and used his full name for the first time. Then he opened, on February 4, 1918, in a rural comedy called *The Little Teacher,* and got himself a pair of good notices. Said *The New York Times* critic: "As the Canuck

friend of the hero, Edward G. Robinson had the best opportunity and made the most of it." Alex Pierce wrote in the *Tribune*: "Edward G. Robinson created an amusing role as Batiste."

A brief tour of duty with the U.S. Navy followed, but Robinson never left New York harbor and was only a subway ride from Broadway. "We were all secluded up there because of the flu epidemic," he recalled, "but the farthest I ever got as a sailor was in a rowboat in Pelham Bay. And when the Armistice was signed, I broke down and cried by myself in a YMCA hut, and I figured, 'Now what have I done to save the world for democracy?'"

Back on Broadway, Robinson was in the comedy *First Is Last,* which had a brief run at the start of the 1919–20 theatre season, and of the young actor's performance Alexander Woollcott commented in *The New York Times*: "The present company, assembled by William Harris, Jr., is quite hopelessly handicapped, so that only Edward G. Robinson flares up in one scene of drink-befuddled oratory." In December of that season, Robinson was Satan in *Night Lodging,* a translation of Gorky's "The Lower Depths." Found the *Tribune*: "Edward G. Robinson carried off a scene in the last act with a true spirit of fire."

Looking back on those early days in the theater, Robinson reminisced: "On the stage, I never had to starve. Occasionally, my brothers would come to my aid. I never indulged myself in luxuries, although my tastes ran in that direction, and I had to be a success to satisfy my appetites. When I started out in a road show, people—actors—of my category would stop at a boarding house, and I would go along, but after a night or two, I didn't like it— the bed I had to sleep in, the kind of food. I wanted a good cigar, so I lived beyond my means. I'd change and go to a hotel and try to get a good dinner. I guess I just couldn't afford to be a failure."

In September 1920, he was Pinsky in Booth Tarkington's *Poldekin,* which starred George Arliss. The play was one of the very earliest to deal with anti-Communism. He followed this with the role of The Director in Sven Lange's *Samson and Delilah,* which brought the great Yiddish Art Theatre actor, Jacob Ben-Ami, to Broadway for the first time. The *Times*'s Alexander Woollcott singled out Robinson for "a fine performance."

With Ben-Ami, Sam Jaffe and Louis Wolheim, among others, Robinson appeared, in December 1921, in the premiere English-language staging of the Peretz Hirshbeim play, *The Idle Inn* (which

Wolheim adapted with Isaac Goldberg). "This was the most heterogeneous conglomerate company one could imagine," Robinson said. "There were Scotsmen, Irishmen, Cockneys and Americans all trying to play Jews. It was a folk story, produced by Arthur Hopkins, but in the translation from the Yiddish, the last act was left out."

The following month, Robinson was seen as Nordling in a revival of *The Deluge,* and then he joined The Theatre Guild and found himself cast as Louis in the French farce, *Banco,* a vehicle for Alfred Lunt. The Woollcott review was a negative finding, though: "The piece is delightfully acted with only Edward G. Robinson rather at a loss."

The actor's notices were substantially better, however, for his next stage outing, Ibsen's *Peer Gynt,* with his friend Joseph Schildkraut in the lead. Robinson played two parts, and Woollcott noted: "There must be a word for the telling performance of Edward G. Robinson as the Button Moulder in the superb last act." Inexplicably (and possibly through a printing error), the actor was billed as *Edgar* G. Robinson when he played Shrdlu in Elmer Rice's "The Adding Machine" in March 1923. The first name notwithstanding, Woollcott singled him out for comment: "Excellent, too, it need hardly be said, is Robinson."

During the late spring of 1923, Robinson made his first motion picture (and his only silent film), playing a Spanish aristocrat in *The Bright Shawl.* Richard Barthelmess, Dorothy Gish and Jetta Goudal had the leads, Mary Astor was his sister, and his AADA classmate, William Powell, also had a part. Said Robinson: "I did *The Bright Shawl* during an interval between plays. I had very few intervals. In order to do a lot of theater in a short time, you had to be in a few failures. Mine I considered distinguished failures. No sooner would one play finish, though, than I was rehearsing another one. But there was a rather long interval, and I had never been to Cuba, and it was right after Christmas time. John Robertson, a distinguished director in silent films, had seen me and thought that I would be great for this vehicle, to play this Spanish Don, an old man—and it was a trip to Havana, where those great cigars were made. That was the only silent part I ever played. I swore off after that because I didn't particularly like it, and I felt that the stage held more of a future for me."

Returning to the stage the following October, Robinson was Louis in Edna St. Vincent Millay's adaptation of Molnar's *Launzi*—and the *Edward*

was back on the playbill but the *G.* was missing! One month later, he turned up in the Zoe Akins comedy, *A Royal Fandango,* starring Ethel Barrymore. Included among the supporting players was a young actor named Spencer Tracy. Ironically, Robinson and Tracy were never again to work together, although a number of Tracy roles four decades later were assumed by Robinson when his long-time friend was indisposed by a series of illnesses.

In 1924, Robinson played Octavius in *The Firebrand,* in which Joseph Schildkraut starred as Benvenuto Cellini, but it was in a pair of G. B. Shaw works in November 1925 that Robinson got his first "money" reviews. He played Caesar in *Androcles and the Lion* and Giuseppe in *Man of Destiny* on one double bill. Writing in *The New York World,* Alexander Woollcott raved: "The role that suddenly, surprisingly, magnificently comes to life for the first time is that of Caesar, played with great gusto by that capital actor, Edward G. Robinson." The critic for *The New York Times* said: "As the Emperor Caesar, the mighty and omnipotent, Mr. Robinson also gave an enjoyable performance running to low comedy." And the *Tribune,* commenting on the second play, found: "It was easily Edward G. Robinson as Giuseppe who carried off histrionic honors."

With The Theatre Guild company (Alfred Lunt, Lynne Fontanne, Dudley Digges, et al), Robinson was next on view in Franz Werfel's *The Goat Song,* in January, 1926, and J. Brooks Atkinson wrote in *The New York Times:* "Mr. Robinson is refreshingly amusing as the peddler Jew." And two months later, he played the Stage Director in the Guild's production of Evreinov's *The Chief Thing.*

Then in August, he appeared in the Lawrence Langner farce, *Henry Behave,* and garnered this review from *The New York Times:* "The honors of the play go to Edward G. Robinson who has strayed from The Theatre Guild to donate a flawless portrayal of the smug oleagenous VP of the realty company." Included among the supporting players were Pat O'Brien, Elisha Cook Jr., and an actress named Gladys Lloyd, who, on January 21, 1927, would become Mrs. Edward G. Robinson.

Miss Lloyd, née Gladys Cassell, was the daughter of the famed artist-sculptor C. C. Cassell, and had had a number of stage roles previously, including a part with the Astaires in *Lady Be Good.* She had also been married previously and had a daughter.

Back with the Guild, Robinson next appeared in three consecutive plays in four months. In October 1926, he was Porfirio Diaz in Werfel's *Juarez and Maximilian;* the following month he played a small role as a New England lawyer in Sidney Howard's *Ned McCobb's Daughter;* and at the start of the new year, he received some nice notices as Smerdiakov, the epileptic in *The Brothers Karamazov.*

And in March, performing in repertory with the Guild, he was Ponza in Pirandello's *Right You Are if You Think You Are.* Talking about the great turnover of roles in this particular period, Robinson recalled: "The runs were fairly short, since The Theatre Guild worked on a subscription audience that guaranteed you six weeks before you went into another play. That was attractive to me, because they [the Guild] were going to establish a repertory company, but they never did. You have a repertory company until you have a hit. Then you just keep running with it. The Guild didn't live up to its obligations in my mind."

Stardom followed with Robinson's next Broadway role.

Establishing him among the great young actors of the stage—and giving him his first starring role —was Bartlett Cormack's sensational play, *The Racket,* which opened on Broadway in November 1927. Robinson played the only gangster part he ever did on the stage—that of Nick Scarsi—in an interpretation which was chillingly close to the public's conception of Al Capone.

Wrote Arthur Ruhl in the *Herald-Tribune:* "Mr. Edward G. Robinson as the villainous boss was the only one whose make-up and manner clicked with pungent 'Theater' the instant he stepped on the scene. He was quite wicked enough to satisfy the hungriest melodrama fan, and it is reassuring to be able to report that he got 'his' in the end."

And this from the *New York World:* "Edward G. Robinson as the crook, stopping at nothing, was great, especially at the last when driven into a corner, threatening, desperate, but cold and calculating." *Theatre Magazine* called his performance "a masterly creation of character."

Robinson's sinister Italian gangster in the Chicago underworld was the forerunner of the Capone-like character he was later to develop on the screen and with which he would virtually single-handedly create a cinematic style to fit the national mood.

"We had a fair run in New York," Robinson recalled, "and we were booked into Chicago about the end of April, but Chicago wouldn't let us in because *The Racket* was much too true." He told film book author Don Shay in *Conversations:* "It was documentary, you see. As a result the season was aborted and disorganized, and some of us were offered a chance to come out for ten weeks to play it in Los Angeles and San Francisco. It was my practice not to leave New York. When a play went on the road, I went into another one, you see, but it was already what you would call 'morte saison'— dead season for the actor. What could you do in April, May and June, and all that, except perhaps try out a play for the following season. So I came out [to Los Angeles] and these motion picture tycoons happened to see me in this particular role. That was my introduction to them. They wanted me to stay and do some pictures then—the pictures had just begun to talk—but I could not divorce myself from the theatre and I went back."

Returning to Broadway where he at last had realized stardom, Robinson opened in November 1928 in what could be termed a three-act grand guignol—as Mr. Crispin in *A Man with Red Hair,* based on the Hugh Walpole novel. Here, in part, is the appraisal of his performance by the critic of *The New York Times:*

"Its titular character—a terrible monstrosity in the book—who is made almost as alarming on stage by Edward G. Robinson—believes in the religion of pain; that by undergoing it one acquires power and learns the innermost meaning of life . . . Mr. Robinson is, of course, an actor who has given some extremely good performances in this metropolis. His characterization of Crispin is not the high spot of his acting career, but it ranks well at the top. He brings out all the insane, demoniacal qualities in this cruelest of his stage portraits, depicting the sadist as among the maddest and most horrific of men."

Writing in *The New York Sun,* Stephen Rathburn said: "Seen last season as the super gangster in 'The Racket,' Mr. Robinson proves in his present characterization of a sadistic lunatic that he is without a peer in this particular field on the legitimate stage. His only rival is Lon Chaney! The highest praise I can give Mr. Robinson is to say that if his acting career were not so well known and anybody had said that he was formerly a prominent member of the Moscow Art Theater, nobody in last night's audience would have doubted the statement."

The following February, Edward G. Robinson,

the playwright, presented himself, leaving his work in the trusted hands of Edward G. Robinson, the actor. In a three-act comedy, *Kibitzer,* which he wrote with Jo Swerling, Robinson starred as Lazarus, an Amsterdam Avenue cigar dealer. Of his role, *The New York Times* found: "The play is almost entirely Mr. Robinson and his performance. The portrayal of The Kibitzer by this actor of finish and variety is full-length, revealing him in nearly all his moods and aspects. . . . For Mr. Robinson, it constitutes a minor triumph; another scalp added to his list of histrionic achievements."

And this from *Theatre Arts Monthly:* "Hardly a season fails to demonstrate Edward G. Robinson's astonishing talent as a character actor."

The film people came knocking at Robinson's door again, this time with an offer to appear in a movie to be shot in New York, and so in 1929 Edward G. Robinson began what would be truly an illustrious cinema career. The vehicle that began it all, *The Hole in the Wall,* was not, however, the skyrocket to make his name a marquee draw. It did mark a number of "firsts" though. It was Claudette Colbert's first sound picture (like Robinson, she had previously made one silent film) ; it was the first feature-length talking motion picture to be shot at Paramount's Astoria Studio on Long Island; it was the first "talkie" to be directed by Robert Florey. In it, Robinson played a crook named The Fox whose love for Miss Colbert gets absolutely no response, primarily because she is too busy seeking retribution from a woman whose lies had sent her (Colbert) to prison for five years. (Although *The Hole in the Wall* was definitely Claudette Colbert's film, Robinson's name appeared first—and quite prominently—when Paramount decided to cash in on the actor's new popularity a few years later and reissue the film.)

Robinson's second talkie, *Night Ride,* starring his friend Joseph Schildkraut, gave him another role as a hood. Schildkraut later wrote in his book, *My Father and I:* "There was the part of a Capone-like gangster in the picture and I suggested my good friend and former classmate at the American Academy of Dramatic Arts, Edward G. Robinson, for the role. Carl Laemmle Jr. had never heard of him, and it took all of my persuasion to make Universal engage him. Robinson was magnificent, perfectly cast, and he 'played me right off the screen,' as the saying goes."

Before *Night Ride* was released in January 1931, Robinson returned to the theater for what turned out to be less than a success and his last legitimate stage appearance for more than two decades. He played the title role in "Mr. Samuel" by E. Fleg and Winthrop Ames, adapted from the Comedie-Française's *The Merchant of Paris.* "Since Edward G. Robinson plays the title part with colorful impetuosity," commented J. Brooks Atkinson in *The New York Times,* "the long stretches in which Mr. Samuel reduces conversation to soliloquy are completely engrossing. For Mr. Robinson is a versatile actor who can make a bootlegger in *The Racket* or a psychopathic busybody in *Kibitzer* or a rough-hewn grandee of business in the current play immediate and vivid figures."

The play ran a brief two weeks on Broadway, and Robinson later said in a *New York Post* article (1940) : "That disaster decided me. I thought, 'What's the good of being true to the theater when in eighteen years, one hasn't built up a following big enough to support one in even his lesser efforts?'"

Irving Thalberg then engaged Robinson to play Tony, the crippled grape-grower, in a new film production of *A Lady to Love,* MGM's sound version of Sidney Howard's *They Knew What They Wanted.* Filmed previously by Paramount as *The Secret Hour* with Pola Negri and Jean Hersholt (and in 1940 by RKO under the original Howard title featuring Carole Lombard and Charles Laughton in the leads) , this talkie version was Thalberg's hope for easing Vilma Banky's transition to sound. The plan was a failure in that respect, but the picture did reveal Robinson to be a powerful screen performer in the role of a love-sick old man who wins over a mail-order bride by enclosing the picture of a younger man so she won't be disappointed. Noted *The New York Times:* "As Tony, Mr. Robinson is capital. . . . The range of acting as offered by [him] is most gratifying." *Cinema* (May 1930) commented: "Mr. Robinson is the life of the picture. . . . It is hard to imagine [the role] better acted."

Robinson also starred in the German-language version of the production which was filmed simultaneously with virtually the same cast (except for Joseph Schildkraut who replaced Robert Ames as the romantic lead) .

The story goes that Irving Thalberg, realizing Robinson's screen potential, called the actor to his office and offered him a generous five-year million-dollar contract. Robinson, who still considered his loyalties to the stage, held out for a six-month pact to allow him time for some Broadway acting, and his agent was called in as intermediary in the negotiations which ended in a standoff. Robinson never again worked in a Thalberg film. (It would be interesting to ponder the direction of Robinson's career had he signed with MGM rather than with Warner Brothers.)

Instead, he returned briefly to Universal, where *Night Ride* had been made; he took on another gangster role in Tod Browning's sound remake of his own 1921 film, *Outside the Law,* and then he played an Oriental half-caste—the chop suey king of San Francisco—in *East Is West.* That, too, was a remake—of a 1923 silent.

He followed that picture with the first of many he would do for Warners, *The Widow from Chicago.* He again played a gangster, but by now he had gained enough of a reputation so that *The New York Times* headed its review: "Edward G. Robinson In New Film."

The role of Caesar Enrico Bandello, "Little Caesar," came next.

Recalled Robinson: "I had the advantage of reading the book by Burnett, and when the script was first submitted to me, it was just another gangster story—the east side taking over the west side, and all that. Finally I was given a version that made some difference, reading more or less like a Greek tragedy. It's a man with a perverted mind, ambitions of a kind, who sets a goal more important than himself—that's what makes him a highly moral character in his perverted way. He is a man who defies society, and in the end is mowed down by the gods and society, and doesn't even know what happened. If Rico had expended his energies in another way, he would have been a great, great fellow. In his own mind, he thought he was doing the right thing, and that's the way you color him. You, as an actor, comment on him—subjectively and objectively. Rico in his way was like Macbeth and Othello and Richard—all of those great characters—and it was like a Greek tragedy or one by Shakespeare. Rico Bandello was not at all like Nick Scarsi [in *The Racket*]. Bandello was very naive, while Scarsi was an extremely sophisticated character. But I think that the picture has sustained itself throughout these years because it was constructed as a Greek tragedy."

Within weeks of the film's release, the legend of the underworld character Robinson had created was already beginning to haunt him. Wherever he went, he was recognized not as Edward G. Robinson the actor, but as "Little Caesar." And for more than twenty years afterwards, critics, in reviewing his performances in any films, would judge his work against his portrayal of Rico Bandello—whether he was playing a gangster, a cop or a doctor, or doing broad comedy or stark drama. Somehow, a reference to "Little Caesar" would find its way into the critique.

(And it is not over yet. *Little Caesar* went into theatrical reissue again in the fall of 1970, receiving another Broadway run nearly forty years after its premiere there.)

Buoyed by the phenomenal success of *Little Caesar,* Warners teamed Robinson with James Cagney, fresh from *his* recent triumph in *Public Enemy,* in the only Robinson–Cagney combination ever put together—*Smart Money.* The film had Robinson playing a small-town barber who becomes a big-time gambler, with Cagney as the good friend he accidentally kills over the affections of costar Evalyn Knapp.

"When I did *Little Caesar,*" said Robinson, "they wanted to star me, put me above the title, but I said to the Warners that despite the fact that I had been starred in many plays on Broadway, this is another field. I suggested that they try another picture, and if the public really accepts me as such, then they could put my name above the title. But once you do, I told them, since I am signing a long-term contract with you, you will continue to do it so long as I am working for you."

Following *Smart Money* came *Five Star Final,* with Robinson cast in a non-gangster part for a change. In this well-remembered attack on Yellow Journalism, he was the managing editor whose get-the-story-at-any-cost policy ruins a number of lives and causes a couple of suicides. The same story turned up five years later as *Two Against the World,* with Humphrey Bogart handling the Robinson role. As *Five Star Final* was playing at the Warner Theatre on Broadway, Edward G. Robinson opened a block and a half away on Seventh Avenue at the Palace (September 18, 1931) on a bill headlined by Kate Smith. Robinson was tagged in the ads and on the marquee as " 'Little Caesar' himself," and got this notice from *Variety:* "Two distinguishing points in the show are the new style MC-ing of Rick Craig and the astonishing adaptability to the two-a-day technique of Robinson. Of the two, the Robinson angle is probably more striking. The tough guy from Hollywood, it is to be remembered, comes to vaudeville on the crest of a wave of fan popularity. His background, except for a short time in pictures, is strictly legit. . . . [In] the Robinson number, which doesn't bear too much repetition, he gives little speeches

Publicity pose for **Five Star Final.**

between screen showing of scenes from 'Little Caesar' and 'Smart Money.'"

Most of Robinson's 1932 film work, while quite profitable for the Brothers Warner, provided the actor with rather routine screen assignments. Robinson was a tong executioner in San Francisco's Chinatown in *The Hatchet Man*—a type of character he does not best essay. *Two Seconds,* in which he is a murderer who recalls his entire life in the seconds preceding his execution, gave him less than he returned to it. (This was his third picture with Mervyn LeRoy, who had also directed him in *Little Caesar* and *Five Star Final.*) In *Tiger Shark,* decked out in a spiffy, well-groomed mustache and a hook where his left hand should be, he played Mike Mascarena, the best tuna fisherman on the west coast ("portrayed splendidly by Edward G. Robinson," reported *The New York Times*), who loses his girl, Zita Johann, to his buddy, Richard Arlen, and his life to a shark.

Silver Dollar gave to Robinson, however, a full-blown role worthy of his talents. Playing the legendary silver-mining senator from Colorado, H. A. W. Tabor, but called Yates Martin in the script, the actor was able to turn in a bravura performance of "Little Caesar" caliber. *The New York Times* headed its review: "Edward G. Robinson In Film Version of David Karsner's Biography of Haw Tabor." And the *Sunday Times* found that "Whatever Mr. Robinson did in 'Little Caesar' is even more convincing here, notwithstanding that Yates Martin is a character from the past." Following the film's premiere on the day before Christmas, 1932, the Warners received this

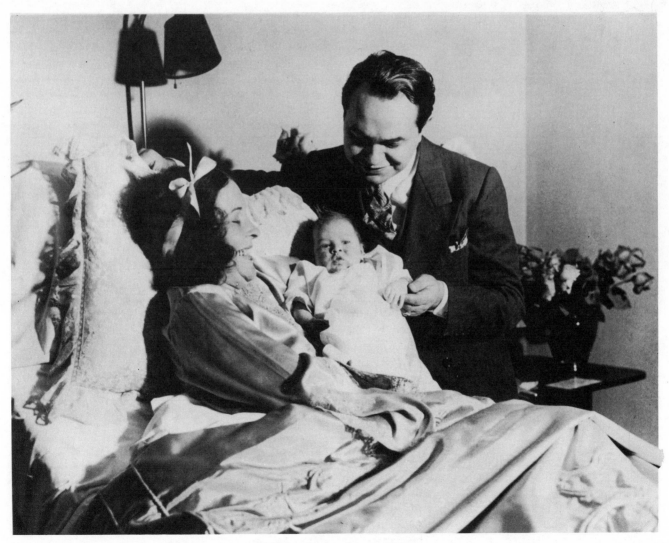

With wife and son, 1933.

congratulatory wire from ex-Governor Al Smith: "Robinson is more Haw Tabor than Tabor himself could have been."

Edward G. Robinson's only son, Emanuel Robinson Jr., known nearly always as Manny (as his father always has been to his friends), was born on March 19, 1933, in Doctor's Hospital in New York. Harry Warner was his godfather.

With wife, 1934.

Robinson's first screen comedy was *Little Giant*, released in May 1933. It was a bit of fluff about a former beer baron who decides to get some culture. In another departure for Robinson, this time he got the girl—Mary Astor.

In *I Loved a Woman*, from another novel by David Karsner, the author of *Silver Dollar*, Robinson played a beef baron who made a fortune selling tainted meat, lost his home when he began playing around with a money-grubbing opera singer (Kay Francis) whom he had promoted to stardom, and had a run-in with Teddy Roosevelt. Then he was a gambler who bets on and goes to the dogs in *Dark Hazard*. It came from a novel by W. R. Burnett, who had also written *Little Caesar* earlier and whose later claim to fame would be *The Asphalt Jungle*. *Dark Hazard*, incidentally, turned up just three years later remade as *Wine, Women and Horses*.

The Man with Two Faces, a film version of the George S. Kaufman and Alexander Woollcott play, *The Dark Tower*, gave Robinson the opportunity to don some bizarre makeup and attempt a French accent, and to play an egotistical actor who murders his brother-in-law to save the sanity of his sister. Louis Calhern was in the former role,

Mary Astor in the latter. It was all done more meaningfully and suspensefully on the stage in the hands of Basil Sydney.

On loan-out to Columbia for John Ford's hilarious comedy, *The Whole Town's Talking* (from another W. R. Burnett novel), Edward G. Robinson hit another peak in his career and accepted rave reviews for his adeptness as a comedian. He played a dual role—as a timid clerk and a look-alike gangster. Curiously, it was the first of only five pictures in which he starred that ever played Radio City Music Hall, and his photo was used for the first time along side *The New York Times* review. It would be nearly thirty years before Robinson would again work with John Ford.

In 1935, he also did another picture on loan-out —this one for Samuel Goldwyn, and the only time since he became a star that he got less than top billing (in deference to Goldwyn regular Miriam Hopkins). The film was called *Barbary Coast*, directed by Howard Hawks from an original screenplay by Charles MacArthur and Ben Hecht. Robinson had the flashy role of Louis Chamalis, the owner of a crooked gambling house in the San Francisco of Gold Rush days, who transforms a naive young lady into the Belle of Frisco and then watches her fall for a handsome, hard-luck Forty-Niner (played by Joel McCrea). Most of the critical attention, though, was focused on a young Walter Brennan, who virtually stole the picture as Old Atrocity—and probably would have won a supporting Oscar had they been awarded in those days. (The Supporting Actor/Actress awards be-

Chatting with Miriam Hopkins and Jim Thorpe in publicity pose.

With Ginger Rogers, c. 1937.

gan in 1936, when Brennan *did* win, repeating the feat in 1938 and in 1940.)

Robinson's next screen portrayal was to have been Duke Mantee in *The Petrified Forest,* and there are two stories of why it was not. This is the more well-known: Leslie Howard, who had starred opposite Humphrey Bogart in the Robert E. Sherwood play on Broadway, had agreed to do the film version on condition that Bogart also re-create his role. Warners, meanwhile, had already settled on Edward G. Robinson as Mantee. When Howard learned of this, he threatened to withdraw unless Bogart played the gangster.

However Robinson told writer Don Shay a few years ago that he had himself turned down the role. "I didn't want to go along and keep doing gangster parts. I was then contracted to Warner Brothers and I kept insisting that I wanted to get away from the gangster category. And it was nice

because it brought Humphrey Bogart back into pictures and then eventually he became a very important star."

He and Bogart made the first of their five films together in *Bullets or Ballots.* Said Robinson in retrospect: "In those days, I would play the leading role, and he [Bogart] would be opposite me, and we would shoot at each other perhaps a reel before the picture finished. Since I happened to be the so-called 'star,' he would die a reel ahead of me, and I would go on with a bullet in me right up to the last scene. In *Key Largo,* the last time we did a picture together, the situation was reversed. He was then their star and I was just a visitor, and we had our shoot-out as usual, but I died first and he went on for another reel."

Bullets or Ballots was the first picture in which Robinson moved over to the right side of the law. The film was based on the life of Johnny Broder-

With (left to right): Bogart, EGR Jr., George E. Stone on the Warner Bros. set, 1937.

ick, one of New York's most famous detectives, and Robinson played the detective who pretended to be kicked off the force to get a line on and infiltrate the rackets. "It's no secret," reported *World-Telegram* film critic Douglas Gilbert in May 1936, "that Mr. Robinson, a sterling stage player, has long tired of his bloody roles and is increasingly apprehensive lest he go down in film history as a type. It is said that he consented to make this film on condition that he be given the role of Beethoven in a contemplated picture of the great composer's life."

What Robinson was given, however, was a chance (by Columbia Pictures) to see London and to again show his comic flair. The project was *Thunder in the City,* an effortless little affair made

in England, which did not materially help nor hinder his career.

On his return to Warner Brothers, he starred in what would rank as another screen classic—*Kid Galahad* (ridiculously retitled *Battling Bellhop* for television), in which he and Humphrey Bogart again faced each other as rival fight managers who kill each other off at the fadeout. It was Robinson's only film with the queen of the Warner lot, Bette Davis (who played his girl friend), and it made a star out of young Wayne Morris in the sensational title role.

(Worthy of note as a sidebar is the infrequency of times Edward G. Robinson was teamed with the other Warner stars or with members of the lot's "stock company," considering the studio's penchant for working out various boxoffice combinations. Robinson, for instance, worked only once with Cagney, Garfield, Raft [while he and Robinson were both at Warners], Bette Davis, Kay Francis and Ida Lupino. He was never teamed with Errol Flynn, Ann Sheridan, Paul Muni or Olivia de Havilland.)

Kid Galahad was reworked in 1941 as *Wagons Roll at Night,* with a carnival background substituted for the fight ring, and with Bogart in the Robinson role. And in 1962 it was resurrected as a vehicle for Elvis Presley, with Gig Young in Robinson's part as the trainer-manager.

MGM then borrowed the actor in 1937 for *The Last Gangster,* but that studio lacked the pizzazz for creating pictures of the social genre Warners had perfected in the thirties. Ironically, though, Robinson's role of Joe Krozac in *The Last Gangster* was the last "serious" gangster part he would do for eleven years.

On October 19, 1937, Robinson began a long run on the weekly CBS radio series, *Big Town,* starring as Steve Wilson, crusading editor of *The Illustrated Press.* Claire Trevor was the original Lorelei Kilburn, and was succeeded by Ona Munson. "It was a very popular program," Robinson told Don Shay, "Jack Benny was number one and we were number two for many years. I played an editor of a newspaper and it dealt with the problems of the day. Then the war came on, and they still confined me to cleaning up the rackets, and I said 'Now this is an enterprising and alive editor. There's a war going on and I'd like to concern myself with some of the day's big questions.' And they said: 'Well, no, we can't do that. We can't have anything either factual or fictional about the war because it becomes controversial and they won't buy our soap' and that kind of thing. And so I got off—dropped it after five years."

On the screen, Robinson was induced by War-

With Wayne Morris and EGR Jr. on set of **Kid Galahad.**

Publicity pose, 1937.

ners to enter the world of Damon Runyon. He played Remy Marco in the screen version of *A Slight Case of Murder*, which Runyon and Howard Lindsay had written for Broadway a few years before. While the play could not be considered one of the great stage triumphs, the films enjoyed a huge success, and Robinson appeared to be thoroughly enraptured with the role of a gangster who made a Prohibition Era fortune with his needled beer, but forgot to stop needling it after he went straight. Warners remade it in 1954 as a semimusical (!) entitled "Stop! You're Killing Me" with Broderick Crawford and Claire Trevor. Of *A Slight Case of Murder*, Howard Barnes commented in the *Herald-Tribune:* " 'Little Caesar' died hard but his passing shouldn't grieve Mr. Robinson unduly if he can get more scripts like this one."

The Amazing Dr. Clitterhouse followed, and Humphrey Bogart was again the nemesis. Robinson had the title role, which Sir Cedric Hardwicke had done on the stage. John Huston and John Wexley wrote the screen adaptation of the Barre Lyndon play, and the star took the part of a psychiatrist who experiments with criminals to study their mentality—and then decides to become one himself "in the interest of medicine." Claire Trevor had the female lead as a lady fence.

Then Robinson was loaned once again to Columbia for *I Am the Law*, playing a law professor-turned-racketbuster (named John Lindsay!) who, at the climax, herds the city's entire criminal population into a circus tent and attempts to reform it through a lecture and visual aids—visual aids that contain films of an actual electrocution.

On the home lot, Warner Brothers cast him as an FBI agent in *Confessions of a Nazi Spy*, a semidocumentary which was a daring film, at the time, having been based on a just-completed exposé and court case. Attempts were made to suppress the film, and its screenings for the press were held behind locked doors in various locations around the country.

Viewed more than thirty years later, Anatole Litvak's *Confessions of a Nazi Spy* is nothing more than an ordinary espionage melodrama in which Robinson's role is no more dominant than any of the others. But the time was 1939, and the picture was selected by the National Board of Motion Picture Review as Best American Film of the Year.

For MGM, Robinson was a fugitive from a chain gang (wrongly convicted, of course, since he was now playing sympathetic roles if not necessarily

stalwart heroes) in *Blackmail*. The man who sent him to prison on a frameup (twice, yet!) was Gene Lockhart, in one of his dastardly villain characterizations.

Then Robinson got four exceptionally strong roles at Warners. The first, *Dr. Ehrlich's Magic Bullet*, considered by the critics one of the truly

Behind the CBS mike (1937).

memorable biographical screen studies, is still thought by many fans as the best thing the actor has ever done on film, and, after *Little Caesar*, it is the one most closely associated with Robinson. As Paul Ehrlich, the bewhiskered, bespectacled Edward G. Robinson was the scientist who discovered 606, the specific against syphilis. "The most dramatic and moving medical film I have ever seen," Howard Barnes wrote in his critique in the *Herald-Tribune*, "due in no small part to the brilliant portrayal of Dr. Ehrlich by Mr. Robinson . . . an understanding performance which is in the first rank of biographical portraits."

Critical acclaim notwithstanding, Robinson was overlooked by the Academy of Motion Picture

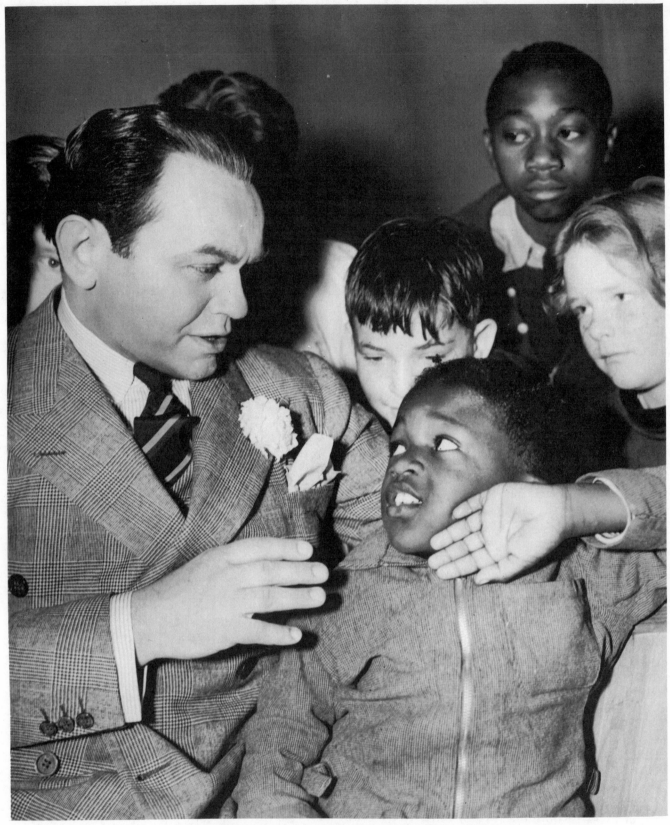

With an assemblage of boys of various ethnic origins, gathered together by Warners to play in an orphanage scene in A Slight Case of Murder.

With Hope Hampton and Herbert Marshall, 1939.

coonut Grove." The next professional meeting between the two would be in 1955, and again they appeared as adversaries.

The fourth and final time Edward G. Robinson and Mervyn LeRoy were on the same picture was in the actor's next film, *Unholy Partners,* at MGM. Three screenwriters toiled on this one, among them Bartlett Cormack, the author of *The Racket.* Like *Manpower, Unholy Partners* was not really worthy of Robinson's talents, to say nothing of the others in the cast: Edward Arnold, Laraine Day, Marsha Hunt, et al. In it, Robinson was an erstwhile reporter who decided to publish his own tabloid, but lack of funds forced him to go into partnership with gangster Edward Arnold. Much of the footage was given over to confrontations between the two.

With *Larceny, Inc.,* Robinson wound up his long association with Warner Brothers. An adaptation of the Laura and S. J. Perelman play, *The Night Before Christmas,* the film comedy had Robinson back in harness—as a gangster named Pressure Maxwell (who ends up as a pillar of society). Among the members of Warners' stock company in support were Jane Wyman, Jack Carson, Broderick Crawford, Anthony Quinn, Edward Brophy, Harry Davenport and Jackie Gleason. Of his three gangster spoofs for Warners, this would be the least successful. A brief announcement accompanying *The New York Times* review of the film noted that Warners had recently purchased an unpublished story by Guy Kilpatric saluting the Merchant Marines. It was to be the basis of a film called *Heroes Without Uniforms* and a vehicle for Robinson, Bogart, Raft and Sydney Greenstreet. When it finally reached the screen as *Action in the North Atlantic,* only Bogart remained from the original proposed lineup.

Publicity pose for **Larceny, Inc.**

Free now from his long-term contract and from his weekly radio series, *Big Town* (which he left on July 2, 1942), Robinson spent some time in Europe on tours of various military installations, and then returned to make appearances in two omnibus films by French director Julien Duvivier, who produced them with Charles Boyer (who also acted in both). In each, Robinson had the opportunity to demonstrate his acting abilities in small parts, developing and socking over three-dimensional characterizations in his briefly allotted screen time.

In *Tales of Manhattan,* a compilation of stories revolving around a man's dress coat and the effect it has on the lives of those who come in contact with it, Robinson, in his portion, was a successful lawyer-turned-Bowery-alcoholic who wears the coat to his graduation class reunion at the Waldorf-Astoria—and is given a second chance at life. (An episode starring W. C. Fields, running approximately twenty minutes, was deleted from the final print because the film was too long and the sequence was the easiest to remove. It now remains a curiosity among Fields fans and cinema buffs.)

In *Flesh and Fantasy,* which has been likened to a cinema program of three one-act plays, Robinson appeared in the second episode, an adaptation of Oscar Wilde's *The Crime of Doctor Saville.* The actor was seen as an American attorney in London who is convinced by palmist Thomas Mitchell that he will commit murder. And he does—he murders the palmist.

The three Robinson cinematic contributions to the war effort were rather weak affairs. *Destroyer,* which Columbia Pictures laughingly attempted to liken to the classic "In Which We Serve," found Robinson in uniform as a real old salt who has his moment in battle and then relinquishes his job as Chief Boatswain's Mate and the hand in marriage of daughter Marguerite Chapman to costar Glenn Ford. In *Tampico,* again playing an old sea dog, Robinson battled a Nazi spy ring, tangled with a young lady (Lynn Bari) who might or might not have been an enemy collaborator, and sparred with First Mate Victor McLaglen.

And as Wilbert Winkle, a tinkerer wed to a shrew, Robinson was an overaged draftee who distinguished himself as a war hero in a film version of Theodore Pratt's novel, *Mr. Winkle Goes to War* (promoted by Columbia Pictures as "In the Great 'Mr. Deeds' Tradition"). It was an unsuccessful melding of comedy and drama, and even

Robinson seemed to agree, through his performance, that he was uncomfortable in the role.

If the preceding three roles can be considered lesser Robinson, the three which followed more than compensated for the unpardonable waste of his talent. Billy Wilder's taut classic, "Double Indemnity," a harsh examination of an almost perfect crime, came first. Wilder and Raymond Chandler fashioned a superb screenplay from a series of stories by James M. Cain, written for *Liberty Magazine* and allegedly based on a murder case of the 1920s. Wilder then convinced Paramount to let him cast their star light comedian, Fred MacMurray, as a villain (which they did since MacMurray was in the process of wrapping up his contract with the studio). Next the writer-director argued a good case with Barbara Stanwyck, who apparently did not relish the idea of playing a murderess—even in a blonde wig. To Edward G. Robinson, Wilder entrusted the role of the insurance investigator who is bothered by a suspicious claim and learns that this colleague is a murderer.

Although the entire film was done in flashback, with MacMurray tipping the plot with his opening line, "I've killed a man," Wilder delicately maintained the suspense to the last frame—and presumably beyond, since a long trial and execution sequence running about twenty minutes was deleted from the final print, which now ends with Robinson calling for a police ambulance to take the wounded MacMurray to the hospital. Recently Robinson said: "That scene that we did shoot but was never seen was good for the character I played in that he witnessed the execution of his only friend (MacMurray), and he feels that he is the one who has killed MacMurray because the gnawing of an inner person forced him [my character] to suspect that the original death was not suicide. And it was the reaction of that character witnessing the execution that was very, very dramatic." Robinson, it is universally agreed, came off best in this film, doing full justice to the role as written by Wilder and Chandler in this intriguing adult drama.

An even greater part came to Edward G. Robinson in his next film, *The Woman in the Window,* the first of two he did under the direction of Fritz Lang. Again blessed with a literate script—this one by Nunnally Johnson from J. H. Wallis's novel, *Once Off Guard*—Robinson was cast as a psychology professor whose drab life is changed when he meets the model whose portrait in the window of a gallery near his club he has admired for some time. With her, he gives in to one moment of emotional weakness (hence the title of the original novel) and becomes involved in murder. Merle Oberon was originally signed to star opposite Robinson, but the role subsequently was taken by Joan Bennett. Most knowledgeable critics agree that the superior melodrama was compromised when director Lang "copped-out" with a trick ending—having Robinson awaken from a dream of all that had gone on before. Lang, however, defended it in an article, "Happily Ever After," he had written in 1948 for Penguin Film Review No. 5. He claimed it was necessary, since "if I had continued the story to its logical conclusion, a man would have been caught and executed for committing a murder because he was one moment off guard." Thought Robinson, in retrospect: "They were thinking, I suppose, of box-office. Why kill him since he was a sympathetic character. Perhaps they thought that would be too morbid—like *Double Indemnity*."

In his third successive Grade-A role, Robinson was Martinus Jacobson, a Norwegian-American farmer in Wisconsin, who helps awaken in his young daughter, played by Margaret O'Brien, the realities of life. The film was *Our Vines Have Tender Grapes*, and the Dalton Trumbo screenplay from George Victor Martin's novel allowed Robinson to create another of his memorable characterizations, and Thomas M. Pryor wrote of it in his review in *The New York Times*: "One of the finest performances of his long and varied career."

During the war years, after leaving "Big Town," Robinson did a variety of dramatic appearances on radio and was selected by *Motion Picture Herald* as "The most effective film personality on radio." In addition, he devoted a great deal of energy to various patriotic and religious causes. On screen, he spoke the English commentary for the feature-length Russian documentary, *Moscow Strikes Back*, in 1942, and the following year he was narrator for a short called "The Red Cross At War." He, Paul Muni and Jacob Ben-Ami, along with a group of other actors, participated on March 9, 1943, at New York's Madison Square Garden, in a mass memorial to the Jews who had lost their lives during the Nazi regime. Entitled *We Will Never Die* and written by Ben Hecht, it was seen by 40,000 people during two performances. Ben-Ami narrated and as described by *The New York Times*: "Paul Muni and Edward G. Robinson, dwarfed by the great stone tablets [in a massive set erected in the Garden], came through the space between the Ten Commandments . . . [and] alternately they recited

the record that Jews have written into world history, from Abraham and Moses down to our time."

During 1944, Robinson was heard as narrator on *Too Long, America,* a radio documentary about racial intolerance; toured France with a U.S.O. troupe; made propaganda broadcasts in various languages for the Voice of America; and, at the invitation of the British Ministry of Information, acted in a feature-length semi-documentary (for which he took no salary) , *Journey Together,* as an American flight instructor involved in the training of R.A.F. pilots. (It was released in the U.S. in 1946.)

Following the war, Robinson was scheduled to star for Paramount in a motion picture called *Bright Journey,* from an original screenplay by Arnold Manhoff to be directed by actor Paul Stewart. The project, in which Robinson was to portray a venal fight promoter, never got off the ground. The later *Body and Soul* was remarkably similar in story-line. John Garfield assumed the lead and Lloyd Goff took the role Robinson was to have played.

Edward G. Robinson's first post-war picture, thus became his second for Fritz Lang: *Scarlet Street.* It was produced independently (since no studio would touch the story because of its "adult" theme) by a company known as Diana Productions, headed by Fritz Lang, Walter Wanger, and his wife, Joan Bennett, and it reunited Robinson, Miss Bennett and Dan Duryea in an attempt to again spark the kind of electricity they had produced in *The Woman in the Window.* The new project had been adapted by Dudley Nichols from Georges de la Fouchardière's play, *La Chienne,* and had been previously filmed (in 1931) by Jean Renoir under that title. Among the problems confronting *Scarlet Street* were the many similarities (probably too many) between it and *The Woman in the Window.* As in the picture it followed, *Scarlet Street* dealt with a middle-aged philanderer with a weakness that involved him with a shady young woman and, later, a murder for which another man is accused. While *Scarlet Street* played more with irony at its climax than with a trick ending, *The Woman in the Window* still towers above it as a tauter, more perfectly rounded melodrama (the fadeout notwithstanding) .

In a lengthy Sunday piece about the film, Bosley Crowther wrote of *Scarlet Street:* "In picturing this slightly noxious story, Walter Wanger and Fritz Lang have combined some rather vivid movie-making with some pretty weak fictitious stuff, so that the whole thing comes out a variably absorbing and irritating show. Edward G. Robinson is mousey—perhaps a little too earnestly so—as the cashier, Dan Duryea is salty as the boy friend, and Joan Bennett makes a rather spiritless cat."

If *Scarlet Street* was not the success all involved had hoped, it was not for lack of publicity. Six weeks before its scheduled New York opening (January 1946), it was slapped with a ban by the Motion Picture Division of the New York State Department of Education. Rather than requesting certain deletions in this "adult drama," the Board of Review banned the entire film, an action taken only rarely against a major Hollywood production (like *The Outlaw*). On appeal, the Board announced that, in consideration of public opinion and the seriousness of the film's intentions (!), the motion picture would be licensed for exhibition if certain unspecified cuts were made—like, allegedly, elimination of six of the seven stabs which Christopher Cross (Robinson) inflicts on Kitty March (Bennett) with an ice pick, as well as certain isolated lines of dialogue. The cuts were made.

Next, Robinson worked for and with Orson Welles in *The Stranger*, from a screenplay by Anthony Veiller and John Huston. Taking the part originally intended for Agnes Moorehead, long a member of Welles's Mercury Players (but presumably without strong enough name value for marquee bait), Robinson was a war crimes commissioner posing as an art collector (type casting?) who tracks down the former commandant of a Nazi prison camp now posing as a school teacher in a Connecticut town. He got the majority of the critical notices on this film, which turned out to be an arch Wellesian exercise, both in cinematic techniques and in acting excesses (with the exception, of course, of Robinson).

Then, with producer Sol Lesser, Robinson formed a new production company called Film Guild Corporation, which turned out only one film—*The Red House,* a memorable chiller paced by the performances of Robinson and Judith Anderson and of four young players: Lon McAllister, Allene Roberts, Julie London and Rory Calhoun. With a screenplay by Delmer Daves (who also directed) from the novel by George Agnew Chamberlain, *The Red House* was embraced by the critics as a true adult hair-raiser, and A. H. Weiler found, in *The New York Times,* that "Edward G. Robinson is excellent as crippled Pete Morgan, whose mind is cracking under the thrall of the horrible secret of The Red House."

Shortly after that film's release, some rather adverse publicity that would seriously affect Robinson's future movie career began appearing in print. Column and magazine items had begun to imply that the actor was a Communist, or at least a Communist sympathizer—or perhaps something less than 100 percent American.

In a series of articles in *The New York Post* (March 1957), entitled "The Edward G. Robinson Story," writers David Gelman and Marcy Elias noted that during the thirties, Robinson was known to all kinds of fund-raisers in Hollywood as the softest touch in town. He had told an interviewer back in 1938, "Everybody on the Coast keeps hollering at me to do something about improving the world either in the movies or out. They want me to stump for this ism or that ism. I would but I don't know anything about isms. I'd rather listen to the worst violinist in the world than be the best politician." Instead, he apparently had lent his name and given his money to a whole spectrum of causes—and this generosity (or naivete) came back to haunt him a decade later. *Newsweek,* for one, bluntly stated: "Edward G. Robinson is persistently found in Communist fronts." And in a news story headed "Civil Rights Group Called Red Front" (August 31, 1947), *The New York Times* said that Edward G. Robinson's name was included on the "initiating committee." The story went on to detail that, when contacted, Robinson did not recall whether he had agreed to be one of the committee, but "if I lent my name, I am sure it was in behalf of the best American ideals. I don't believe in Communism and I never lend my name to any organization that smacks of Communism."

In their article on Robinson, Gelman and Elias went on: "In 1950, *Red Channels* listed Robinson as having been connected with eleven alleged Communist fronts. The publication made no mention of the more than 300 other groups he had patronized in one way or another."

Robinson insisted upon appearing before the House Un-American Activities Committee to clear his name ("I couldn't let anyone call me a Communist," he explained), and subsequently testified three times. On October 27, 1950, he submitted a twelve-page list of contributions over a ten-year period and detailed a full record of his war activities. Two months later, he again appeared, answering questions fully, repeating his war record, and telling members of the committee that he had sent a transcript of his earlier testimony to J. Edgar Hoover.

He also told the hearing: "You are the only tribunal we have in the United States where an

In the early 1950s.

American citizen can come and ask for this kind of relief. . . . I am sorry if I have become a little bit emotional . . . because I think I have not only been a good citizen, I think I have been an extraordinarily good citizen and I value this above everything else."

Robinson made a final committee appearance on April 30, 1952, reading again into the record his war activities and his list of contributions. He was finally cleared with this finding from HUAC: "According to the evidence to this committee, you are a good, loyal and intensely patriotic American citizen."

The actor's friend, writer Jo Swerling, later said: "Eddie was terribly hurt by the Congressional hearings professionally. This is a very cool industry, unfriendly to anybody in trouble. He was broken up by it. It almost ruined his life. It cost him a fortune. Eddie spent, I'd say, $100,000 in legal fees and for trips to Washington." Swerling also recalled that after the hearings had begun, producers stopped offering Robinson "the type of parts he was accustomed to getting."

The effect of all of Robinson's well-documented problems did not immediately reflect on the actor's career. Following *The Red House*, there had been four other films in the works before the HUAC investigation of Hollywood got under way.

First, there was the Chester Erskine screen adaptation of Arthur Miller's powerful play, *All My Sons*, with Robinson portraying the corrupt airplane-parts manufacturer who had caused the death of twenty-one flyers including his own son. The critical notices were mixed on the film version, but most agreed that Robinson came off well in his interpretation of Joe Keller, the part that Ed Begley had originated on Broadway.

Key Largo reunited him with Bogart back at the old lot (where Bogart was now the company's ace attraction just as Robinson had been a decade earlier), and Robinson gave another memorable performance as the ruthless Johnny Rocco. As Bosley Crowther put it in his review, "an expertly timed and timbered scan of the vulgarity, corruption and egoism of a criminal mind." In his book, *Agee on Film*, critic James Agee made this observation: "The first shot of Edward G. Robinson in 'Key Largo,' mouthing a cigar and sweltering naked in a tub of cold water ('I wanted to get a look at the animal with its shell off') is one of the most powerful and efficient 'first entrances' of a character on record." And Robinson's scene forcing his alcoholic mistress, Gaye Dawn (Claire Trevor), to sing "Moanin' Low" before giving her the drink for which she had been begging, and then refusing to give it to her, further demonstrated that he had not lost his sadistic touch in the years since he played Rico Bandello. This was John Huston's followup to his superb *The Trea-*

sure of Sierra Madre, and he and Richard Brooks had virtually rewritten Maxwell Anderson's free-verse play. For her performance in the film, Claire Trevor won an Oscar.

Night Has a Thousand Eyes, with Robinson an ex-vaudevillian who finds himself endowed with clairvoyant powers and attempts to prevent a murder he has foreseen, turned out a rather tepid, unsuccessful cinemazation of Cornell Woolrich's interesting novel.

The final film in this phase of Robinson's career, however, gave him wide latitude for another carefully etched and memorable characterization—as Gino Monetti, the barber from New York's Little Italy who had become a successful banker, and whose three sons fight to take over the empire he had created while the fourth, who had gone to prison for him, returns to avenge his father. The picture, *House of Strangers,* was shown at the 1949 Cannes Film Festival, and for his performance in it Robinson was chosen Best Actor of the Year. Twice since, 20th Century-Fox has remade

With his son in 1952, during court hearings.

the film. In 1954, it turned up as a western, *Broken Lance,* with Spencer Tracy in the Robinson role, and seven years later, it was reworked as *The Big Show,* with a circus atmosphere.

Robinson also made a brief appearance spoofing his familiar gangster interpretation in Warners' Doris Day musical, *It's a Great Feeling.* Then he found his services were no longer in demand, and he went to Europe to seek roles.

He found only one, in the English film, *My Daughter Joy* (shown in the United States as *Operation X*). It was an adaptation of Irene Nemirowsky's novel, *David Golder,* and had been filmed under that title by Julien Duvivier in France in

Publicity pose for **Black Tuesday.**

1931 with Harry Bauer in the leading role. In the new version, directed by Gregory Ratoff and minus its political and racial inferences (about a Jewish conspiracy to rule the world), Robinson was cast as a power-hungry millionaire who rose from bootblack in this study of megalomania.

Then he returned to the United States and asked HUAC to hear his testimony. Between his second and third appearances before the committee, Robinson returned to the stage for the first time in more than twenty years, as Rubashov, the disenchanted Communist, in *Darkness at Noon*. While Claude Rains was playing the role on Broadway, Robinson headed the national company for a 26-week tour (September 28, 1951–April 26, 1952). Supposedly, Sidney Kingsley, the play's producer and co-author (with Arthur Koestler), had originally offered the role of Rubashov to Robinson, but the actor turned it down because it was too exhausting a part, requiring him to be on stage through every single minute of the action.

Until he was finally cleared by HUAC, the only motion picture work Robinson could obtain was in *Actors and Sin*, an independent two-part film written, produced and directed by his friend, Ben Hecht. Robinson appeared in the first story, "Actor's Blood," playing a fading star who attempts an odd revenge upon the boy friends of his actress daughter (Marsha Hunt) by making her suicide appear to be murder so that each will be a suspect.

The Hollywood work he at last *was* able to locate provided him with a series of rather undistinguished roles in some dreary B films. *Vice Squad* revolved around a routine day in the life of a big city police official and was told in semi-documentary style; *The Big Leaguer* had Robinson in a baseball uniform, playing the part of Hans Lobert, a real-life scout for the New York Giants who was put in charge of the organization's training camp in Florida, and was the first picture in his screen career which did not have a regular play-date in Manhattan (and odd, since it was produced by MGM—certainly a major studio—and since it dealt with baseball as played by a New York team); *The Glass Web* found him as a television researcher who is played off against TV writer John Forsythe by their mutual girlfriend, Kathleen Hughes, an enterprising young would-be actress. *The Glass Web* was, incidentally, Robinson's sole 3-D movie —and hardly worth the effort.

In *Black Tuesday*, he was once again a vicious, snarling killer (to the joy both of critics and fans), and in *The Violent Men*, playing Barbara Stanwyck's crippled husband who finds himself cuckolded by his younger brother (Brian Keith), Robinson appeared in the first western of his career. The only apparent reason for *A Bullet for Joey* was the teaming again of Robinson and George Raft.

Tight Spot, a rather stagey film version of Lenard Kantor's play *Dead Pigeon*, had Robinson star as a U.S. attorney trying to keep material witness (Ginger Rogers) alive to testify against a gangster (Lorne Greene), with most of what action there was confined to a hotel room. And in *Illegal*, Robinson was a former District Attorney who makes a comeback as a defense lawyer for a crime syndicate. The film was Warners' remake of its *Mouthpiece* (1932) and its *The Man Who Talked Too Much* (1940); it was thought to be vaguely similar in structure to *The Asphalt Jungle* of W. R. Burnett (who, by coincidence, co-authored the screenplay of "Illegal").

The Robinson of the prime years surfaced, though, in Warners' *Hell on Frisco Bay*. He was cast as Victor Amato, the vicious waterfront boss whose nemesis is an ex-cop he had framed (Alan Ladd). This was the Robinson of *Little Caesar*, older by 25 years, but excitingly alive in a meaty, incisive role, spiced with sharp dialogue (by Martin Rackin and Sydney Boehm), sardonic wit, and the perfect opportunity—with one snarl wrapped behind him—to act rings around the entire cast. And Edward G. Robinson was never one to let a good role slip by unmolded.

Nightmare, alas, was something else again—a weak programmer from another story by Cornell Woolrich (who wrote it under his pen name, William Irish), and previously filmed by Paramount in 1947 as *Fear in the Night* by the same director, Maxwell Shane. Again Robinson was a detective.

And, in a brief but telling role as a cruel Hebrew overseer who uses every opportunity to make points with the Egyptians by betraying Moses, Robinson closed out another phase of his film career in DeMille's massive new version of *The Ten Commandments*. Replying to a comment about how, as the Hebrew leader Dathan, he looked as though he had just stepped from the pages of the Bible, Robinson said: "You sort of have to get into a role—to feel it and sense it and dwell on it and get inside it. Something I've always believed in: you may *look* the part but that doesn't

As Dathan in DeMille's **The Ten Commandments.**
Makeup artist Paul Malcolm (r) puts finishing
touches on EGR's beard, while Frank Westmore (1)
supervises.

mean you're going to play it. But if you *feel* the part, you'll look it. Sensing that role made me take on the look."

Also disappearing at this stage of Robinson's career was the Hollywood in which he ranked as the least star-like (in appearance) of all the major stars. He was asked to comment on the changing system, with businessmen replacing the moguls who had been absolute czars. "In retrospect," he felt, "seeing these college-bred men now, functioning on their own, I think the Mayers and the Goldwyns and the Warners served a great purpose. You can get any number of college men, but they don't often become very good picture-makers who are great gamblers and who have an intuitive feel-

ing for what should be done on the screen. A great many of those older producers were very illiterate —I'm not going to mention names—but somehow they had that special something to produce pictures and to assemble the many, many talents that go into a production."

During this period, Robinson also began dabbling in television. He made his network debut (as did Bing Crosby) in a guest appearance on an NBC telethon for the U.S. Olympic Committee which was hosted by Bob Hope (June 21, 1952). His first dramatic work on the medium was in a pilot film for a proposed weekly series, *For the Defense* (1954), in which he had planned to star as a former police captain turned criminal defense

With fellow art colletcor Vincent Price at a Los Angeles gallery in 1957.

painting for two dollars at a 1913 auction. (He has rebuilt much of his art treasury in the ensuing years since the divorce.) A page-one story in *The New York Times* (February 26, 1957) was headlined: "Edward G. Robinson Art Brings $3,000,-000." Its purchaser was later identified as Greek shipping magnate Stavros Niarchos, who bought 58 paintings and a Degas bronze. "I had put everything into pictures," Robinson explained, "and couldn't afford to buy my wife's share of their value."

Less than three weeks before the divorce announcement, Edward G. Robinson had returned to Broadway in Paddy Chayefsky's first stage play, *Middle of the Night,* and, as The Manufacturer, a middle-aged widower in love with a younger woman (Gena Rowlands), the star was in top form and scored a personal artistic triumph. Wrote *The New York Times*'s Brooks Atkinson: "It seems like old times to have Edward G. Robinson back. . . . [He] gives a winning and skillful performance, and no one could be more relaxed about a part. But no one could give the character more warmth or kindness, or make an undistinguished man so notable. If the years have done nothing else to him, they have supplied him with a quarter

attorney. The series never materialized and whether this single half-hour episode was ever shown is undetermined.

He *was* seen, though, late in 1954 in a TV adaptation of Eric Ambler's *Epitaph for a Spy* for the CBS *Climax* series. Robinson played an unsuspecting Iron Curtain refugee who is used as a pawn by a pair of French traitors while vacationing in Southern France. In January 1955, and again the following December, he appeared in teleplays on NBC's *Ford Theater,* and in late 1956, Robinson and Vincent Price, both acknowledged art authorities, put their expertise on the line over a four-week period on the popular, pre-scandal-plagued *The $64,000 Challenge.*

On February 25, 1956, Robinson's wife of 29 years sued for divorce, and in August they arranged a settlement of $3.5 million in community property, plus 25 percent of all of the actor's future earnings. To meet these terms, Robinson was forced to sell what has been considered one of America's finest privately owned art collections, which he had begun when he purchased his first

Following wedding to Jane Adler, January 16, 1958.

With son on the set of TV's Zane Grey Theatre in 1959.

With Frank Sinatra and director Frank Capra on the
set of Hole in the Head.

century of living, which leaves its mark on the soul of everyone who is perceptive.

"If there is any technical difference that can be noted by a theatergoer with a short memory," Atkinson continued, "it is a deepening of authority. His acting is effortless. . . . It is good to be reminded of his easy skill and to have him back with us again."

And Richard Watts, commenting in *The New York Post,* said: "Thanks in great part to the superb acting and moving performance of Edward G. Robinson in the leading role, the result is a touching and interesting drama that combines realism with sentiment in expertly showmanlike proportions."

The show ran for 479 performances on Broadway, and then Robinson took it on tour during the 1957–58 season. Ironically, as happened with the film version of *Death of a Salesman,* which he very much had wanted to do, Robinson lost the role of The Manufacturer to Fredric March when *Middle of the Night* reached the screen in 1959.

Edward G. Robinson married again on January 16, 1958, while *Middle of the Night* was being performed in Washington, D.C. His new wife, Jane Adler (née Jane Bodenheimer), 26 years his junior, was with the production end of the show in which Robinson was starring.*

The following October, he made his only appearance on the prestigious CBS-TV series, *Play-*

* She, too, shares her husband's love of art, and in 1971, she authored with Leonard Spigelgass a chatty book about his collection, "Edward G. Robinson's World of Art."

Arriving in Israel to film *Israel*, 1959.

house 90, in Ernest Kinoy's "Shadows Tremble." Robinson was a retired toy manufacturer who decided to buy the historic Vermont home in which he had regularly summered, but the tradition-bound villagers did not take kindly to "immigrants" and he found himself virtually ignored by them. Early the next year, he made a pair of dramatic television appearances in fairly rapid succession. He starred on the *Goodyear Theater* in "A Good Name" (as a clothing manufacturer) in March, and four weeks later, he was seen on an episode of the *Zane Grey Theater*, acting opposite his son in a Civil War story called "Loyalty." This was the first time the two Robinsons had worked together professionally and followed a long, well-documented estrangement between the two which first became public in 1952. The younger Robinson talked freely of it in his autobiography, *My Father, My Son,* published in 1957.

Robinson's return to the screen was as Frank Sinatra's older brother in the film version of Arnold Shulman's play, *A Hole in the Head.* It was originally written for television and aired in 1955 under the title, *The Heart Is a Forgotten Hotel.* It was expanded for the Broadway stage where it opened in February 1957 as *A Hole in the Head,* and was turned into the musical *Golden Rainbow* eleven years later. For the film, the characters were changed from Jews to Italians with the leading role refashioned to fit the personality of Sinatra (who co-produced with director Frank Capra), but the best lines went to Edward G. Robinson and to Thelma Ritter who played the latter's wife. Bosley Crowther, writing in *The New York Times,* felt that "As the brother, a narrow-minded dullard, Edward G. Robinson is superb; funny while being most officious and withering while saying the drollest things." The role proved a good beginning to the latest part of Robinson's film career —as a superlative character actor. Together with *Hell on Frisco Bay,* it provided him with the best screen part he had during the 1950s.

He began the next decade by playing Daniel Webster in an hour-long television adaptation (by

Phil Reisman Jr.) of Stephen Vincent Benet's *The Devil and Daniel Webster* (David Wayne was The Devil) on NBC—and rerun, curiously, on CBS two years later.

Robinson was seen on the wide screen in 1960 twice. In *Seven Thieves*, he took the part of an old-time crook who masterminds a $4 million robbery of the Casino at Monte Carlo and dies of a heart attack from the excitement of the caper. The film was a screen version of Max Catto's novel, *Lions at the Kill*, and was the first of many in which Robinson would blueprint a complicated crime for others to execute—like *The Biggest Bundle of Them All, Grand Slam, Never a Dull Moment* and *Mad Checkmate*.

Next he turned up as a "guest star" in *Pepe*,

which was an overblown, overlong movie written to exploit the talents of the Mexican star Cantinflas, but which virtually destroyed that brilliant clown's career in this country. Robinson was seen as a film producer (named Edward G. Robinson) who gives a down-and-out director (Dan Dailey) his comeback chance and who returns to Cantinflas a horse the diminutive Mexican had doggedly followed for 195 screen minutes (plus intermission).

Robinson was off the screen until mid-1962 (part of the time filming in Japan and in Italy), but he was seen on television in 1961 first on the *General Electric Theater* in a story called "The Drop-Out" and then in an episode of Robert Taylor's series, *The Detectives*, entitled "The Legend of Jim Riva." In "The Drop-Out," Robinson was

***With Kirk Douglas and director Vincente Minnelli on location in Rome for* Two Weeks in Another Town.**

a salesman who welcomes his high school drop-out son (played by Billy Gray) into the business and is satisfied to learn at the fadeout that the boy has doubts about leaving school after making the rounds with his father. And as "Big Jim Riva," the last of the big-time gangsters, Robinson was a man who is released from prison and who plans a quiet retirement. At his homecoming party,

With Princess Margaret and Lord Snowden, 1963.

though, he and his wife are wounded by a young hood and he decides to round up his old mob to avenge his shooting.

The following March, he narrated "Cops and Robbers," a documentary in NBC-TV's *Project 20* series, which combined old still photos and rare film footage to trace the growth of American law-breaking from the days of Colonial piracy through the workings of contemporary syndicate operations.

In 1962, again playing a movie producer, Robinson appeared in a visually beautiful but rather lightweight comedy-drama called *My Geisha,* with Shirley MacLaine and Yves Montand (whom producers were still intent on making an American

"star"). In *Two Weeks in Another Town,* he was cast not as a movie producer but, for a change of pace, as a movie director. The best thing about the film—in which almost none of the characters are either likeable or believable—is that he was reteamed with Claire Trevor (as his wife) for the first time since *Key Largo,* and they played, as *Variety* concluded, "the only lifelike people in the story."

While on location in Nairobi, Kenya, in June 1962, filming *Sammy Going South* (shown in the United States in mid-1965 under the title *A Boy Ten Feet Tall*), Robinson suffered a heart attack, but returned to complete his role in that motion picture. Back in the United States, he narrated, with Betty Hutton, Cornel Wilde and Barbara Stanwyck, *The World's Greatest Showman,* a ninety-minute television tribute to Cecil B. De-Mille in December 1963. Interestingly, the show was produced not by Paramount, where DeMille created his most memorable spectaculars, but by MGM; it has the unique distinction of being introduced by the familiar logos of both companies—the MGM lion and the Paramount mountain.

In transit in the mid 1960s. (Cesar Romero is in the background).

His next motion picture role, in 1964, was in MGM's *The Prize*, which Mark Robson directed from Ernest Lehman's screenplay of the Irving Wallace novel. Robinson played a dual role—a Nobel Prizewinning German physicist who is kidnapped on the eve of the awards ceremonies and the twin brother who, years before, had defected to the East, and who is substituted for the good doctor. As inane as *The Prize* was on the screen, it proved to be a fun movie and Paul Newman's presence in practically every scene helped insure it huge boxoffice success. It also marked the American film debut of Elke Sommer.

Good Neighbor Sam the same year was a 1960s attempt at screwball comedy with Jack Lemmon as an advertising account-executive whose coup was obtaining the business of a straight-laced, middle-American, Bible-spouting dairy magnate, played with good humor by Edward G. Robinson. And in *Robin and the Seven Hoods*, Robinson, in a gag appearance sans screen credit, played his briefest role in films, reprising his by-now personal gangster characterization and being killed off two minutes and twenty seconds into the story. A life-sized painting of him hung prominently, though, through much of the film as a reminder of who the boss was. And for Warner Brothers, yet!

Billed simply as Con Man, Robinson was then in *The Outrage*, Martin Ritt's westernized version of Akira Kurosawa's *Rashomon*, perhaps the most famous of all Japanese films (at least in the Western world). Said A. H. Weiler in *The New York Times*: "Edward G. Robinson's portrayal of the bearded, seedy, cocky con artist is earthy and direct." And Wanda Hale wrote in the *Daily News*: "(He) is delightful as the cruddy old man, a cynic who hears the various versions of the crimes and believes none." He was next reunited with John Ford after three decades, turning up briefly in *Cheyenne Autumn* as Secretary of the Interior Carl Shurz, a role Spencer Tracy was originally to have played. As with his previous two or three screen appearances, this role could be considered not much more than a cameo.

Early in 1965, Robinson did more television, beginning with a dramatic reading on *Hollywood Palace*. Then he was seen in the TV drama *Who Has Seen the Wind?* as the captain of a tramp steamer whose passengers include a family of stateless wanderers in the backlash of World War II, forced to spend their lives on shipboard because their country no longer exists. The program was the second in a series of ninety-minute dramas pro-

duced for the United Nations by Telsun Productions and underwritten by the Xerox Corporation. An international cast was featured (among the players: Stanley Baker, Maria Schell, Theodore

In mid 1960s with art collection.

Bikel, Gypsy Rose Lee, Victor Jory, Lilia Skala, Simon Oakland) and it marked the debut television assignment of director George Sidney.

And, at the end of 1965, he made an appearance on the popular TV game show, *What's My Line?*

A Boy Ten Feet Tall, which he had made in 1962 and in which he was the sole American, finally received an American release in May, 1965. In it, Robinson looked, as *Variety* noted: "like a slightly junior Ernest Hemingway," playing a grizzled diamond smuggler who helps a ten-year-old war orphan on his 2000-mile trek from Port Said to Durban in search of relatives. In New York to promote the film, Robinson was interviewed by Howard Thompson of *The New York Times*, and the actor made these observations about his profession and about film-making in general:

There are certainly more jobs [for actors], but more problems from the standpoint of rounding one's talent.

With art collection, 1966.

And acting is such a chaotic, haphazard profession, anyway, requiring so much careful handling and management. I searched deeply inside myself before I decided on it. When I was a kid of twelve, I first thought about the pulpit, then got over it. Then I thought about law. Then I did some amateur theatricals and finally made up my mind.

The danger today is being catapulted into an important decision too quickly. These people fall harder and more rapidly. I fought against the idea of being billed as a star here on Broadway before I went to Hollywood, and I fought again when *Little Caesar* came up. I told them to wait. The picture was a big hit. Still, I said to wait for a couple of more. I told them to go ahead, finally, on *Five-Star Final*. And I was a star.

As for film technique—well, I try to soak myself in the character. Sometimes it's strange and hard. You go over your lines, look for the key. Maybe it's in some little inflection. And it's not easy if you're handed a script on Friday and told to come in ready on Monday. I wanted to be loaded with my people. They talk about

actors filling the screen. I think what they really mean is that loaded *character* filling it.

The director? That depends entirely upon him. But not many are helpful to we poor actors, I don't mind saying. You do maybe one or two takes, then they move the camera for new angles and you're frightened to death left all alone out there, knowing your sins are about to be recorded from generation to generation—and for television. Now, when I see some of my old pictures, I say to myself that I could have done this or that. I want to say, "Let's do that one again."

Although Robinson had gotten sole above-the-title billing in *A Boy Ten Feet Tall,* the starring role actually went to young Fergus McClelland, an unknown. Robinson had his best role in years, though, in his next film—and it was a starring part. Playing Lancey Howard, the suave, wily old gentleman cardshark in *The Cincinnati Kid,* he brought

Publicity pose for **Grand Slam.**

sharply to life a thoughtfully etched and finely honed portrait of The Man as author Richard Jessup had created him in his novel, and once again acted a part originally destined for Spencer Tracy. Wearing an immaculate suit, sporting a carefully barbered white goatee, lighting expensive cigars incessantly, Robinson battles Steve Mc-Queen (in the title role), studying his young opponent through a stoic mask and through nothing more than slits where his weary, wary eyes should be. In one of the most suspenseful showdowns ever filmed, in a lengthy game of stud poker, The Kid, holding a full house, has to decide whether The Man holds a straight flush, and The Man must choose the exact moment to make the wrong move, as he is fond of saying, at the right time.

In *The Cincinnati Kid,* Robinson again worked with Joan Blondell—for the first time since *Bullets or Ballots* nearly thirty years before. He was then to remain off the screen for almost three years, although he had a small role as an American CIA agent in a French film called *La Blonde de Pekin,* shot in late 1966 and first released in Europe in

Dramatic readings, c. 1968.

1968. (It has never been shown theatrically in the United States.)

During the time he was away from American screens, Robinson's total professional exposure in the United States was a twenty-second walk-on (or head-out-the-window gag bit) on the *Batman* TV

series in 1966. Late in 1967, after *Bonnie and Clyde* had gone into release and had begun to create the lingering controversy over violence in films and the current resurgence in gangster movies, Edward G. Robinson was asked to give his thoughts about the trend in a *Los Angeles Times* interview.

"Violence has always been a prevalent element in drama and all the performing arts, even ballet," he said. "I guess it's paradoxical to say that violence is entertaining, but it's practically impossible to create meaningful conflict without it. Besides, we all get a vicarious kick out of the violence we see on the screen. We live a great repression and this is one way to vent our feelings, to unwind by seeing violence depicted. My concern with this whole question is from the assertion that the gangster pictures of the 1930s were the first step toward the alleged glamorization of violence to pictures like *Bonnie and Clyde.* There is no place in motion picture history that we can point our finger to and say 'Violence started here' because violence is a fact of life, and therefore of drama, and has been an integral part of films since the beginning."

Robinson was seen in cameo roles in 1968 in two Italian-made pictures with a similar theme—the perfect crime. He was the mastermind in both *The Biggest Bundle of Them All* (in which he was asked by a gangster friend, Vittorio De Sica, to set up the big platinum heist, which he did— through the use of visual aids: the "Madison Avenue touch," as he, as Professor Samuels, noted) — and in *Grand Slam* (where he was the architect and financier of an intricate diamond theft to be executed by younger, more agile confederates—all hand-picked specialists—during Carnaval in Rio de Janeiro).

His other two 1968-made films have had only spotty European release; and were sold directly to television in the United States. He was the brains behind another seemingly perfect bank robbery in an Italian-Spanish coproduction, *Uno scacco tutto matto (Mad Checkmate),* and he was involved in the theft of Michelangelo's *Pieta* in *Operation St. Peter's* for an Italian-French-German motion picture combine.

His role in *Never a Dull Moment,* for the Walt Disney organization, was somewhat larger. Robinson was Leo Smooth, urbane arch-gangster, who has devised an ingenious art theft from the Los Angeles County Museum (where, ironically, many of his own personal paintings are on permanent loan). The robbery is foiled by an at-liberty actor (Dick Van Dyke) who has stumbled onto the plans

With Efrem Zimbalist Jr. on set of **The F.B.I.**

by error and who institutes a zany chase throughout the gallery.

In June 1968, Robinson was seriously injured in an automobile accident when his car hit a tree. "I must have fallen asleep," he told reporters when he was able. His hospitalization forced him to relinquish to Jose Ferrer the scheduled role of Hassan Bey, a Turkish war lord, in a film variously entitled *Cervantes* and *The Young Rebel* (Horst Buchholz played the lead), but the loss of the part was of not much consequence since the picture was poorly distributed and passed virtually unnoticed.

Robinson celebrated his 75th birthday in the company of close to 20,000 people at a Madison Square Garden salute which was tied in with the annual Hanukkah Festival in 1968, and he witnessed the world premiere of a new ballet dedicated to him.

In films, Robinson has a brief part in *Mackenna's Gold,* a big, rambling, seemingly out-of-hand western, which was produced by Carl Foreman. The actor appeared as a blind old prospector who is the only link to the exact location of the fabulous gold lode the rest of the disparate cast is seeking in the heart of Apache country. And in television, he starred, in April 1969, in a two-hour pilot film called "U.M.C." (for University Medical Center), which became a series during the 1969–70 season without him. He played an old doctor who is given a heart transplant by his close friend and protege, the skilled young house surgeon (Richard Bradford in the feature; Chad Everett in the weekly series).

On the set of Mackenna's Gold.

With Burgess Meredith, John Garfield Jr., and Ray-mond Massey on the set of Mackenna's Gold.

At testimonial dinner to Jack L. Warner, November 1969, with (left to right): Bette Davis, Mervyn LeRoy, Warner, Rosalind Russell and Ted Ashley.

In late 1970, he appeared briefly as a friendly piano dealer who sells one of the instruments to the wife of Edvard Grieg in the elaborate musical,

At a premiere in February 1970.

Song of Norway, and he was seen on television in two dramatic roles which were aired in the span of ten days. In the first, "The Old Man Who Cried Wolf," on the ABC *Movie of the Week* anthology, Robinson was an aged gentleman who witnesses the murder of an old friend (played by old friend Sam Jaffe) but cannot convince the authorities or even his own family that a crime had been committed. Possibly because his was the only truly developed role in the teleplay, Robinson acted circles around the rest of the cast, and *Variety* called him "a tower of acting strength," while *The Hollywood Reporter* noted: "Robinson's performance is strong and moving." Percy Shain, television critic for the *Boston Globe,* felt that "Edward G. Robinson gave movies made for TV a boost with his outstanding performance," and Anthony LaCamera, who reviews television for the Boston *Record American,*

decided: "Edward G. Robinson deserves an award for his tremendous performance in 'The Old Man Who Cried Wolf.'"

Said Robinson later: "I've gotten so much mail on *The Old Man Who Cried Wolf,* and they absolutely objected to the ending, saying 'Why did you have to die?' I say, people do die for their courage, determination and the things they see that the rest of the world doesn't see."

On the NBC series, *Bracken's World,* Robinson starred as a Hemingway-like character in a story entitled "The Mary Tree," which revolved around the documentary filming of the life of a famed author whose daughter suddenly appears to debunk the image he had so carefully built up over the years. Edward G. Robinson Jr. played a brief role in the episode and spoke a few lines. "We shot it in seven days," Robinson recalled, "which doesn't exactly give you too much rehearsal time. At least if your role is the lead, you have a chance to look at the script before you start and you have time for a conference with the writer and the producer and can suggest changes and discuss values and work on the relationships of the characters." Ironically, Robinson was appearing simultaneously on a competing program, *The Tom Jones Show,* doing a few dramatic readings.

On the eve of these aforementioned excursions into television in late 1970, Robinson looked forward to the beginning of a more active career in the medium. After complaining, with a chuckle, about television commercials, and admitting that "the only one I look at is that Maxwell House Coffee spot which I did [in the late 1950s]," he told Kay Gardella of the New York *Daily News:* "Where I hesitated before, I wouldn't hesitate now to take on a TV role. I think they can do some wonderful things now. One always begins again, and I'm hopelessly in love with spring."

And, to *The Boston Globe's* Percy Shain he confided: "For many years I had turned up my nose to television. I feared I would have to make too many compromises. But I finally said to myself, 'Look, you have to make compromises in everything you do. At this stage of your life, what do you have to lose?' So I decided to get my feet wet. I tried making the pilot of 'Medical Center.' Not bad, I said. So I decided to make the big plunge, do a 'Movie of the Week,' to see if I could stand the gaff. Well, we worked on it for ten days, and when I say 'work,' I mean it. We worked days and nights, long hours. It was a little too much, I thought, but we got it done."

*With son in publicity pose for "The Mary Tree" on
NBC's Bracken's World.*

Publicity pose for "The Mary Tree."

Edward G. Robinson in 1971.

When Edward G. Robinson was honored by the Masquers after sixty years of acting in the theater, on radio and in films, he spoke of himself as an actor and what it means to be one. "An audience identifies with the actor of flesh and blood, and heartbeat," he said, "as no reader or beholder can identify with even the most artful paragraphs in books, or the most inspired paintings. There, says the watcher, but for some small difference in time, or costume, or inflection, or gait, go I. And so the actor becomes the catalyst: he brings to bright ignition that spark in every human being that longs for the miracle of transformation."

He continued: "Every night the actor bears the stigmata which his imagination inflicts upon him and bleeds from a thousand words. I don't know that I have bled very much. If I have I feel no debility from that loss, perhaps because it has been more than balanced by my satisfactions. Now, in the twilight of my long days of acting, I feel invigorated, proud of the calling of player. I am sure it was not in vain. If mummer I was, it was not mere mummer, no more than any actor is mere, no more than any person who gives of himself to the enrichment of other is mere. Only to that degree will I look back."

Edward G. Robinson died on January 26, 1973.

STAGE APPEARANCES

TITLE	ROLE	THEATRE	OPENING DATE
PAID IN FULL	SATO	at Binghamton, N.Y.	April, 1913
Stock Tour of Canada			1914
UNDER FIRE	ANDRE LEMAIRE	Hudson Th. NYC	Aug. 12, 1915
UNDER SENTENCE	FAGAN	Harris Th. NYC	Oct. 3, 1916
THE PAWN	HUSHMARU	Fulton Th. NYC	Sept. 8, 1917
THE LITTLE TEACHER	BATISTE	Playhouse Th. NYC	Feb. 4, 1918
FIRST IS LAST	STEVE	Maxine Elliott Th. NYC	Sept. 17, 1919
NIGHT LODGING	SATAN	Plymouth Th. NYC	Dec. 22, 1919
POLDEKIN	PINSKY	Park Th. NYC	Sept. 9, 1920
SAMSON AND DELILAH	THE DIRECTOR	Greenwich Village Th. NYC	Nov. 17, 1920
THE IDLE INN	MENDEL	Plymouth Th. NYC	Dec. 20, 1921
THE DELUGE	NORDLING	Plymouth Th. NYC	Jan. 27, 1922
BANCO	LOUIS	Ritz Th. NYC	Sept. 20, 1922
PEER GYNT	THE BUTTON MOULDER and VON EBERKOPF	Garrick Th. NYC	Feb. 5, 1923
THE ADDING MACHINE	SHRDLU	Garrick Th. NYC	Mar. 19, 1923
LAUNZI	LOUIS	Plymouth Th. NYC	Oct. 10, 1923
A ROYAL FANDANGO	PASCUAL	Plymouth Th. NYC	Nov. 12, 1923
THE FIREBRAND	OCTAVIUS	Morosco Th. NYC	Oct. 15, 1924
ANDROCLES AND THE LION	CAESAR	Klaw Th. NYC	Nov. 23, 1925
THE MAN OF DESTINY	GIUSEPPE		
THE GOAT SONG	REB FEIWELL	Guild Th. NYC	Jan. 25, 1926
THE CHIEF THING	THE STAGE DIRECTOR	Guild Th. NYC	Mar. 22, 1926
HENRY BEHAVE	WESCOTT P. BENNETT	Nora Bayes Th. NYC	Aug. 23, 1926
JUAREZ AND MAXIMILIAN	PORFIRIO DIAZ	Guild Th. NYC	Oct. 11, 1926
NED McCOBB'S DAUGHTER	LAWYER GROVER	John Golden Th. NYC	Nov. 29, 1926
THE BROTHERS KARAMAZOV	SMERDIAKOV	Guild Th. NYC	Jan. 3, 1927
RIGHT YOU ARE IF YOU THINK YOU ARE	PONZA	Guild Th. NYC	Mar. 2, 1927
THE RACKET	NICK SCARSI	Ambassador Th. NYC	Nov. 22, 1927
A MAN WITH RED HAIR	MR. CRISPIN	Ambassador Th. NYC	Nov. 8, 1928
KIBITZER	LAZARUS	Royale Th. NYC	Feb. 18, 1929
MR. SAMUEL	SAMUEL BRISACH	Little Th. NYC	Nov. 10, 1930
DARKNESS AT NOON	RUBASHOV	(on tour) McCarter Th., Princeton, N.J.	Sept. 28, 1951
		closed: Cox Th., Cincinnati, Ohio	Apr. 26, 1952
MIDDLE OF THE NIGHT	THE MANU-FACTURER	ANTA Th. NYC	Feb. 8, 1956
		(on tour) Shubert Th., New Haven, Conn.	Oct. 9, 1957
		closed: Curran Th., San Francisco, Calif.	Mar. 29, 1958

In **The Firebrand.**

In Peer Gynt.

In Goat Song.

With George Gaul, Alfred Lunt and Morris Carnovsky in **The Brothers Karamazov.**

In **The Kibbitzer.**

With Nancy R. Pollock and Betty Walker, in Middle of the Night.

In Middle of the Night.

FILMOGRAPHY

THE BRIGHT SHAWL (First National, 1923) 80 M.

Director, John S. Robertson; based on the novel by Joseph Hergesheimer; screenplay, Edmund Goulding; camera, George Folsey.

CHARLES ABBOTT .... Richard Barthelmess
LA CLAVEL .... Dorothy Gish
LA PILAR .... Jetta Goudal
CAPTAIN CASPAR DE VACA .... William Powell
NARCISSA ESCOBAR .... Mary Astor
ANDRES ESCOBAR .... Andre de Beranger
DOMINGO ESCOBAR .... Edward G. Robinson
CARMENCITA ESCOBAR .... Margaret Seddon
CAPTAIN CESAR Y SANTACILLA .... Anders Randolf
VINCENTE ESCOBAR .... Luis Alberni
JAIME QUINTARA .... George Humbert

Synopsis

Wealthy young American adventurer Charles Abbott intrudes into Spanish-oppressed Cuba of the 1850s. He falls in love with his friend's sister Narcissa and simultaneously wins the affection of La Clavel, a fascinating dancer and the idol of Havana, also the mistress of the infamous Spanish despot, Captain Santacilla. Asked to obtain valuable information regarding the Spaniards, Abbott makes a play for La Clavel and is decoyed to her home where he and Santacilla have a desperate struggle. La Clavel suddenly returns and springs at Santacilla with a knife, but in the melee she is stabbed by the Spaniard. Meanwhile, Santacilla is felled by a heart attack.

The dying dancer gives Abbott her bloodstained bright shawl as a token of her love. The shawl is later stolen by a Chinese spy, La Pilar, who, while wearing the shawl one night, kills Abbott's friend Escobar, a young Cuban patriot. In protest, Abbott duels the Spanish authority represented by Captain De Vaca and is badly wounded.

Regaining consciousness aboard a ship bound for the United States, Abbott finds a note from De Vaca explaining to him that the Spanish authorities so admired his courage that they decided to free him and return him to his own country with all his belongings, including the shawl—and with Narcissa and her mother.

THE HOLE IN THE WALL (Paramount, 1929) 73 M.

Director, Robert Florey; based on the play by Fred Jackson; screenplay, Pierre Collings; camera, George Folsey; editor, Morton Blumenstock.

JEAN OLIVER .... Claudette Colbert
"THE FOX" .... Edward G. Robinson
GORDON GRANT .... David Newell
MADAME MYSTERA .... Nelly Savage
GOOFY .... Donald Meek
JIM .... Alan Brooks
MRS. RAMSAY .... Louise Closser Hale
MRS. CARSLAKE .... Katherine Emmet
MARCIA .... Marcia Kagno
DOGFACE .... Barry Macollum
INSPECTOR .... George McQuarrie
MRS. LYONS .... Helen Crane

Synopsis

Seeking retribution from Mrs. Ramsey, the woman responsible for sending her to prison on a false theft charge, Jean Oliver poses as a fortune teller named Madame Mystera, and plans to kidnap the woman's young granddaughter. Her scheme is to teach the youngster the fine art of stealing and then, in later years when the girl is caught, to reveal herself to Mrs. Ramsay as the granddaughter's tutor in crime.

Jean's plan hits a temporary snag when the

With (from left) Richard Barthelmess, Andre de Be-
ranger, Margaret Seddon and Mary Astor in **The**
Bright Shawl.

infamous gangster known as The Fox falls in love
with her, but the single-mindedness of her purpose
leaves no time to reciprocate his amorous advances.
Neither does she have time for Gordon Grant, a
newspaper reporter who loves her and whom she
had secretly loved since their school days.

One day, while Jean is in her "reading room,"
HOLE IN THE WALL, busily studying her crystal ball
at the behest of Mrs. Ramsey, who, of course, has
failed to recognize the thickly-veiled phony
"gypsy," the dastardly Fox absconds with the already once-kidnapped child as ransom against his
love for Jean. He has one of his accomplices take
the young girl to a railway dock, but, in the process
of tying the youngster to a pillar, the hood tumbles
into the water and drowns, leaving the bound
girl to the oncoming tide.

Meanwhile, through the work of reporter Gor-

don Grant, the police close in on the gypsy parlor,
not realizing that it is Jean who is posing as
Madame Mystera. The Fox intervenes and strikes
a bargain with the police—the disclosure of the
young girl's whereabouts for the freedom of Jean,
so that she might marry the reporter.

Reviews

The New York Times, April 15, 1929

"[One] unfortunate feature of this production is
that able Claudette Colbert was called upon to act
in it. So was Edward G. Robinson. Both are competent so far as their lines and actions permit."

Variety, April 17, 1929

"Edward G. Robinson as the sinister 'Fox' gives a

With Mary Astor, Margaret Seddon, Luis Alberni and
Andre de Beranger in **The Bright Shawl.**

better account through shading his mastermind
crook with a thoroughly sympathetic touch.''

NIGHT RIDE (Universal, 1929)

Director, John Robertson; based on a story by Henry
La Cossit; screenplay, Edward T. Lowe, Jr.; editor, A. Ross
and Milton Carruth.

JOE ROOKER	Joseph Schildkraut
RUTH KEARNS	Barbara Kent
TONY GAROTTA	Edward G. Robinson
BOB O'LEARY	Harry Stubbs
CAPT. O'DONNELL	DeWitt Jennings
BLONDIE	Ralph Welles
MAC	Hal Price
ED	George Ovey

Synopsis

With the marriage ceremony uniting him with
Ruth Kearns barely completed, reporter Joe
Rooker is called out to cover the story of a double
murder during a bank robbery. Rooker finds the
butts of a special brand of cigarettes at the scene
of the crime and traces them to Tony Garotta, a
gangland leader. With these, and other evidence,
Rooker is certain he can prove that it was Garotta
who pulled the trigger and he files his story at the
paper, outlining the incriminating facts.

The gangster, meanwhile, has successfully eluded
the police, and goes gunning for Rooker. Garotta
kidnaps him and takes a fellow reporter along as
a second hostage, intending to kill them after a

one-way night ride and then make his escape. During the ride, he tells Rooker that he has bombed the house where his (Rooker's) bride is staying with her mother. Ironically, they are at the hospital where the mother was taken after drinking too much at her daughter's wedding. Rooker presumes they are dead, but is powerless at the moment to avenge the supposed murders.

Before Garotta can make good on his threat to do away with the two reporters, however, he is caught in a police trap and arrested. Rooker gets the exclusive story to his paper and learns that his wife and mother-in-law are safe.

He returns to Ruth and they begin a belated honeymoon.

Reviews

The New York Times, January 20, 1930

"Edward G. Robinson is excellent as Tony Garotta."

Variety, January 22, 1930

"Edward G. Robinson is a finished and polished actor, ideal for the character he enacts."

A LADY TO LOVE (MGM, 1930) 92 M.

Director, Victor Seastrom; based on the play *They Knew*

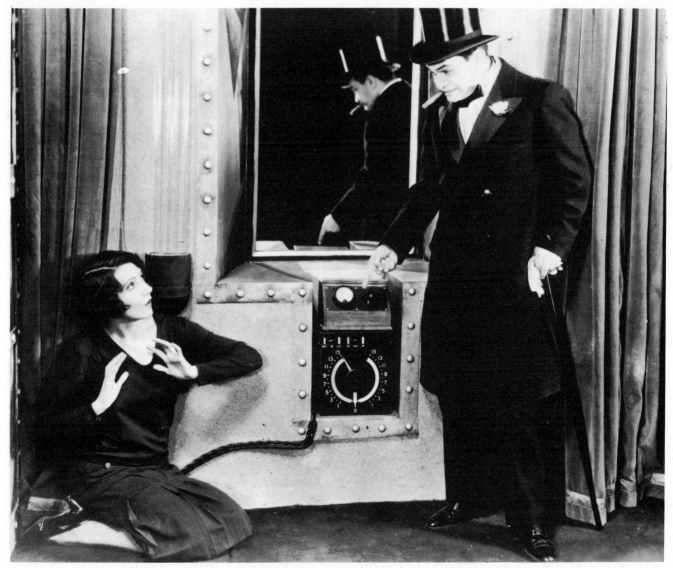

With Claudette Colbert in The Hole in the Wall.

With Joseph Schildkraut and players in **Night Ride.**

What They Wanted by Sidney Howard; screenplay, Howard; sound, Douglas Shearer; camera, Merritt B. Gerstad; editor, Conrad A. Nervig and Leslie Wilder.

LENA SHULTZ .... Vilma Banky
TONY .... Edward G. Robinson
BUCK .... Robert Ames
POSTMAN .... Richard Carle
FATHER McKEE .... Lloyd Ingraham
DOCTOR .... Anderson Lawler
AH GEE .... Gum Chin
ANGELO .... Henry Armetta
GEORGIE .... George Davis

Synopsis

After spotting Lena Shultz, a young Swiss waitress, while dining in San Francisco, Tony—a successful, aging grape grower in the Napa Valley—sends her a marriage proposal by mail, and as they have never met, he encloses a photograph. Afraid she will spurn his offer if she knows he is middle-aged and a cripple, Tony puts in the envelope a picture of his handsome young assistant, Buck.

Led by a desire for a home and affection, Lena quits her job and goes to Tony's vineyard. When she arrives at the train station, no one is there to meet her. She journeys out to the ranch and is about to leave, when Tony is brought in on a stretcher. On the way to meet her, he has been hurt in an automobile accident.

Lena is at first shocked to discover that Tony is fifty years old—not the man she saw on the photograph. However Lena is so impressed by Tony's honest, loving character that she marries him, despite their differences in age.

Before long, Lena's daily encounters with Buck at the farm sparks a romance between them, and one night he seduces her.

Tony eventually learns of Lena's deception, but after his initial anger, he forgives her. Lena, accepting the childlike worshipping of Tony, decides to stay with him. Buck has left the farm, too guilty over his behavior to stay on there.

Reviews

The New York Times, March 1, 1930

"[It has] at least one performance, that of Edward G. Robinson, arising out of the mist of only fair direction, and a striving by the other players toward realism that just misses being excellent. As Tony, Mr. Robinson is capital. His happiness at discovering Lena and his joy at her willingness to remain . . . are both ably portrayed with sufficient touches of pathos and imagination to bring him definitely forward as a player of no mean dramatic ability. The picture lacks mobility, but the range of acting, as offered by Mr. Robinson . . . is most gratifying."

Quinn Martin, *New York World,* March 3, 1930

"A somewhat effortful and highly seasoned performance by J. G. Robinson [sic] as the crippled, lovesick Italian, Tony."

Cinema, May, 1930

"Mr. Robinson is the life of the picture as the Italian grape-grower in search of a wife. . . . It is not a conventionally romantic role, but that of a man bubbling over with romance and Latin lovableness. It is hard to imagine it better acted."

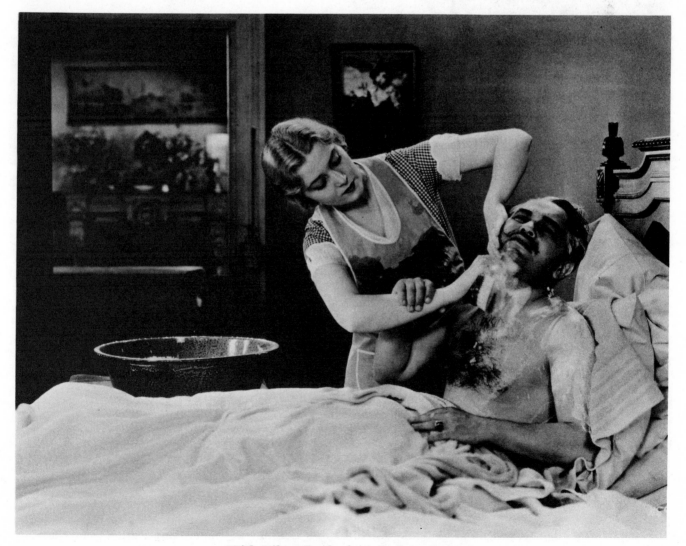

With Vilma Banky in **A Lady to Love.**

In **A Lady to Love.**

in the bank's window, letting the police get a good look at him.

When gang leader Cobra Collins learns about the upcoming $500,000 bank heist in his territory, he wants to be cut in on a 50–50 basis. Fingers's moll, Connie, tries to bluff Cobra by telling him that the robbery is scheduled for next week, but a call comes through saying that the heist is now in progress.

At the robbery site, Fingers has hidden himself in the building's locker room then, after blowing open the safe, he escapes and hides out in an apartment, opposite one owned by a cop.

Eventually the police and the double-crossed Cobra arrive on the scene. During the shootout Cobra is killed. Connie and Fingers are sent to jail.

Reviews

The New York Times, September 1, 1930

"Edward G. Robinson imparts a good deal of strength to his interpretation of Collins."

Variety, September 3, 1930

"The acting may be summed up as 90% pitiful. . . . As the result, Robinson, Miss Nolan and Owen Moore work the angle of talking out of the corner of the mouth with such consistency and such exaggerated gusto as to provoke the sensibilities and patience of the most easygoing fan."

OUTSIDE THE LAW (Universal, 1930)

Director, Tod Browning; screenplay, Browning and Garrett Fort; sound, C. Roy Hunter; camera, Roy Overbaugh; editor, Milton Carruth.

COBRA COLLINS . . . . Edward G. Robinson
CONNIE . . . . Mary Nolan
"FINGERS" O'DELL . . . . Owen Moore
JAKE . . . . Edwin Sturgis
HUMPY . . . . John George
THE KID . . . . Delmar Watson
POLICE CHIEF . . . . DeWitt Jennings
POLICE CAPTAIN . . . . Rockliffe Fellowes
and: Frank Burke, Sydney Bracey.

Synopsis

As part of his plan to knock over a bank, crook Fingers O'Dell poses as an advertising mannequin

EAST IS WEST (Universal, 1930) 75 M.

Director, Monta Bell; based on the play by Samuel Shipman and John Hymer; screenplay, Winifred Eaton Reeve and Tom Reed; sound, C. Roy Hunter; editor, Harry Marker.

MING TOY . . . . Lupe Velez
BILLY BENSON . . . . Lewis Ayres
CHARLIE YONG . . . . Edward G. Robinson
LO SANG KEE . . . . E. Allyn Warren
HOP TOY . . . . Tetsu Komai
MR. BENSON . . . . Henry Kolker
MRS. BENSON . . . . Mary Forbes
THOMAS . . . . Edgar Norton

Synopsis

The Love Boat comes into a Chinese port with Billy Benson, a young American, on board. On shore, where an auction is in progress a lovely girl

In **Outside the Law.**

named Ming Toy is being placed on the sale block by her father. Billy intervenes and saves the girl.

A kindly Chinese patriarch, Lo Sang Kee, takes Ming Toy to San Francisco where her vivacious conduct gets her into assorted difficulties with a waterfront do-good missionary society.

To save Ming Toy from deportation, Lo Sang Kee sells her to Charlie Yong, who is known as the Chop Suey King. Billy appears on the scene and kidnaps Ming Toy. He wants to marry her despite the potential repercussion of his social position as heir to the family fortune.

Ming Toy eventually learns that she really is not Chinese, but was taken from a murdered missionary as a baby and raised by a local family. Charlie Yong allows her to go to Billy with his blessings.

Reviews

The New York Times, November 1, 1930

"Edward G. Robinson appears in his first talker [sic] as Charlie Yong, the chop suey 'king' of San Francisco's Chinatown, and provides most of the entertainment with his amusing characterization of an egocentric half-caste. . . . Both Mr. Robinson and Miss Velez liven the rambling narrative with many amusing moments, but their task is a heavy and thankless one."

Waly., *Variety,* November 5, 1930

"Edward G. Robinson, as the suey king, is allowed too much footage for mugging and repetitious action."

With Mary Noland in **Outside the Law.**

THUNDER IN THE CITY (Columbia, 1937) 76 M.

Producer, Alexander Esway; director, Marion Gering; screenplay, Robert Sherwood and Aben Kandel; camera, Al Eilks; editor, Arthur Hilton.

DAN ARMSTRONG .... Edward G. Robinson
LADY PATRICIA .... Luli Deste
THE DUKE OF GLENAVON .... Nigel Bruce
THE DUCHESS OF GLENAVON .... Constance Collier
HENRY GRAHAM MANNINGDALE ....
.... Ralph Richardson
LADY CHALLONER .... Annie Esmond
SIR PETER CHALLONER .... Arthur Wontner
DOLLY .... Elizabeth Inglis
JAMES .... Cyril Raymond
EDNA .... Nancy Burne
BILL .... Billy Bray
SNYDERLING .... James Carew
MILLIE .... Everley Gregg

CASEY .... Elliott Nugent
REPORTER .... Terence De Marney
FRANK .... Roland Drew

Synopsis

Dan Armstrong, a salesman whose techniques are a bit too high-pressure for his staid employers, is sent to their London offices to observe how English business is able to flourish with more sedate methods. On his arrival, Armstrong is met by two distant relatives, Lord and Lady Challoner, impoverished owners of Challoner Hall. Dan accepts their invitation to spend the weekend with them and their other guests, the Duke and Duchess of Glenavon and their daughter Lady Patricia, and wealthy stockbroker Henry Manningdale. While

With Henry Kolker, Lew Ayres and Lupe Velez in
East Is West.

In **East Is West.**

With Nigel Bruce in **Thunder in the City.**

posits of mangalite, a miracle metal. Manningdale is willing to develop it, if Patricia marries him.

Dan gives the impression that he is well-to-do and the Glenavons ask him to back their project. He in turn suggests that they float a new company making the Duke chairman of the board. With this scheme, they acquire the necessary funds. To get even, Manningdale acquires the only process by which mangalite can be manufactured. When the time comes for the company to start work, Dan discovers the maneuver and is told by Manningdale that the only alternative to the company's bankruptcy is the transfer of all Dan's stock interest.

Dan makes the inevitable but profitable sacrifice and prepares to leave England. At the airport, however, he finds a large, enthusiastic crowd there to bid him goodbye. Among the throng is Patricia, who has sacrificed marriage to Manningdale for a flight to America with Dan.

there, Dan learns that the only part of the Glenavon estate that has any value is an unexploited mine property in Rhodesia containing large de-

With Luli Deste and Nigel Bruce in **Thunder in the City.**

Reviews

Bosley Crowther, *The New York Times*, April 23, 1937

"The British are having a bit of good wholesome fun at their own expense in *Thunder in the City* [. . .] whether you have fun, too, will depend largely on how you feel about the Edward G. Robinson brand of Napoleonics. . . . Our Robinson reflex is normal: we cringe at the rasping voice, genuflect when the great man pounds the table, feel involuntary tears start when he stands before hysterically admiring or dramatically hostile throngs to make his grand gesture of success or renunciation grander than success, but all the time we are emotionally thinking: Please, for goodness sake, somebody give him a tricorne hat."

Howard Barnes, *New York Herald-Tribune*, April 23, 1937

"Edward G. Robinson is brilliantly comic in *Thunder in the City* as he was sinisterly forbidding in his memorable gangster roles."

Variety, January 27, 1937

"Story is splendid vehicle for Edward G. Robinson as an American go-getter salesman who comes to London and confronts the dignified, but nevertheless shrewd, business methods and sterling qualities of the nobility who have titles handed down for generations and 'play the game.' "

THE WIDOW FROM CHICAGO (First National, 1930) 64 M.

Director, Edward Cline; screenplay, Earl Baldwin; camera, Sol Polito; editor, Edward Schroeder.

POLLY HENDERSON .... Alice White
SWIFTY DORGAN .... Neil Hamilton
DOMINIC .... Edward G. Robinson
SLUG O'DONNELL .... Frank McHugh
CRIS JOHNSTON .... Lee Shumway
MULLINS .... Brooks Benedict
DET. LT. FINNEGAN .... John Elliott
CORA .... Dorothy Mathews
MAZIE .... Ann Cornwall
CAPT. DAVIS .... E. H. Calvert
EHELN .... Betty Francisco
JIMMY HENDERSON ..... Harold Goodwin
DESK MAN .... Mike Donlin
PATROLMAN .... Robert Homans
JOHNSTON .... Al Hill
NEIGHBOR WOMAN .... Mary Foy
SGT. DUNN .... Allan Coran

Synopsis

Veteran New York cop Lt. Finnegan and Detective Jimmy Henderson, following a tip, board an inbound train hoping to nab Chicago hood Swifty Dorgan who has come East seeking to "do a job" for Dominic, a notorious vice baron. As the detectives approach, Swifty leaps from the train as it roars across a bridge and is apparently killed.

Planting a news story that Swifty Dorgan has escaped from the police, Jimmy assumes the gangster's identity and joins Dominic's gang, none of whom knew Dorgan.

One day as Jimmy waits for a gangland car to pick him up, his sister Polly sees him shot down in the doorway, and an automobile speeding away. Determined to avenge her brother's death, Polly poses as Swifty Dorgan's widow and obtains a job in Dominic's nightclub.

Later the real Swifty Dorgan shows up at the nightclub, and Polly has to persuade him to play dumb. Soon, he has fallen in love with her and thinks of quitting the rackets.

When Dominic and his gang attempt to hold up a rival nightclub, a detective tries to gun down Swifty. Polly shoots the detective and the gang makes its getaway. Back at his office Dominic comforts Polly, and tells her that he previously has killed several policemen, including her brother Jimmy. Unknown to Dominic, Polly had arranged the telephone on his desk so that detectives at the police station could hear the boasting confession.

As Dominic completes the account of his slayings, he notices the phone off the hook and tries to escape, but the police are everywhere. Using Polly as a shield, Dominic nearly gets free. However, Swifty arrives and he and Dominic have a shootout, Dominic surrenders and Polly and Swifty leave together.

Reviews

The New York Times, December 20, 1930

"The endless variety of Edward G. Robinson's particular world of make believe is demonstrated once again in *The Widow from Chicago*, which presents him as an agreeably despicable gang leader in the metropolitan beer racket. . . . Mr. Robinson gives

With Lee Shumway and Al Hill in Widow *from* Chicago.

an interesting and authentic characterization as Dominic, a resourceful and intelligent underworld power. It is not his fault that he is made to provide a denouement by falling into the most puerile of traps."

New York Herald-Tribune, December 21, 1930

"Mr. Robinson plays the underworld king in the best Nick Scarsi manner, and, as usual, presents a vivid and striking portrait of a coldly malignant killer."

Variety, December 22, 1930

"Edward G. Robinson's gang leader is the poorest such characterization he has turned in. . . . Some of the things Robinson has to say sound all out of proportion. Miss White's exaggerated eye-rolling is just as bad. Neil Hamilton is miscast."

LITTLE CAESAR (First National, 1931) 80 M.

Director, Mervyn LeRoy; based on the novel by William R. Burnett; screenplay, Francis E. Faragoh; camera, Tony Gaudio.

CESARE BANDELLO (Rico) .... Edward G. Robinson
JOE MASSARA .... Douglas Fairbanks Jr.
OLGA STASSOFF .... Glenda Farrell
"BIG BOY" .... Sidney Blackmer
POLICE SERGEANT FLAHERTY .... Thomas Jackson
PETE MONTANA .... Ralph Ince
TONY PASSA .... William Collier Jr.
ARNIE LORCH .... Maurice Black
SAM VETTORI .... Stanley Fields
OTERO .... George E. Stone

Synopsis

Anxious to work on bigger things, small time hood Cesare Bandello, alias Rico, joins Sam Vettori's gang, one of the two rival mobs in the city. Both are under the direct supervision of Pete Montana, lieutenant of the crime czar known as "Big Boy."

Rico plans to take over a cafe that is under the protection of the rival gang, but in doing so, he kills Crime Commissioner McCleve. Sam is horrified at this, and Rico, thinking he is weakening, overthrows him as leader of the gang.

The first step in his rapid rise in the underworld is when Arnie Lorch, the rival gang leader, bungles an assassination attempt on him and Rico

hunts him down, outbluffs him and warns him to leave town. Lorch goes to Detroit.

Rico now faces Montana to explain his actions, and asks for and gets Archie's former territory as well as his own. Rico determines to get Montana's job. Later, Rico is called in by "Big Boy" himself and is offered Montana's position, which he accepts jubilantly, still keeping his eye on the biggest job in the underworld. Rico turns on his pal, Joe Massara, who has a dance act with his girlfriend Olga Strassof. In a showdown, Rico demands that Joe, who has been trying to leave the gang, drop Olga, but Joe refuses. When Rico threatens to kill the girl, Joe turns state's evidence to save Olga and himself. Rico tries to shoot Joe, but finds he is unable to pull the trigger. Beaten by his own

With Alice White and Neil Hamilton in **The Widow from Chicago.**

In Little Caesar.

In Little Caesar.

With George E. Stone (far left), Noel Madison (with tommygun) and Douglas Fairbanks, Jr. (second from right) in Little Caesar.

With Douglas Fairbanks Jr. and Glenda Farrell in
Little Caesar.

psychology, he flees, but later returns, hurt by unknown pride, to turn himself in. At first the police
do not believe him, but when they finally catch on
to his identity, Rico panics and commits suicide.

Reviews

The New York Times, January 10, 1931

"The production is ordinary and would rank as
just one more gangster film but for two things. One
is the excellence of Mr. Burnett's creditable and
compact story. The other is Edward G. Robinson's
wonderfully effective performance. Little Caesar
becomes at Mr. Robinson's hands a figure out of
Greek epic tragedy, a cold, ignorant, merciless
killer, driven on and on by an insatiable lust for
power, the plaything of a force greater than himself."

SMART MONEY (Warner Bros., 1931) 90 M.

Director, Alfred E. Green; screenplay, Kubec Glasmon,
John Bright, Lucien Hubbard and Joseph Jackson; camera,
Robert Kurrle; editor, Jack Killifer.

NICK (THE BARBER) VENIZELOS	Edward G. Robinson
JACK	James Cagney
IRENE GRAHAM	Evalyn Knapp
SLEEPY SAM	Ralf Harolde
MARIE	Noel Francis
DISTRICT ATTORNEY'S GIRL	Margaret Livingstone
THE GREEK BARBER	Maurice Black
SPORT WILLIAMS	Boris Karloff
DISTRICT ATTORNEY BLACK	Morgan Wallace
SALESMAN-GAMBLER	Billy House
ALEXANDER AMENOPPOPOLUS	Paul Porcasi
LOLA	Polly Walters
HICKORY SHORT	Ben Taggart
CIGAR STAND CLERK	Gladys Lloyd
BACK-TO-BACK SCHULTZ	Clark Burroughs

Synopsis

Nick Venizelos runs a barber shop in Irontown. He has two weaknesses: gambling and blondes.

One of Nick's blonde friends hits him for $100, which almost immediately turns up in the hands of Sport Williams, who comes to gamble in Nick's backroom establishment. Nick's luck holds and he beats Sport.

The boys, including Jack, a barber in Nick's shop, think Nick should try his luck in the big city. They raise a $10,000 pool for him to gamble with against the syndicate. On his way to the train station, Nick runs into Sport, who insists the barber take his $1000 stake.

In the big city, Nick picks up Marie, a cigar counter girl, and she tells him where Hickory Short is having his big game in the hotel. Nick goes and blows the whole bundle. He soon learns he had been taken by the others in the game, all of whom were connected with Hickory, a recent parolee. Nick vows revenge on hood Sleepy Sam and Marie who tricked him.

Biding his time, he takes a barbering job in the city. Jack joins him, and they go back to $2.00 horse betting. A wealthy Greek notes Nick's luck at the track and stakes him to a big game. Nick beats Sleepy Sam at his own tricks. To complete his revenge, he takes Marie from Sam and forces her to live with him.

After encountering Hickory on a train and taking him for a bundle at poker, Nick moves on to become the biggest figure in the gambling world, running a huge gaming place with a barber shop as a front. His posh club becomes so notorious that the District Attorney goes after him, preying on Nick's prime weakness—blondes.

Irene comes into Nick's life. Although Jack is convinced she is a D.A. plant and warns Nick, the latter is entranced with the girl, and soon is pro-

posing marriage. Irene has a blackmailing record and is forced by the D.A. to help snare Nick. She slips a racing form into Nick's coat pocket at the casino, and when he is caught in a police raid, he is carrying the gambling paraphernalia, an offense punishable by six months. In the meantime, Jack has seen Irene stuff the paper into Nick's coat, confronts her and is wrestling with her, when

In Smart Money.

Nick comes in—Nick battles Jack and accidentally kills him.

Nick gets a ten-year prison sentence, and, on his way to the penitentiary, he reverts to his old bluff and jauntily poses for photographers. Irene is at the station and promises to wait for him. Nick is ready to gamble on anything.

Reviews

The New York Times, June 19, 1931

"Mr. Robinson gets all that is humanly possible out of the part of Nick the Barber, who, aside from

With James Cagney in **Smart Money.**

his penchant for gambling, also has a weakness for blondes, canaries and meticulously polished finger nails."

The Sunday New York Times, June 28, 1931

"Edward G. Robinson, who added to his histrionic laurels by his clever work in the title role of *Little Caesar,* contributes another expert portrayal in (this picture)."

FIVE STAR FINAL (First National, 1931) 89 M.

Director, Mervyn LeRoy; based on the play by Louis Weitzenkorn; screenplay, Byron Morgan; camera, Sol Polito; editor, Frank Ware.

JOSEPH RANDALL . . . . Edward G. Robinson
MICHAEL TOWNSEND . . . . H. B. Warner
JENNY TOWNSEND . . . . Marion Marsh
PHILLIP WEEKS . . . . Anthony Bushell
NANCY (VORHEES) TOWNSEND . . . . . . Frances Starr
KITTY CARMODY . . . . Ona Munson
ZIGGIE FEINSTEIN . . . . George E. Stone
BERNARD HINCHECLIFFE . . . . Oscar Apfel
ROBERT FRENCH . . . . Purnell Pratt
MISS TAYLOR . . . . Aline MacMahon
T. VERNON ISOPOD . . . . Boris Karloff
BRANNEGAN . . . . Robert Elliott
MISS EDWARDS . . . . Gladys Lloyd
GOLDBERG . . . . Harold Waldridge
MRS. WEEKS . . . . Evelyn Hall
MR. WEEKS . . . . David Torrence
TELEPHONE OPERATOR . . . . Polly Walters
REPORTER . . . . James Donlin
SCHWARTZ . . . . Frank Darien

Synopsis

To build-up his paper's circulation, Hinche-

With Oscar Apfel in Five Star Final.

In Five Star Final.

With Oscar Apfel, Robert Elliott and Purnell Pratt
in **Five Star Final.**

cliffe, owner of *The New York Gazette,* wants his staff to dig up information on a 20-year-old murder in which Nancy Vorhees shot her lover. Randall, the city editor, puts his top reporter on the case. Among the newsmen involved is a defrocked minister called Isopod.

Nancy is now married to Michael Townsend, who gave up his social position to wed her soon after she was cleared by the police. The Townsends now live in the Bronx with their daughter, Jenny, who is engaged to marry Philip Weeks. Isopod visits the Townsends and Nancy gives him a photo of Jenny, thinking he is the minister who will officiate at the pending marriage.

Nancy soon learns that it was a reporter who had visited her, and she calls Randall, begging him not to rehash old matters and ruin her daughter's future. However, Randall insists that news is news.

Failing in her plea, Nancy shoots herself, and when Townsend comes home and finds his dead wife, he commits suicide.

Meanwhile, *The Gazette's* circulation has skyrocketed with the sensational headlines and stories. Randall suddenly gains a sense of conscience and tells off Hinchecliffe; he loses his job.

Returning to his office, Randall finds Jenny there with a gun, waiting to kill him. When he explains his new sensibility, she calms down and eventually leaves.

Reviews

The New York Times, September 11, 1931

"Edward G. Robinson . . . gives another strong performance as the editor of a muck-raking tabloid

With Ona Munson in **Five Star Final.**

in the pictorial translation of Louis Weitzenkorn's play. . . . It is a picture which in the matter of production and acting takes its place beside the film of *The Front Page*. . . . With a big cigar in the corner of his mouth most of the time, Edward G. Robinson as Randall, the editor of the New York Gazette, makes the most of every line."

London Times, December 28, 1931

"As Randall, Mr. Edward G. Robinson succeeds in the best way an actor can—he succeeds, that is, in endowing the character he is playing with a definite personality. Randall is a far finer man than the people for whom he works, but familiarity with the methods of cheap newspapers has given him a protective armor of cynicism."

THE HATCHET MAN (First National, 1932) 74 M.

Director, William A. Wellman; based on the play *The*

Honorable Mr. Wong" by Achmed Abdullah and David Belasco; screenplay, J. Grubb Alexander; camera, Sid Hickox; editor, Owen Marks.

WONG LOW GET	Edward G. Robinson
TOYA SAN	Loretta Young
NAG HONG FAH	Dudley Digges
HARRY EN HAI	Leslie Fenton
YU CHANG	Edmund Breese
LONG SEN YAT	Tully Marshall
CHARLEY KEE	Noel N. Madison
MADAME SI-SI	Blanche Frederici
SUN YAT SEN	J. Carrol Naish
MISS LING	Toshia Mori
LI HOP FAT	Charles Middleton
MALONE	Ralph Ince
CHUNG HO	Otto Yamaoka
WAH LI	Evelyn Selbie
SOO LAT	E. Allyn Warren
FOO MING	Eddie Piel
FUNG LOO	Willie Fung
FAN YI	Gladys Lloyd
SING GIRL	Anna Chang
TONG MEMBER	James Leong

Synopsis

Wong Low Get, hatchet man of the Lem Sing Tong in San Francisco, follows the society's edict that Sun Yet Sen, a boyhood friend, must be executed. Knowing that Wong must keep his word, Sen, just before meeting his death, wills the hatchet man all his property. Wong promises that he will marry Sen's daughter when she grows up.

Years pass, with an Americanized Wong becoming a powerful figure in the Chinese community. Toya Sen dutifully marries Wong, although she secretly loves the evil, handsome, young half-cast, Harry En Hai, whom she first met at a dance hall.

Tong wars rage again in San Francisco, although Wong pleads for restraint. When his confidential clerk is murdered, however, he supports group leader Chung Ho who unburies the avenging hatchet. Chung Ho eloquently wins over the loyalty of the opposing tong, except Malone, the white leader. Wong kills him.

With Noel Madison in The Hatchet Man.

Returning home, Wong finds Toya in the arms of Harry En Hai. Despite the girl's explanations, Wong sends the pair away. Shunned by his friends for this anti-traditional act, he sells his shops and becomes a farmer.

When Wong later learns that the young Harry En Hai has been deported to China for selling drugs, taking Toya with him, Wong follows overseas. He traces Toya to the Hanghow Sing House where she is virtually a slave. Wong informs the owner that Toya is his wife, and with his honorable hatchet he kills En Hai. Wong and Toya leave together, unmolested.

Reviews

The New York Times, February 4, 1932

"Although Wong, played by Mr. Robinson, is clad

With Loretta Young and Leslie Fenton in The Hatchet Man.

most of the time in Chinese silks, his voice, like the voices of others in this tale, is decidedly American, something which is accounted for through the years the characters have spent over here. All the same, Mr. Robinson is a better barber, gambler, gangster and tabloid writer than he is a Chinese Hatchet Man."

TWO SECONDS (First National, 1932) 68 M.

Director, Mervyn LeRoy; based on the play by Elliott Lester; screenplay, Harvey Thew; camera, Sol Polito; editor, Terrill Morse.

JOHN ALLEN	Edward G. Robinson
BUD CLARK	Preston Foster
SHIRLEY DAY	Vivienne Osborne
TONY	J. Carrol Naish
BOOKIE	Guy Kibbee
ANNIE	Adrienne Dare
JUDGE	Frederick Burton
LIZZIE	Dorothea Wolbert
THE DOCTOR	Edward McWade
THE WARDEN	Berton Churchill
A COLLEGE BOY	William Janney
REPORTER	Lew Brice
REPORTER	Franklin Parker
REPORTER	Frederick Howard
MRS. SMITH	Helen Phillips
FAT GIRL	June Gittleson
TART	Jill Dennett
TART	Luana Walters

With Vivienne Osborne in **Two Seconds.**

JUSTICE OF THE PEACE	Otto Hoffman
DOCTOR	Harry Beresford
MASHER	John Kelly
MASHER	Matt McHugh
EXECUTIONER	Harry Woods
WOMAN	Gladys Lloyd

Synopsis

Newspaper reporters are gathered in the death-house at the State Penitentiary to witness the execution of a murderer named John Allen, who insists that he is dying for the wrong crime. In the last two seconds of his life he recalls the events leading up to the present time. John Allen and Bud Clark are riveters working on a skyscraper girder. Allen is rather sour on life, but Bud is optimistic as he has just cashed in at the races. That night the two have dates, but Allen is not interested, and after work he wanders off to a dance hall where he meets Shirley Day. They begin seeing each other quite regularly and one night when he gets drunk, she takes him to a justice of the peace, and they get married.

While Allen is at work, But has learned that Shirley has been seeing Tony, proprietor of the dance hall. When Bud informs Allen of this, Allen gets angry and swings at Bud, who loses his balance and falls to his death.

Allen goes to pieces. Shirley taunts him, stating that she had to borrow money from Tony to pay for rent and food. Allen resolves to avenge his friend's death himself, hiding away his few dollars until he has enough to bet on the races. When he wins a fairly big stake he takes only enough to pay off his debts. Allen then goes out looking for Shirley and finds her with Tony. After stuffing the money that Shirley had borrowed from Tony in Tony's hand, Allen turns and shoots his wife.

Back in the deathhouse, Allen repeats that if he had been sentenced for Bud's death, that would have been fair, but it is an injustice for him to die for killing Shirley.

Reviews

The New York Times, May 19, 1932

"Edward G. Robinson contributes a remarkably forceful portrayal in the picture version of Elliott Lester's play. . . . When Mr. Robinson depicts the nerve-racked condition of Allen or delivers a heated talk to the judge who sentences him, his acting is unusually impressive."

William Boehnel, *New York World-Telegram,* May 19, 1932

"With *Two Seconds* . . . the distinguished screen career of Edward G. Robinson encounters a temporary lapse. With the excellent Mervyn LeRoy as director, and with several experienced players to support him, Mr. Robinson, whose Little Caesar still stands as his finest screen portrayal, moves indifferently, and at times almost amateurishly, through a picture of incredibly meagre purpose. . . . I had no idea that Mr. Robinson, whose flair for choosing good parts for himself is well known, could be caught so empty handed and that he would ever allow himself to indulge in such over-acting as he does here."

TIGER SHARK (First National, 1932) 80 M.

Director, Howard Hawks; based on the story "Tuna" by Houston Branch; screenplay, Wells Root; assistant director, Richard Rosson; camera, Tony Gaudio; editor, Thomas Pratt.

With Vivienne Osborne in **Two Seconds.**

With Richard Arlen and Vince Barnett in **Tiger Shark.**

MIKE MASCARENA .... Edward G. Robinson
QUITA .... Zita Johann
PIPES BOLEY .... Richard Arlen
LADY BARBER .... Leila Bennett
ENGINEER .... Vince Barnett
THE MAN .... J. Carrol Naish
MANUEL .... William Ricciardi

Synopsis

Capt. Mike Mascarena is the best tuna fisherman on the Pacific coast, although he was crippled years before, losing a hand to a shark while rescuing a buddy, Pipes Boley. Mike's tough exterior masks a complex that women laugh at him because of his hook and that he will not be allowed in heaven when he dies because he is not whole.

On one cruise, old Manuel, a member of Mike's crew is killed, leaving an orphan his daughter, Quita. When Mike comes ashore, he looks her up, saving the girl from suicide. Eventually, he asks her to marry him, and out of gratitude for his kindness, she feels she cannot refuse. Pipes resents the marriage, thinking Quita is a golddigger, but Mike is so happy in his new married life that he does not notice Pipes and Quita falling in love. On the next voyage out, Pipes falls ill and is taken ashore. Mike has him taken to his home where Quita nurses him back to health. Pipes wants to leave before things between him and Quita get out of hand, but Quita won't let him go. One day, Mike happens in on them while they are embracing. Instantly, friendship turns to hate, and Mike forces them both onto his ship. At sea, Mike knocks Pipes unconscious and tosses him into an open boat. He drives a harpoon into the craft intending to sink it. He throws another harpoon into a man-eating shark. As the shark swims away, the harpoon rope catches around Mike's foot and he is dragged overboard. Sailors rescue Pipes but fail to reach Mike in time. He dies in Quita's arms.

Reviews

The New York Times, September 23, 1932

"This fisherman is portrayed splendidly by Edward G. Robinson, who makes the character both sympathetic and fearsome according to what is happening."

New York World-Telegram, September 23, 1932

"Mr. Robinson gives a fine, finished performance as Mike, blending love and hatred in exactly the right manner."

SILVER DOLLAR (First National, 1932) 84 M.

Director, Alfred E. Green; based on the biography of H. A. W. Tabor by David Karsner; screenplay, Carl Erickson and Harvey Thew; camera, James van Trees; editor, George Marks.

YATES MARTIN	Edward G. Robinson
LILY OWENS	Bebe Daniels
SARAH MARTIN	Aline MacMahon
POKER ANNIE	Jobyna Howland
MINE FOREMAN	DeWitt Jennings
COL. STANTON	Robert Warwick
HAMLIN	Russell Simpson
ADAMS	Harry Holman
JENKINS	Charles Middleton
GELSEY	John Marston
MRS. ADAMS	Marjorie Gateson
PRES. CHESTER A. ARTHUR	Emmett Corrigan
MINER	Wade Boteler
MINER	William Le Maire
MARK	David Durand
RISCHE	Lee Kohlman
MRS. HAMLIN	Teresa Conover
SECRETARY	Leon Waycott (Ames)

With Zita Johnson in **Tiger Shark**.

EMMA ABBOTT .... Virginia Edwards
HOOK .... Christian Rub
GENERAL GRANT .... Walter Rogers
WILLIAM JENNINGS BRYAN .... Niles Welch
  and: Wilfred Lukas, Alice Wetherfield, Herman Bing,
    Bonita Granville, Walter Long, Willard Robertson,
    Frederick Burton, Charles Coleman.

Synopsis

Yates Martin, a Kansas farmer, gets caught up in the Colorado gold rush, and with his wife, Sarah, opens a general store in one of the boom towns. However, Yates goes broke extending credit to the miners, who pay him in shares to their mines.

The Martins are about to return to Kansas and farming when two miners come in with silver bags. Martin becomes the richest of them all. Soon Martin becomes a leading town figure, and enters politics, being elected in turn mayor, postmaster, sheriff and eventually lieutenant governor. He has so much money he is literally throwing it away. He buys a mansion in Denver, erects a big opera house, donates land for a post office, and is the first to give charity on any occasion.

Martin meets Lily, a beautiful woman who delights in diamonds and pearls, and adores the limelight—a complete contrast to his wife. Martin

With Bebe Daniels and Emmett Corrigan in Silver Dollar.

leaves Sarah for Lily. The resulting scandal almost ruins his chance for running for the U.S. Senate, but he manages to win a vacant seat. He weds Lily in Washington with the President and Senators attending the nuptials.

Returning to Denver, Martin continues his reckless spending and when silver is demonetized due to the gold standard, he is ruined.

Now destitute and alone, he visits the Grand Opera House which he had once built. There he is found dying of heart failure.

Reviews

The New York Times, December 23, 1932

"This screen translation, in which Edward G.

In **Silver Dollar.**

Robinson gave a conspicuously able performance, opened last night. . . . The role of Tabor, who in this offering is called Yates Martin, is especially well-suited to Mr. Robinson's talent. His characterization is compelling and convincing, and he succeeds admirably in delivering the complex nature of the man who, in the film, is invariably more fortunate than clever. (He) makes the most of Martin's egoism and of his confidence in the power of wealth he derives from silver mines."

The Sunday New York Times, January 8, 1933

"Whatever Mr. Robinson did in *Little Caesar* is even more convincing here, notwithstanding that Yates Martin is a character from the past."

Richard Watts Jr., *New York Herald-Tribune,*
  December 24, 1932

"Directed and written with the proper vigor and quite brilliantly played by Edward G. Robinson, the film presents what is perhaps a fairly neglected

With Russell Simpson and Harry Holman in **Silver Dollar.**

period in the national life with raciness and authenticity."

Regina Crewe, *New York American,* December 23, 1932

"The picture provides Edward G. Robinson with one of the most vibrant of all the lively parts he has portrayed. And, needless to say, he creates a character rich and full and colorful, vivid in all its dimensions. It is an achievement, perhaps the finest in all his cinematic career, at least comparable to any."

THE LITTLE GIANT (First National, 1933) 74 M.

Director, Roy Del Ruth; story, Robert Lord; screenplay, Lord and Wilson Mizner; music conductor, Leo F. Forbstein; art director, Robert Hans; camera, Sid Hickox; editor, George Marks.

JAMES FRANCIS "BUGS" AHEARN	Edward G. Robinson
POLLY CASS	Helen Vinson
RUTH WAYBURN	Mary Astor
JOHN STANLEY	Kenneth Thomson
AL DANIELS	Russell Hopton
EDITH MERRIAM	Shirley Grey
GORDON CASS	Donald Dillaway
MRS. CASS	Louise Mackintosh
DONALD HADLEY CASS	Berton Churchill
FRANKIE	Helen Mann
VOICE OF RADIO ANNOUNCER	Selmur Jackson
BUTCH ZANWUTOSKI	Dewey Robinson
(ED) TIM	John Kelly
BUTLER	Sidney Bracey
JOE MILANO'S HOODS	Bob Perry Adrian Morris

*With Harry Holman, Teresa Conover and Russell
Simpson in Silver Dollar.*

WAITER	Rolfe Sedan
CHARTERIS	Charles Coleman
GUEST	Bill Elliott
INGLEBY	Leonard Carey
MAID	Nora Cecil
INVESTMENT CLERKS	Lester Dorr
	Lorin Raker
DETECTIVE	Guy Usher
D.A.	John Marston
PULIDO	Harry Tenbrook

Synopsis

Seeing the end of Prohibition on the horizon and his bootlegging racket about to collapse, Chicago beer baron Bugs Ahearn decides to go to California and break into society. With his pal, Al Daniels, he signs in at a swanky west coast hotel and joins a polo club.

Bugs is ignored by the best citizens, however, and is about to give up in disgust, when Polly Cass, whom he believes to be a wealthy society girl, falls from her horse. Bugs helps her up and takes her home. She invites him to tea where he is ribbed about his manners—until Polly's brother, Gordon, discovers that Bugs is a millionaire; then the entire family adopts him.

Bugs inquires about renting a home so that he can entertain properly, and Ruth Wayburn, a society girl whose father died broke, leases him hers. Bugs in return engages Ruth as his social secretary.

The Cass family and their horsey set make Ahearn's house their headquarters. Ruth knows they are frauds but she cannot convince Bugs, who becomes engaged to Polly. Shortly thereafter Polly's father sells Bugs some phony stocks. The District Attorney is after Mr. Cass because of the stock deal, but Bugs persuades the D.A. to give him a few days to return the money. He then sends for his boys from Chicago to strong-arm the people who sold him the fraudulent stocks and get his money back.

Bugs then goes to Polly's house, retrieves his money from her father and forcibly takes back the engagement ring from his fiancee. He returns to Ruth.

Reviews

The New York Times, May 25, 1933

"Edward G. Robinson, as the prime player, reveals himself as no mean comedian, and yesterday afternoon, the audience roared when the gangster, who is known here as Bugs Ahern, tackles a French menu and when he turns up at an informal afternoon party in full regalia. . . . [He] is alert and forceful even in this light affair."

The Sunday New York Times, May 29, 1933

"Mr. Robinson is as sure of his ground as a comedian as he has been in heavy roles. He makes Ahern quick-witted and quite natural, so long as the story permits."

Marguerite Tazelaar, *New York Herald-Tribune,* May 26, 1933

"*The Little Giant* is an amusing bit of fluff which gives Mr. Robinson a chance to reveal unsuspected comedy talents."

William Boehnel, *New York World-Telegram,* May 27, 1933

"This fast moving and thoroughly entertaining picture shows Mr. Robinson at his best and is one

With Ben Taggart and Russell Hopton in **The Little Giant.**

of the really worthwhile films that have come along during the last few weeks. . . . [He] is excellent as the erstwhile racketeer."

John S. Cohen Jr., *New York Sun*, May 27, 1933

"Edward G. Robinson undoubtedly finds himself

With Mary Astor in Little Giant.

with another success on his hands. . . . [He], it goes without saying, is forceful, right and genuinely amusing."

I LOVED A WOMAN (First National, 1933) 90 M.

Director, Alfred E. Green; based on the book by David Karsner; screenplay, Charles Kenyon and Sidney Sutherland; camera, James Van Trees; editor, Bert Levy.

LAURA McDONALD	Kay Francis
JOHN HAYDEN	Edward G. Robinson
MARTHA LANE HAYDEN	Genevieve Tobin
SHUSTER	J. Farrell MacDonald
SANBORN	Henry Kolker
CHARLES LANE	Robert Barrat
HENRY	George Blackwood
DAVENPORT	Murray Kinnell
LARKIN	Robert McWade
OLIVER	Walter Walker
FARRELL	Henry O'Neill
MAID	Lorena Layson
WARREN	Sam Godfrey
THEODORE ROOSEVELT	E. J. Ratcliffe
HOTEL PROPRIETOR	Paul Porcasi
BOWEN	William V. Mong

Synopsis

John Hayden, wealthy Chicago scion, is forced to interrupt his art studies in Greece and take over his father's meat packing business when his father dies. John is attracted by Martha Lane, daughter of his father's biggest competitor. Only after marrying her however does John discover that she is nothing but a social climber.

Despite her ridicule, John retains his high ideals and insists that his firm handle only top quality meats and maintain good working conditions for the men. When his rivals underbid him and his firm sinks to second rate, Martha's taunting becomes unmerciful.

One evening at the opera, he meets Laura McDonald, a beautiful young singer, and offers to finance her musical education abroad. When John asks for a divorce so he can marry Laura, his wife refuses. Then too, Laura pleads that marriage would interfere with her career—so John and Laura continue meeting secretly. Laura's success in the musical world and her ambition to even greater glory encourages John onward to become champion in the meat industry, and his sense of values undergo a big change.

During the Spanish American War, he outbids all his rivals and secures major army contracts; then he supplies the Army with tainted beef. Col. Teddy Roosevelt charges him with the deaths of many soldiers and threatens to prosecute him when he gets into power. When Roosevelt becomes President, John is tried for manslaughter, but acquitted.

Martha meantime has hired detectives to follow John and Laura, but they report back that Laura has been seeing other men. John is told and reluctantly leaves Laura whom he still loves. As years pass, John undertakes increasingly bigger gambles and efforts to match the rising peaks of Laura's career. Indicted for fraud when his company faces bankruptcy, he flees to Greece.

A broken man, deserted by his friends, John is alone until Laura learns of his plight. She begs Martha to go to him, but Martha refuses. So Laura goes to John herself, offering him the comfort he needs.

With Kay Francis in **I Loved a Woman.**

Reviews

The New York Times, September 22, 1933

"Edward G. Robinson's latest picture . . . is a worthy offering . . . concerned with the crimes of Chicago meat-packers both during the Spanish-American and World Wars, and in it, Mr. Robinson has an excellent opportunity for a definite characterization, of which, it need hardly be said, this efficient actor takes full advantage. . . . [His] portrayal rivals his splendid interpretation in *Silver Dollar.*"

The Sunday New York Times, October 1, 1933

"Mr. Robinson gives an excellent portrayal as a gentle and sympathetic individual who becomes a ruthless beef baron."

New York Herald-Tribune, September 22, 1933

"A careful and conscious account of the life of a zestful American character, effectively acted by Edward G. Robinson."

New York American, September 22, 1933

"A dull and lifeless picture, with the virile Edward G. Robinson badly miscast."

John S. Cohen, Jr., *New York Sun,* September 22, 1933

"Mr. Robinson is never so admirable as in portraying what may be described as a ruthless rise to power, and thus he has another personal success on his hands."

DARK HAZARD (First National, 1934) 72 M.

Director, Alfred E. Green; based on the novel by William R. Burnett; screenplay, Ralph Block and Brown Holmes; camera, Sol Polito; editor, Herbert Levy.

JIM "BUCK" TURNER .... Edward G. Robinson
MARGE MAYHEWS .... Genevieve Tobin
VALERIE .... Glenda Farrell
TEX .... Robert Barrat
JOE .... Gordon Westcott
GEORGE MAYHEW .... Hobart Cavanaugh
PRES BARROW .... George Meeker
SCHULTZ .... Henry B. Walthall
BRIGHT .... Sidney Toler
MRS. MAYHEW .... Emma Dunn
FALLEN .... Willard Robertson
MISS DOLBY .... Barbara Rogers
PLUMMER .... William V. Mong

Synopsis

Jim Turner is a born gambler, capable of winning and losing $20,000 in one evening. To stay close to the betting scene he takes a job as cashier at a small racetrack in a little Ohio town. There he meets Marge Mayhew at a boarding house run by her mother, who has tried to match-mate her daughter with Pres Barrow, one of the town's leading citizens. However, Jim sweeps Marge off her feet and she marries him on condition that he give up gambling. Jim and Marge go to Chicago where he becomes a clerk in a cheap hotel. He is eventually offered a job managing a California dog track. He gambles occasionally, causing a rift at home.

Valerie Wilson, an old flame of Jim's, turns up at the racetrack one day, and renews her acquaintance with him. When she pops in at Jim's home somewhat intoxicated, Marge is angered and locks Jim out. Resentful, Jim goes off with Valerie to a gambling house where he wins more than $20,000. Jim returns home remorseful and again promises Marge that he will quit gambling. She doesn't believe him and while Jim is asleep she takes his money and departs for home, leaving a note telling him he can come for her when he swears off gambling permanently.

Jim knocks around the country for a few years and then decides to go back to Marge. She takes him in but admits that she now is in love with Pres Barrow, who has been courting her again.

When the dog races come to town Jim is lured back to the track, where he sees Dark Hazard, one of the dogs he had bred in California. Dark Hazard is injured in a race and is about to be shot when Jim interferes and buys him for a song. Jim takes the dog home but Marge will not let him keep it in the house. Jim becomes more disgruntled and one night, finding Marge in Pres's arms, he goes out and gets drunk. After sobering up, he realizes that it is the small town stuff that has changed Marge. He and Pres get into a fight, but seeing Marge's concern for him, Jim realizes the true situation, and leaves with Dark Hazard.

Dark Hazard recovers and Jim comes into the money again. Sometime later in Australia, Jim is back betting at the race tracks and making a killing. That night he again goes broke at roulette.

Reviews

The New York Times, February 23, 1934

"Jim Turner, the hunch gambler, spills himself noisily on the screen in Edward G. Robinson's familiar style of alternately shy and snarling moods. Mr. Robinson provides a hearty cartoon character which is admirably suited to the unexpected guffaw and the well-timed hook to the chin."

Marguerite Tazelaar, *New York Herald-Tribune,* February 23, 1934

"Again the combination of Edward G. Robinson and W. R. Burnett results in that singular emotional quality which was the touchstone of *Little Caesar.* While the latter was a far more sensational and melodramatic piece, the star's performance in *Dark Hazard* is just as true to type and as poignantly drawn. . . . It is the contrast in Mr. Robinson's characters which give them much of their fascination. His heroes are never completely heroic and his villains are never altogether unsympathetic."

New York Sun, February 23, 1934

"Edward G. Robinson adds one more portrait to his gallery of quaint likeable misfits."

Variety, February 27, 1934

"It's an unusual portrayal for Robinson, despite the fact that he's cast as a gambler. A big shot for a few moments, a bum most of the time, he's always dominated by those around him and near him, instead of, as in his past pictures, being the head man."

THE MAN WITH TWO FACES (First National, 1934) 72 M.

Director, Archie Mayo; based on the play "The Dark Tower" by George S. Kaufman and Alexander Woollcott; screenplay, Tom Reed and Niven Busch; camera, Tony Gaudio; editor, William Holmes.

DAMON WELLS	Edward G. Robinson
JESSICA WELLS	Mary Astor
BEN WESTON	Ricardo Cortez
DAPHNE MARTIN	Mae Clarke
STANLEY VANCE	Louis Calhern
BARRY JONES	John Eldredge
DR. KENDALL	Arthur Byron
INSPECTOR CRANE	Henry O'Neill
WILLIAM CURTIS	David Landau
HATTIE	Emily Fitzroy
MARTHA TEMPLE	Margaret Dale
PATSY DOWLING	Dorothy Tree
MORGUE KEEPER	Arthur Aylesworth
PEABODY	Virginia Sale
DEBUTANTE	Mary Russell
MATRON	Mrs. Wilfred North
MR. JONES	Howard Hickman
MRS. JONES	Maude Turner Gordon
CALL BOY	Dick Winslow
DOORMAN	Frank Darien
DRIVER	Bert Moorhouse
BELL BOY	Ray Cooke
NEWSBOY	Jack McHugh
LIEUTENANT OF DETECTIVES	Douglas Cosgrove
DETECTIVE	Wade Boteler
WEEKS	Guy Usher
REWRITE MAN	Milton Kibbee
EDITOR	Joseph Crehan

Synopsis

Damon Wells is the most brilliant actor and director of the New York stage, while his sister Jessica is the top actress of the day until a mysterious mental and physical breakdown sends her into oblivion. It is discovered that she is under the Svengali-like influence of her husband, Stanley

In Dark Hazard.

With Louis Calhern in **The Man With Two Faces.**

Vance. When Vance strangely vanishes, Jessica re-gains her health and soon stages a theatrical come-back. Then Vance returns—he had been in prison—and Jessica again begins to break down. One day Vance takes Jessica to the suite of a fashionable hotel, intending to sell her honor and her rights in the show to a theatrical producer named Chautard. Later, Jessica turns up at home inco-herent and Vance is found in a closet of the hotel suite, murdered.

Chautard has vanished, leaving no trace. The police are completely baffled and give up the case. One detective, however, refuses to quit, and dis-covers that Vance had murdered his former wife for her money and had been involved in other criminal activities. A false moustache the detective finds in a Gideon Bible in the murder room con-vinces him that Chautard is really an actor. He recalls seeing a play many years before which had a character similar to Chautard in the cast. He be-

gins to haunt the theatres, especially the dressing room of Damon Wells.

Wells begins to get uneasy and bursts into a sweat when, one night, the detective hands him the false moustache and advises the actor to be more careful in the future. Wells is completely non-plussed until the detective states that the world was well rid of the scoundrel Chautard, and that he has officially given up the case. The only person knowing of the crime is Ben Weston, a theatrical producer, who loves Jessica. It was in Weston's office that Wells had changed into his Chautard character.

Freed of her husband, Jessica rises to new heights of professional success. Weston proposes marriage and she is ideally happy.

Reviews

Andre Sennwald, *The New York Times,* July 12, 1934

"Mr. Robinson, as the self-confessed best actor in America and the self-appointed executioner of a first-class knave, maintains the comic mood successfully, which is a considerable help to the story."

The Sunday New York Times, July 22, 1934

"Edward G. Robinson, in the Basil Sydney role, concealed himself admirably behind a set of whiskers, a wig, false eyebrows, and a putty nose, but the snarl of Little Caesar occasionally slipped through his French accent."

Richard Watts Jr., *New York Herald-Tribune,* July 12, 1934

"Edward G. Robinson, Mary Astor, Louis Calhern and other members of the cast perform with moderate effectiveness."

William Boehnel, *New York World Telegram,* July 12, 1934

"Edward G. Robinson's impression of Jessica's brother is a suave bit of acting, done in the best tradition of good actors impersonating good actors."

New York American, July 13, 1934

"Edward G. Robinson, who is nothing if not ver-

With Margaret Dale and Emily Fitzroy in **The Man With Two Faces.**

satile, is seen in the role of Damon Wells, the excellent and slightly egotistical actor. The role gives Robinson plenty of opportunity to exercise his recognized bent for character work and disguise."

THE WHOLE TOWN'S TALKING (Columbia, 1935) 93 M.

Producer, Lester Cowan; director, John Ford; based on the novel by William R. Burnett; screenplay, Jo Swerling and Robert Riskin; assistant director, Wilbur McGaugh; camera, Joseph August; editor, Viola Lawrence.

ARTHUR FERGUSON JONES/KILLER MANNION
.... Edward G. Robinson
WILHELMINA "BILL" CLARK .... Jean Arthur
DET. SGT. MIKE BOYLE .... Arthur Hohl
HEALY............................. Wallace Ford
DISTRICT ATTORNEY SPENCER ..... Arthur Byron
HOYT .... Donald Meek
J. G. CARPENTER .... Paul Harvey
BUGS MARTIN .... Edward Brophy
SEAVER .... Etienne Girardot
DET. SGT. PAT HOWE .... James Donlan
WARDEN .... J. Farrell Macdonald
AUNT AGATHA .... Effie Ellsler
POLICE LT. MAC .... Robert Emmett O'Connor
MANNION'S HENCHMEN .... John Wray
Joseph Sauers (Sawyer)
RUSSELL .... Frank Sheridan
PRESIDENT OF THE CHAMBER OF COMMERCE ...
.... Clarence Hummel Wilson
RIBBER .... Ralph M. Remley
SEAVER'S PRIVATE SCERETARY ..... Virginia Pine
MAYOR .... Ferdinand Munier
RADIO MAN .... Cornelius Keefe
REPORTER AT DOCK .... Francis Ford
BIT GIRL .... Lucille Ball
DETECTIVE .... Robert E. Homans
SOB SISTER .... Grace Halo
CONVICT .... Walter Long
TRAFFIC COP .... Ben Taggart
GANGSTER .... Al Hill
BIT MAN .... Gordon DeMain
CITY OFFICIAL .... Sam Flint
REPORTER .... Emmett Vogan
SECRETARY .... Bess Flowers
LANDLADY .... Mary Gordon
GUARD .... Tom London
BIT MAN .... Charles King

Synopsis

Arthur Jones, a milquetoast clerk in a hardware company, is lunching with "Bill" Clark, a girl in the office (he loves her but does not have the nerve to tell her) when he is suddenly surrounded by the police and arrested. Apparently he bears more than a passing resemblance to Killer Mannion, Public Enemy No. 1, who had earlier in the day broken out of prison. Luckily, Jones is able to prove his identity, although the publicity makes him famous. When he returns home that night, he finds Mannion in his room. The killer forces him to surrender the passport given him by the D.A. for identification should he again be picked up. Mannion plans on using the identification passport while on jobs at night—Jones is to keep the document during the daytime.

When Jones's Aunt comes to visit, Mannion has his gang kidnap her and for protection they also take Bill along. Meanwhile, the rash of holdups continue. Afraid of mistakenly shooting Jones, the police decide to place him in jail for safekeeping. To settle an old score, Mannion poses as Jones, so that he can get inside the prison and kill Bugs Martin, a former gang member who had double-crossed him. Planning to have Jones killed and identified as the escaped convict, Mannion sends his meek double to the bank with a bundle, supposedly containing stolen money. Jones misplaces the parcel and returns home, where he overhears the gang joking about how easily he (Jones) had been framed.

Jones enters, posing as Mannion, and when the real killer returns, Jones orders the gang to eliminate him. Then he grabs a gun and holds the gangsters for the police. Collecting both the reward money and his new found courage, he asks Bill to marry him.

Reviews

Andre Sennwald, *The New York Times,* March 1, 1935

"Pungently written, wittily produced and topped off with a splendid dual performance by Edward G. Robinson, it may be handsomely recommended as the best of the new year's screen comedies. . . . Mr. Robinson, while he succeeds in being unbelievably downtrodden in the wistful little man who looks like Public Enemy No. 1, has not forgotten how to play Little Caesar, and he stifles the laugh in your throat when he is being Killer Mannion. . . . With a splendid narrative like this, he returns with a rush to the front line of film players."

Richard Watts Jr., *New York Herald-Tribune,* March 1, 1935

"After a number of recent cinema adventures in a minor key, Edward G. Robinson returns to the

With Jean Arthur in The Whole Town's Talking.

In The Whole Town's Talking.

With Jean Arthur in The Whole Town's Talking.

In The Whole Town's Talking.

days of his Hollywood glory in a lively and satisfactory combination of farce and melodrama. . . . The work manages to supply a one-man carnival for its star, and, with Mr. Robinson taking every advantage of its side-show possibilities, you have the opportunity to enjoy good acting and to have the soul-satisfying pleasure of watching the shrewd and resourceful performer on one of the happiest times of his life. Here, Mr. Robinson enjoys the vast blessing of a picture which enables him to perform in two contrasting roles without the necessity of a scene wherein he must pretend to make embarrassed love to the wife of his double. . . . The picture is, of course, always a Robinson field day and the star takes proper and unashamed advantage of all his opportunities."

Eileen Creehan, *New York Sun,* March 1, 1935

"Mr. Robinson, turning in a performance that goes up near the top of the comedy list for this year, plays a dual role."

Regine Crewe, *New York American,* March 1, 1935

". . . the Best thing Mr. Robinson has done since the unforgettable *Little Caesar.* . . . [He] is twin star of the picture, for he portray both clerk and killer, and delivers two separate and distinct characterizations which never once overlap or intrude one upon another. No one need be told how thrilling [he] can impersonate an underworldling, and his Killer Mannion ranks with the finest of these conceptions. . . . The entire piece is a field day for Robinson."

Land., *Variety,* March 6, 1935

"Robinson will derive a heap of benefits from this assignment. It hands him some dazzling moments of acting . . . notably, his characterization of the submerged, overpolite and indecisive office worker is human and believable. Always having been a swell actor, because he makes you believe him in various roles, this picture is a great break for him."

BARBARY COAST (United Artists, 1935) 91 M.

Producer; Samuel Goldwyn; director, Howard Hawks; screenplay, Ben Hecht and Charles MacArthur; musical director, Alfred Newman; camera, Ray June; editor, Edward Curtis.

MARY RUTLEDGE (SWAN)	Miriam Hopkins
LOUIS CHAMALIS	Edward G. Robinson
JIM CARMICHAEL	Joel McCrea
OLD ATROCITY	Walter Brennan
COL. MARCUS AURELIUS COBB	Frank Craven
KNUCKLES JACOBY	Brian Donlevy
PEEBLES	Otto Hoffman
WIGHAM	Rollo Lloyd
SAWBUCK McTAVISH	Donald Meek
SANDY FERGUSON	Roger Gray
OAKIE	Clyde Cook
JED SLOCUM	Harry Carey
JUDGE HARPER	J. M. Kerrigan
BRONCO	Matt McHugh
AH WING	Wong Chung
SHERIFF	Russ Powell
SHIP'S CAPTAIN	Frederik Vogeding
FIRST MATE	Dave Wengren
McCREADY, THE SECOND MATE	Anders Van Haden
PILOT	Jules Cowles
STEWARD	Cyril Thornton
DRUNK	Clarence Wertz
LOOKOUT	Harry Semels
HELMSMAN	Theodore Lorch
BIT SAILORS	Olin Francis
	Larry Fisher
LEAD LINE SAILOR	George Simpson
BIT PASSENGERS	Bert Sprotte
	Claude Payton
	Frank Benson
	Bob Stevenson
SAILOR (thrown out of saloon)	David Niven
BILL	Edward Gargan
FISH PEDDLER	Herman Bing
RINGSIDER	Tom London
GAMBLERS	Heinie Conklin
	Charles West
	Constantine Romanoff
	Art Miles
	Sammy Finn

Synopsis

In the Frisco Gold Rush days of the 1850s, no white woman—no woman of gentility—lived in the town until Mary Rutledge arrived to marry Dan Morgan, only to discover that he is dead. Col. Marcus A. Cobb, who has come west to establish San Francisco's first newspaper, offers Mary his protection and urges her to return to New York. However, she is determined to stay out west.

At the Bella Donna Club, Mary meets its owner, Louis Chamalis, reputed to be the most powerful man in San Francisco. Soon the transformation of Mary into the woman known as Swan is complete. Hard and brittle, bedecked in diamonds, she presides at Chamalis's crooked roulette wheel. When miner Sandy Ferguson loses his year's digging there and is killed for all of his protests, Cobb prepares to print a true account of the murder. Chamalis gives orders to demolish his plant, but Swan intervenes in Cobb's behalf. Chamalis then insists that Swan either show some love for him or get out.

Riding in the gold fields one day, Swan meets Jim Carmichael, a young Easterner, who has just made a big strike, and they are instantly attracted to one another. Swan suddenly sees her life at the Bella Donna as hideous. One night, Jim wanders into the Bella Donna, and, disillusioned at discovering Swan's identity, he recklessly gambles and loses everything.

When violence breaks loose, following the death of Ferguson's partner, who tried to avenge his friend's murder, and the killing of Cobb who printed an expose of Chamalis and his crooked dealings, the community forms a vigilante committee to clean up Frisco and close down Chamalis.

Chamalis meanwhile learns that Swan let Jim win back his money at the Bella Donna, and vows to kill the young miner. Keeping just ahead of the gambling king, Jim and Swan declare their mutual love and escape together in the fog, hoping to reach the *Flying Cloud*, laying at anchor in the bay.

When Jim is shot by one of Chamalis's cronies, Swan promises to go back with Chamalis if he will let Jim go. Chamalis knows he is beaten and decides to let the two go off together. Turning, he finds himself facing the vigilantes with drawn guns. He walks off to meet his fate while Swan races to the ship—and Jim.

Reviews

Andre Sennwald, *The New York Times*, October 14, 1935

"Edward G. Robinson is an effective Chamalis although the gangster pictures have made his snarl overly familiar."

Kate Cameron, *Daily News*, October 14, 1935

"In Chamalis, Edward G. Robinson has again found a character that suits him from the top of his black thatch to his laquered toes. He hasn't been able to get his teeth into such a juicy role

With (from left) Leo Wills, EGR, Bob Wilbur (?)
Jimmie Dime (?), Harry Tenbrook and Ed Gargan
in Barbary Coast.

since his appearance on the screen in *Little Caesar*, and he gives us this Barbary Coast dictator with a relish."

Richard Watts Jr., *New York Herald-Tribune*, October 14, 1935

"Mr. Robinson is a Little Caesar of the middle nineteenth century as the criminal boss of the town."

Regina Crewe, *New York American*, October 14, 1935

"A gaudy, gripping melodrama of guns and gold . . . made colorful by the histrionics of Edward G. Robinson, played against a background of San Francisco's rough and tumble glitter in the days of Forty-Nine. It's a thoroughly satisfying entertainment and you'd better mark it 'must.' . . . Ed-

ward G. Robinson dominates every instant of the drama with a superlative conception of the sinister spoilsman . . . and he manages, with ineffable artistry, to be so appealing a rogue that one regrets to see his final desserts meted out with such inexorable justice."

New York Sun, October 14, 1935

"Not since his memorable performance in *Little Caesar* . . . has Mr. Robinson been as convincingly tough."

BULLETS OR BALLOTS (First National, 1936) 81 M.

Associate producer, Louis F. Edelman; director, William Keighley; story, Martin Mooney and Seton I. Miller; screenplay, Miller; assistant director, Chuck Hansen; art director, Carl Jules Weyl; special effects, Fred Jackman Jr. and Warren E. Lynch; sound, Oliver S. Garretson; music, Heinz Roemheld; camera, Hal Mohr; editor, Jack Killifer.

JOHNNY BLAKE	Edward G. Robinson
LEE MORGAN	Joan Blondell
AL KRUGER	Barton MacLane
NICK "BUGS" FENNER	Humphrey Bogart
HERMAN	Frank McHugh
CAPTAIN DAN McLAREN	Joseph King
ED DRISCOLL	Richard Purcell
WIRES	George E. Stone
NELLIE LaFLEUR	Louise Beavers
GRAND JURY SPOKESMAN	Joseph Crehan
BRYANT	Henry O'Neill
THORNDYKE	Gilbert Emery
HOLLISTER	Henry Kolker
CALDWELL	Herbert Rawlinson
SPECIALTY	Rosalind Marquis
VINCI	Norman Willis
GATLEY	Frank Faylen
OLD LADY	Alice Lyndon
TICKET SELLER	Victoria Vinton
ANNOUNCER'S VOICE	Addison Richards
SECOND KID	Harry Watson
THIRD KID	Jerry Madden
FIRST MAN	Herman Marks
SECOND MAN	Benny, The Gouge
PROPRIETOR	Ray Brown
FIRST MAN	Al Hill
SECOND MAN	Dutch Schlickenmeyer
TRUCK DRIVER	Eddie Shubert
FIRST MAN	George Lloyd
SECOND MAN	Jack Gardner
THIRD MAN	Saul Gross
ACTOR IMPERSONATING KRUGER	Max Wagner
JUDGE	Ed Stanley
JURY FOREMAN	Milton Kibbee
CRAIL	William Pawley
CIGAR CLERK	Jack Goodrich
FIRST BEAUTY ATTENDANT	Alma Lloyd
KELLY	Ralph M. Remley
BANK SECRETARIES	Anne Nagel
	Gordon (Bill) Elliott
KRUGER'S SECRETARY	Carlyle Moore Jr.
MARY	Virginia Dabney

Synopsis

Political pressure has forced Johnny Blake, former detective and head of New York's famous strong-arm squad, to be transferred to a patrolman beat in the Bronx. Resigned to his fate, he marks time until his friend Captain Dan McLaren is made police commissioner.

When McLaren is at last promoted, Blake goes to him expecting to be reinstated. Instead, McLaren discharges him. Later, when the two meet, Blake knocks the police commissioner down.

This act convinces Al Kruger, the city's rackets boss, that McLaren and Blake are through, and he hires Blake to show him how to defeat the law. "Bugs" Fenner, one of the gang, refuses to accept Blake as an ally, suspecting him of being a police undercover agent.

When Blake slugs another cop and is jailed, McLaren comes to see him. It is revealed that Blake really is working for the police.

Fenner becomes suspicious of Kruger and kills him. Blake takes over the numbers game for the syndicate and undercuts Kruger's girl friend, Lee Morgan, who has been operating the rackets in Harlem. With Kruger gone, the big bosses send for Blake and promote him, giving him Kruger's job.

With Frank McHugh in Bullets or Ballots.

Having learned the identities of the men behind the rackets, Blake sets up a police raid on the gang's headquarters. Meanwhile, Fenner learns positively that Blake is working for the police and forces Lee to lead him to Blake's apartment. In a shootout there, Fenner is killed, and Blake mortally wounded. Lee, learning the truth, comes to Blake's rescue and finds him staggering on the sidewalk, satchel in hand. She drives him to the gang leaders' office and there, when Blake enters through a series of doors—which are opened only for him—the police rush in and arrest the criminals. Blake dies in Lee's arms.

Reviews

Frank Nugent, *The New York Times*, May 27, 1936

"The Brothers Warner who have been making

With Joan Blondell in **Bullets or Ballots.**

crime pay (cinematically, of course) ever since they produced *Little Caesar* have turned out another crackling underworld melodrama in *Bullets or Ballots* . . . [with] a crisp, cohesive and fast-moving script which has been capitally served by such Warner crime experts as Edward G. Robinson, Humphrey Bogart, Barton MacLane and Joan Blondell. Although Mr. Robinson's detective, Johnny Blake, figures in some wild-eyed melodrama as the film races along, the character at least has been taken from life. . . . It is a top-notch performance, his best in fact since *Little Caesar.*"

Howard Barnes, *New York Herald-Tribune,* May 27, 1936

"With Edward G. Robinson in an engagingly tough and slugging role, a proficient supporting cast and crafty direction, it is a taut and compelling melodrama. . . . [He] gives a powerful and persuasive performance that dominates the show. As a demoted detective who is asked by a crusading commissioner to join the gangsters and then double-cross them, he has ample opportunities to be menacing."

Douglas Gilbert, *New York World-Telegram,* May 27, 1936

"The role of Johnny Blake . . . is a natural for Edward G. Robinson, and it is a tribute to [his] art that he tosses his studio differences into the ashcan and throws himself wholeheartedly into the part for a performance unequalled since his Little Caesar."

New York American, May 27, 1936

"Mr. Robinson emerges from milquetoast roles
to bring all the forcefulness, the dynamic power of
his vivid histrionicism to bear in a piercing, pungent portrait such as only he can conceive and
execute. . . . He dominates the drama with the
sheer strength of his characterization. Never for
an instant does he lose control. He knows his man
and limns him in clear, incisive colors. The character has its shades and moods and vagaries. Mr.
Robinson registers each with keen, accurate artistry of a super-craftsman in the theatre."

Variety, June 3, 1936

"Edward G. Robinson bows out of his Warner
contract in this picture by one of his most virile
he-man characterizations . . . a tough but honest
dick."

KID GALAHAD (Warner Bros., 1937) 101 M.

Associate producer, Samuel Bischoff; director, Michael
Curtiz; based on the novel by Francis Wallace; screenplay,
Seton I. Miller; assistant director, Jack Sullivan; special
effects, James Gibbons and Edwin B. DuPar; music, Heinz
Roemheld and Max Steiner; art director, Carl Jules Weyl;
sound, Charles Lang; camera, Tony Gaudio; editor, George
Amy.

NICK DONATI	Edward G. Robinson
LOUISE (FLUFF) PHILLIPS	Bette Davis
TURKEY MORGAN	Humphrey Bogart
KID WARD GUISENBERRY	Wayne Morris
MARIE DONATI	Jane Bryan
SILVER JACKSON	Harry Carey
CHUCK McGRAW	William Haade
MRS. DONATI	Soledad Jiminez
JOE TAYLOR	Joe Cunningham
BUZZ STEVENS	Ben Welden
EDITOR BRADY	Joseph Crehan
REDHEAD AT PARTY	Veda Ann Borg
BARNEY	Frank Faylen
GUNMAN	Harland Tucker
SAM McGRAW	Bob Evans
JIM BURKE	Hank Hankinson
TIM O'BRIEN	Bob Nestell
DENBAUGH	Jack Kranz
REFEREE	George Blake
SECOND	Charlie Sullivan
GIRL ON PHONE	Joyce Compton
LOUIE (PIANIST)	Eddie Foster
BARBER	George Humbert
RING ANNOUNCER	Emmett Vogan
RINGSIDER	Stan Jolley
REPORTERS AT PRESS CONFERENCE	
	Harry Harvey

	Horace MacMahon
	John Shelton
REPORTERS	Don Brodie
	Milton Kibbee
REPORTER AT DINNER	Ralph Dunn
TITLE FIGHT ANNOUNCER	Eddie Chandler
TIME KEEPER	Lane Chandler
RINGSIDER	Don DeFoe (DeFore)

Synopsis

Nick Donati, a prizefight manager, has just lost

*With Wayne Morris, Harry Carey, Bette Davis and
Jane Bryan in* Kid Galahad.

his best boy—and most of his money—on a bout in
which his fighter has sold out to Nick's crooked
rival, Turkey Morgan. With the remainder of his
bankroll, Nick throws a big party in his hotel
suite, with his girlfriend Fluff acting as hostess.
Helping to serve drinks at the party is bellhop
Ward Guisenberry. When Ward knocks down
Chuck McGraw, Turkey Morgan's star attraction,
who has insulted Fluff, Nick realizes that with
proper grooming he might have a new champ on
his hands. Fluff dubs him Kid Galahad for his
gallant behavior. With Fluff and trainer Silver
Jackson, Nick takes Ward out to his country place,
where the young potential fighter meets and falls
in love with Nick's sister Marie.

The bellhop's first big fight is against a tough
brother of McGraw, and Galahad knocks him cold.
Following a barnstorming tour in which he gets
plenty of experience, mostly by knockouts, he is
given a shot at McGraw himself for the championship.

With Bette Davis in **Kid Galahad.**

Nick decides to double-cross his own boy and have him lose to McGraw. He orders Ward to go in and slug with McGraw—which is the worst advice he could give, since McGraw is an exceptional puncher. Nick meanwhile bets his money on McGraw. Morgan, in on the deal, warns Nick that if there is any double-crossing, there will be a killing. As the big fight starts, Ward goes in slugging and takes a bad beating. Marie and Fluff look on in amazement and appeal to Nick to change Ward's style. Nick yields to their pleas and tells Ward to box and not to slug. In the eleventh round, he nails McGraw and knocks him out.

Back in the dressing room, Morgan storms in and begans shooting. He himself is killed while mortally wounding Nick. As Nick dies, he gives Ward his blessing to marry Marie, and boasts to Fluff that he has developed a champ.

Reviews

Frank Nugent, *The New York Times,* May 27, 1937

"Assisted no little by the comforting presence of Edward G. Robinson, Bette Davis and Harry Carey in his corner, young Wayne Morris, the Warners' latest astronomical discovery, comes through with a natural and easy performance."

Howard Barnes, *New York Herald-Tribune,* May 27, 1937

"The stars of the photoplay are Edward G. Robinson and Bette Davis, and they contribute steady impersonations that add immeasurably to its power. The power is at his nervous best in the part of a manager who grooms a nobody for the world's championship but turns on the boy when the latter falls in love with his sister."

Rose Pelswick, *New York Journal-American*, May 27, 1937

"Robinson has here his best role since the Little Caesar days, that of Nick Donati, a racketeering fight promoter who insists upon being the brains of the boy he handles."

THE LAST GANGSTER (MGM, 1937) 81 M.

Director, Edward Ludwig; story, William A. Wellman and Robert Carson; screenplay, John Lee Mahin; art director, Cedric Gibbons, Daniel Cathcart and Edwin Willis; montage effects, Slavks Vorkspick; camera, William Daniels; editor, Ben Lewis.

JOE KROZAC	Edward G. Robinson
PAUL NORTH, SR.	James Stewart
TALYA KROZAC	Rose Stradner
CURLY	Lionel Stander
PAUL NORTH, JR.	Douglas Scott
CASPER	John Carradine
SAN FRANCISCO EDITOR	Sidney Blackmer
FATS GARVEY	Edward Brophy
FRANKIE "ACEY" KILE	Alan Baxter
WARDEN	Grant Mitchell
SID GORMAN	Frank Conroy
SHEA	Moroni Olson
WILSON	Ivan Miller
BRODERICK	Willard Robertson
GLORIA	Louise Beavers
BILLY ERNST	Donald Barry
BOTTLES BAILEY	Ben Welden
LIMPY	Horace MacMahon
BROCKETT	Edward Bowley
RED	John Kelly
BOYS	David Leo Tillotson
	Jim Kehner
	Billy Smith
	Reggie Streeter
BOY	Dick Holland

With Rose Stradner and Lionel Stander in **The Last Gangster.**

With (from left) Victor Adams, Edward Pawley, George Magrill, Jerry Jerome, Horace MacMahon and Lionel Stander in The Last Gangster.

With Alan Baxter, Moroni Olsen and Lionel Stander in The Last Gangster.

With Douglas Scott and Lionel Stander in The Last Gangster.

EDITOR .... Pierre Watkin
REPORTER .... Douglas McPhail
EDITOR .... Cy Kendall
REPORTER .... Ernest Wood
FIRST REPORTER .... Phillip Terry
OFFICE BOY .... William Benedict
BOSTON EDITOR .... Frederick Burton
TRAIN GUARD .... Lee Phelps
JO KROZAC .... Larry Simms
TURNKEY .... Wade Boteler
MIKE KILE .... Walter Miller

Synopsis

Returning from Europe with his young bride Talya, aging American gangster Joe Krozac finds that rival gangs have usurped much of his territory while he was away. Quickly assuming charge again, he orders the most troublesome of his competitors rubbed out, but one of them survives and leads the police to him. Joe goes to prison, telling his wife who has just given birth to a son, that he is innocent. She believes him, but her periodic visits to the prison eventually show her the true incorrigible nature of Joe.

In San Francisco, where the newspapers try to crucify Talya and her child, reporter Paul North is fired for writing articles sympathetic to the pair. He and Talya become quite close and he finally persuades her to divorce Joe. Shortly thereafter, they are married and move to Massachusetts where he becomes a prosperous newspaper editor. He adopts Talya's child.

Ten years later, Joe gets out of prison and begins tracking down Talya for deserting him and taking their son. One of Joe's old henchman, Curley, persuades him to come East and again head the old gang. When he arrives the guys beat him up, attempting to find out where he had hidden the gang's cache of money. When Curley has Joe's boy kidnapped and threatens to torture the kid, Joe discloses where the money is hidden. The gang then rushes out to retrieve the money while Joe escapes with his son, but during their flight Joe becomes enraged when the boy refuses to acknowledge him as his father.

The boy takes Joe to his house where the old man intends to kill Talya and her new husband, Paul North. Once there, however, Joe sees that the boy has a good home and life, and he changes his mind.

Joe is soon shot by Acey Kile, an old racketeer rival he once had tried to kill, and he dies holding a merit badge his son had won in school.

Reviews

Frank Nugent, *The New York Times*, December 10, 1937

"Had Warners been doing it, it would have read: 'Mr. Edward G. Robinson in "The Life of The Last Gangster." ' . . . Mr. Robinson's crime lord is a natural family man with a warped desire to create a Public Enemy No. One, Jr. [His] snarls and menace and brooding hate eminently qualify him to be not only 'The Last' but the very first gangster of filmdom. Mr. Robinson, in brief, is the gang cycle by himself. We refuse to believe that *The Last Gangster* is really his epitaph. . . . [He] plays it with an assurance born of long practice."

Howard Barnes, *New York Herald-Tribune*, December 10, 1937

"It is eminently fitting that Edward G. Robinson should be the hero of what we fervently hope is the last Hollywood gangster film, *The Last Gangster*. A lot of water has flowed under the bridge since *Little Caesar* but Mr. Robinson has breasted the tides to make his impersonation of a 1937 thug as persuasive as was his portrait of a killer in that earlier classic of rats and rackets. In the new offering, he creates a bitterly effective impersonation of a beaten hoodlum, which should put a definite period after the cycle of public enemy melodramas. Just as in *Little Caesar*, the film pivots surely around [his] performance. Accept his highly psychological projection of Joe Krozak and you'll find *The Last Gangster* a sociological thriller. . . . [He] does a showy job with the role of Krozak, keeping the thug human, recognizable and pathological."

A SLIGHT CASE OF MURDER (Warner Bros., 1938) 85 M.

Producer, Hal B. Wallis; associate producer, Sam Bischoff; director, Lloyd Bacon; based on the play by Damon Runyon and Howard Lindsay; screenplay, Earl Baldwin and Joseph Schrank; music-lyrics, M. K. Jerome and Jack Scholl; art director, Max Parker; camera, Sid Hickox; editor, James Gibbon.

REMY MARCO .... Edward G. Robinson
MARY MARCO .... Jane Bryan
DICK WHITEWOOD .... Willard Parker
MORA MARCO .... Ruth Donnelly
MIKE .... Allen Jenkins
POST .... John Litel

Lobby Card for A Slight Case of Murder.

RITTER .... Eric Stanley
GIUSSEPPE .... Harold Huber
LEFTY .... Edward Brophy
MR. WHITEWOOD .... Paul Harvey
DOUGLAS FAIRBANKS ROSENBLOOM ....
.... Bobby Jordan
INNOCENCE .... Joseph Downing
MRS. CAGLE .... Margaret Hamilton
EX. JOCKEY KIRK .... George E. Stone
SAD SAM .... Bert Hamilton
REMY'S SECRETARY .... Jean Benedict
THE SINGER .... Harry Seymour
LORETTA .... Betty Compson
NO NOSE COHEN .... Joe Caites
LITTLE BUTCH .... George Lloyd
BLACKHEAD GALLAGHER .... John Harmon
A STRANGER .... Harry Tenbrook
CHAMP .... Duke York
CHAMP'S MANAGER .... Pat Daly
RADIO COMMENTATOR .... John Hiestand
SPEAKEASY PROPRIETOR .... Bert Roach
PESSIMISTIC PATRON .... Harry Cody
FIRST POLICEMAN .... Ben Hendricks

With Willard Parker and Jane Bryan in A Slight
Case of Murder.

SECOND POLICEMAN .... Ralph Dunn
THIRD POLICEMAN .... Wade Boteler
NURSES .... Myrtle Stedman
                                      Lola Cheeney

Synopsis

Beer Baron Remy Marco informs his mob that he is going legitimate when the repeal of Prohibition knocks the bottom out of his bootlegging business. No more police blotter stuff; from now on, it is the Social Register. Marco is a right guy, for a beer runner, but his beer tastes terrible. He has never tasted his own brew, so he does not know how really bad it is, but the public cannot stomach his product and Marco's millions dwindle.

Meanwhile, Marco's daughter Mary falls for a rich man's son, but she refuses to marry him until he gets a job. The best he can do is to become a motorcycle cop. When an ambush, intended for Marco in his own home, backfires the hoods end up shooting each other. Marco returns to his home to find four dead gangsters and their $500,000 racetrack haul. Mary's young cop also arrives on the scene and shoots the dead gangsters all over again, accidentally killing another hood.

In the heat of the excitement, Marco gets a taste of his own beer. He gives the public a new deal, saves his business, and loses his daughter to a cop.

Reviews

Frank Nugent, *The New York Times*, February 28, 1938

"We haven't laughed so much since Remy Marco's Mike found four parties shot to death in the back bedroom of the Saratoga house his boss had rented for the season. . . . For a Runyonesque panel, the casting director had the marvelous good fortune to find Edward G. Robinson and Ruth Donnelly to play Mr. and Mrs. Marco; Bobby Jordan to be the problem child, Douglas Fairbanks Rosenbloom; (etc.) ."

Howard Barnes, *New York Herald-Tribune*, February 28, 1938

"One of the funniest and most satisfying farces which has come out of Hollywood in some time. For Mr. Robinson, the show is a major dispensation. After *The Last Gangster*, it was fairly obvious that straight variations on the Little Caesar role had been exhausted. *A Slight Case of Murder* gives him a burlesque underworld big-shot to portray and he handles the assignment with comical efficiency. As a prohibition needled-beer baron who turns square but forgets to stop needling his beer,

he realizes a nice blend of ruthlessness and clowning. . . . Little Caesar has died hard but his passing shouldn't grieve Mr. Robinson unduly if he can get more scripts like this one."

THE AMAZING DR. CLITTERHOUSE (Warner Bros., 1938) 87 M.

Associate producer, Robert Lord; director, Anatole Litvak; based on the play by Barre Lyndon; screenplay, John Wexley and John Huston; assistant director, Jack Sullivan; art director, Carl Jules Weyl; sound, C. A. Riggs; music, Max Steiner; camera, Tony Gaudio; editor, Warren Low.

DR. CLITTERHOUSE	Edward G. Robinson
JO KELLER	Claire Trevor
ROCKS VALENTINE	Humphrey Bogart
NURSE RANDOLPH	Gale Page

With Gale Page and director Anatole Litvak on set of The Amazing Dr. Clitterhouse.

INSPECTOR LANE	Donald Crisp
OKAY	Allen Jenkins
GRANT	Thurston Hall
PROSECUTING ATTORNEY	John Litel
JUDGE	Henry O'Neill
BUTCH	Maxie Rosenbloom
RABBIT	Curt Bois
PAL	Bert Hanlon
TUG	Ward Bond
POPUS	Vladimir Sokoloff
CANDY	Billy Wayne
LIEUT. JOHNSON	Robert Homans
BIT GUESTS	William Worthington
	Ed Mortimer
WATCHMAN	William Haade
CONNORS	Thomas Jackson
SERGEANT	Edward Gargan

With Gale Page in **The Amazing Dr. Clitterhouse.**

BIT POLICEMEN .... Ray Dawe
                                           Bob Reeves
MRS. GANSWOORT .... Winifred Harris
DR. AMES .... Eric Stanley
NURSE DONOR .... Lois Cheaney
CAPT. MacLEVY .... Wade Boteler
BIT GUEST .... Larry Steers
MRS. JEFFERSON .... Libby Taylor
PATROLMAN .... Edgar Dearing
CHEMIST .... Sidney Bracy
FOREMAN OF JURY .... Irving Bacon
WOMAN JUROR .... Vera Lewis
BAILIFF .... Bruce Mitchell

Synopsis

In order to complete his studies of the mentality and interactions of the criminal mind, Dr. Clitterhouse, the prominent psychologist, decides to be-come a professional criminal to obtain first hand information. Soon he is a successful jewel thief, and, through Jo Keller, a lady fence, he becomes involved with Rocks Valentine's safe-cracking gang. All the while, he is making meticulous notes for his psychological study. Rocks resents Clitterhouse's attempts to take over the leadership of the mob from him, as well as Jo's wavering affections, since Rocks himself is in love with her. During a fur warehouse heist, Dr. Clitterhouse is locked in a storage vault by Rocks, but is freed by Jo's friend Butch.

His researching virtually completed, Clitterhouse plans one last great job. He is determined to leave the gang because Jo is falling in love with him, and he fears he is beginning to like criminal life.

When Rocks demands that the doctor stay on with the gang, Clitterhouse realizes that the one facet of criminal mentality he has not researched is the act of murder. He poisons Rocks with paradictinol chloride, and studies his reactions as the gang leader dies.

Inspector Lane and the police close in on the gang, and Clitterhouse is put on trial. Pleading insanity as his defense, he is acquitted by the jury, which was convinced that any man doing so, and then insisting he was sane during the crimes, must be insane.

Reviews

Frank Nugent, *The New York Times,* July 21, 1938

"As a primary fault in an otherwise smooth and satisfying melodrama, we have Edward G. Robinson being *The Amazing Dr. Clitterhouse.* Mr. Robinson plays him well enough, but hardly as effective as Cedric Hardwicke did in the play. . . . Little Caesar keeps coming through the dignified veneer. It is easier to think of him as a criminal masquerading as a physician than as a medico fronting as a gang lord . . . he never quite succeeds in shaking the role free from the shadowy public enemies, numbers one to ten, which have been the larger part of his past."

Howard Barnes, *New York Herald-Tribune,* July 21, 1938

"A deft and amusing job of screen transcription has been done with *The Amazing Dr. Clitterhouse.* . . . Edward G. Robinson would not have been my choice for the Clitterhouse role, but he performs the assignment capably. Perhaps it is because he has been so clearly identified with gangster roles that he has trouble in underlining the Jekyll and Hyde quality which Cedric Hardwicke accomplished so suavely in the drama. In any case, he never fails to give the picture dramatic punch when it requires it, whether he is calmly stealing or murdering, or testing the reflexes of his henchmen in the very act of lawbreaking."

I AM THE LAW (Columbia, 1938) 83 M.

Producer, Everett Riskin; director, Alexander Hall; based on magazine articles by Fred Allhoff; screenplay, Jo Swerl-ing; music director, Morris Stoloff; camera, Henry Freelich; editor, Viola Lawrence.

JOHN LINDSAY	Edward G. Robinson
JERRY LINDSAY	Barbara O'Neil
PAUL FERGUSON	John Beal
FRANKIE BALLOU	Wendy Barrie
EUGENE FERGUSON	Otto Kruger
TOM ROSS	Arthur Loft
EDDIE GIRARD	Marc Lawrence
BERRY	Douglas Wood
MOSS KITCHELL	Robert Middlemass
INSPECTOR GLEASON	Ivan Miller
LEANDER	Charles Halton
J. W. BUTLER	Louis Jean Heydt
BROPHY	Emory Parnell
CRONIN	Joseph Downing
MARTIN	Theodore Von Eltz
PRISONER	Horace McMahon
GOVERNOR	Frederick Burton
ROBERTS	Lucien Littlefield
WITNESSES	Ed Keane
	Robert Cummings Sr.
	Harvey Clark
	James Flavin
MRS. BUTLER	Fay Helm
STUDENTS	Kane Richmond
	James Bush
	Anthony Nace
PROFESSOR PERKINS	Walter Soderling
GRADUATE LAW STUDENTS	Scott Colton
	(Steve) Gaylord Pendleton
WITNESS	Harry Bradley
AUSTIN	Ed Fetherston
BARTENDER	Bud Jamison
GIRARD'S GIRL	Iris Meredith
STUDENT	Robert McWade Jr.
POLICE SERGEANT	Lee Shumway
SECRETARY	Bess Flowers
POLICEMEN	Bud Wiser
	Lane Chandler
PHOTOGRAPHERS	Reginald Simpson
	Cyril Ring

Synopsis

At the request of prominent civic leader Eugene Ferguson, law professor John Lindsay becomes a special prosecutor in order to clean out the racketeers dominating his city. He chooses as his aide Ferguson's son Paul, one of his former students.

Newspaper columnist Frankie Ballou, draws Lindsay's attention to an underworld character who is promptly gunned down shortly after promising to tell what he knows about the rackets. Suspicious of Frankie, Lindsay does some investigating and learns that despite her denials she knows Eugene Ferguson—in fact she is actually his assistant.

Lindsay's wife, Jerry, meanwhile, persuades an

*With James Millican, John Beal and Barbara O'Neil
in* **I Am the Law.**

extortion victim to testify with a promise of special protection from the prosecutor, but before he
can talk, the man is killed by Eddie Girard, a
Ferguson gunman. Lindsay suspects a leak in his
own office and fires his entire staff, recruiting a
new one from among his former students.

During the next six months two more murders
are committed, and with apparently nothing being
accomplished, the D.A. fires Lindsay. Determined
to continue his investigations as a private citizen,
Lindsay and his men move their files into his home
and work with funds borrowed from loan sharks.
In this way, Lindsay and his team uncover another
racket with the trail leading them closer to Eugene
Ferguson, although Paul is still unaware of it.
Lindsay pits rival gangs against each other by
means of his tapped telephone, and Eddie Girard
is murdered. Another of Ferguson's men tells Paul
of his father's complicity in the racket and is him-

self murdered. Lindsay stops Paul from exposing
his father until there is sufficient concrete evidence.

Ready at last to blow the rackets apart, Lindsay,
with a picked force of policemen, herds all the
criminal elements in the city into a circus tent
where they are shown actual films of an electrocution. Then Ferguson is shown a special reel where
he is conferring with known criminals. Frankie
Ballou is also shown a filmed record of a murder
she had committed. Frankie confesses and Ferguson signs a will leaving his fortune to the perpetuation of crime control. He then borrows Lindsay's
car—knowing full well that one of his henchmen
had previously affixed a bomb to the starter.

Reviews

Bosley Crowther, *The New York Times,* August
26, 1938

"It isn't so much that we feel Mr. Robinson is limited in his screen roles since the night he died, clutching dramatically at his throat, behind a billboard in Chicago; it's just that he strains the imagination a little trying to play both ends of the criminological scale, so to speak, against—or let us say, for the amusement of—the middle. . . . The fact that [he] seems slightly miscast, however, is no reflection on *I Am the Law*, which is still the liveliest melodrama in town."

Howard Barnes, *New York Herald-Tribune*, August 26, 1938

"That the motion picture pays more attention to a racket-buster than racket busting is obviously due to the fact that this particular crusading prosecutor is none other than Edward G. Robinson. It seems evident that he is determined to make film-goers forget that he was once the archtype of the genius gangster. Here he plays a law professor who bucks crooked politics and a blonde gun moll as well as menacing racketeers. It is my hunch, though, that he is still not at home in heroic roles. In *I Am the Law*, he is at his best when he is mussing up three thugs to show his staff how yellow they really are. He delivers a number of speeches about law and order crisply if not very convincingly, dances the 'Big Apple' to lead on the blondes, and acts extremely executive. It's still hard for me to keep in mind that he is a cleaner-upper rather than Little Caesar."

CONFESSIONS OF A NAZI SPY (Warner Bros., 1939) 102 M.

Director, Anatole Litvak; based on the book *The Nazi Spy Conspiracy in America* by Leon G. Turrou; screen-

With Kane Richmond (3rd left) and Gaylord (Steve) Pendleton in I Am the Law.

play, Milton Krims and John Wexley; camera, Sol Polito; editor, Owen Marks.

ED RENARD	Edward G. Robinson
SCHNEIDER	Francis Lederer
SCHLANGER	George Sanders
DR. KASSEL	Paul Lukas
D. A. KELLOGG	Henry O'Neill
ERIKA WOLFF	Lya Lys
MRS. SCHNEIDER	Grace Stafford

In Confessions of a Nazi Spy.

SCOTLAND YARD MAN	James Stephenson
KROGMAN	Sig Rumann
PHILLIPS	Fred Tozere
HILDA	Dorothy Tree
MRS. KASSEL	Celia Sibelius
RENZ	Joe Sawyer
HINTZE	Lionel Royce
WILDEBRANDT	Hans Von Twardowsky
HELLDORF	Henry Victor
CAPTAIN RICHTER	Frederick Vogeding
KLAUBER	George Rosener
STRAUBEL	Robert Davis
WESTPHAL	John Voigt
GRUETZWALD	Willy Kaufman
CAPT. VON EICHEN	William Vaughn (Von Brincken)
McDONALD	Jack Mower
HARRISON	Robert Emmett Keane
MRS. MacLAUGHLIN	Eily Malyon
STAUNTON	Frank Mayo
POSTMAN	Alec Craig
KASSEL'S NURSE	Jean Brooks
KRANZ	Lucien Prival
U. S. DISTRICT COURT JUDGE	Frederick Burton
AMERICAN LEGIONAIRE	Ward Bond
U. S. INTELLIGENCE	Charles Trowbridge
ARMY HOSPITAL CLERK	John Ridgely
HOTEL CLERK	Emmett Vogan
FBI MAN	Edward Keane
GOEBBELS	Martin Kosleck
CUSTOMS OFFICIAL	Selmer Jackson

NAZI AGENT	Egon Brecher
NARRATOR	John Deering

Synopsis

In a small Scottish town, a secretive woman resident has been receiving a flow of mail from all over the world. A local philatelist asks her for the foreign stamps on the envelopes she receives, but she vehemently refuses. Her peculiar reaction causes him to alert Scotland Yard, and British Intelligence learns that she is part of a Nazi spy network. Intercepting a letter sent from Schneider in America detailing plans to kidnap an American air force general, the U.S. government is alerted and Ed Renard, a G-Man, is called into the case to investigate Nazi activities in America.

Schneider, the prime link in the case, is a German-American with strong Nazi sympathies who had been recruited to obtain Allied government military secrets. Apprehended and interrogated by Renard, he is persuaded to divulge the name of the Nazi spy ring leaders in the United States. Among them: Erika Wolff, posing as a German hair dresser aboard a trans-Atlantic liner; Dr. Kassell, head of the local bund in the New York area; Schlanger, the liaison officer in German Intelligence; and Hilda, Erika's American-based accomplice.

Through painstaking investigation, virtually throughout the western world, and with the co-operation of various international police agencies,

With Francis Lederer in Confessions of a Nazi Spy.

the spy network is closed down after the various contacts are picked up in the United States, South America and Europe.

Reviews

Frank Nugent, *The New York Times*, April 29, 1939

"As melodrama, the film isn't bad at all. Anatole Litvak has paced it well, and key performances of Edward (G-man) Robinson as the Federal Man, Mr. Lederer as the weak link in the Nazi spy network, and Mr. Lukas as the propaganda agent are thoroughly satisfactory."

Howard Barnes, *New York Herald-Tribune*, April 29, 1939

"Edward G. Robinson is eloquently persuasive as the investigator of spy ring doings."

New York Journal-American, April 29, 1939

"It is one of Robinson's finest roles, one which he plays with neither bluster nor ranting heroics, but with a quiet and authoritative conviction."

BLACKMAIL (MGM, 1939) 81 M.

Producer, John Considine Jr.; director, H. C. Potter; based on the story by Endre Bohem and Dorothy Yost; screenplay, David Hertz and William Ludwig; camera, Clyde De Vinna; editor, Howard O'Neill.

JOHN INGRAM .... Edward G. Robinson
HELEN INGRAM .... Ruth Hussey
WILLIAM RAMEY .... Gene Lockhart
HANK INGRAM .... Bobs Watson
MOOSE McCARTHY .... Guinn Williams

With (from left) Arthur Hohl, John Wray, Blackie Whiteford and Ed Brady in Blackmail.

With Ruth Hussey, Harry Strang and James C. Morton in **Blackmail.**

DIGGS	John Wray
RAWLINS	Arthur Hohl
SARAH	Esther Dale
ANDERSON	Joe Whitehead
BLAINE	Joseph Crehan
WARDEN MILLER	Victor Kilian
KEARNEY	Gil Perkins
1st WORKMAN	Mitchell Lewis
2nd WORKMAN	Ted Oliver
3rd WORKMAN	Lew Harvey
SUNNY	Willie Best
DRIVER	Art Miles
DESK SERGEANT	Robert Middlemass
WEBER	Ian Miller
DESK CLERK	Hal K. Dawson
LOCAL TROOPER	Philip Morris
1st DEPUTY	Charles Middleton
3rd DEPUTY	Trevor Bardette
COLORED PRISONER	Everett Brown
JUAN	Ed Montoya
PEDRO	Joe Dominguez

With Ruth Hussey and "Bobs" Watson in **Blackmail.**

With Gene Lockhart and Guinn Williams in **Blackmail.**

BOSS BROWN	Eddy Chandler
GUARD	Lee Phelps
SHERIFF	Cy Kendall
POLICE SERGEANT	Wade Boteler
OIL WORKER	Harry Fleischmann

Synopsis

In prison for a crime he did not commit, John Harrington escapes and assumes the identity of John Ingram, building a lucrative, if dangerous, business of putting out oil fires. Helen, his wife, knows of his past, but furthers his ambitions and bears him a son, Hank.

A newsreel photograph reveals Ingram's identity to William Ramey, the real criminal for whom Ingram was serving time. Down on his luck, Ramey offers to clear John for $25,000, to be used supposedly to purchase a farm in Maine. Ingram gives Ramey part of the money in cash and signs a note for the balance. However, Ramey destroys the confession and turns Ingram over to the police. Ingram is sent back to prison and Ramey escapes with a mortgage on Ingram's oil property.

Having promised his wife that he will serve his term and then return to her clean-handed, Ingram is driven to desperation when he learns that because Ramey holds his note, Helen and his son Hank have been forced out of their home and that his business is being ruined.

With the aid of Moose McCarthy, his former helper, Ingram eventually escapes again. When Ramey reads of the escape he skips town and tries to negotiate the sale of a rich oil well which has come in on Ingram's former property.

Ingram now conceives the idea of firing Ramey's well to bring the culprit back. Then he finds his wife in the cheap suburb to which she has been forced to move. To Helen, though, Ingram is now a fugitive who has done the one unforgivable thing. Ramey arrives by plane from New York to find Moose and his crew unsuccessful at extinguishing the blazing well. Ingram manages to get Ramey onto the field near the well, and extracts from him a confession which Moose and the men overhear. Helen and Ingram are reconciled—and Ingram blasts the well and saves his property.

Reviews

Bosley Crowther, *The New York Times*, September 15, 1939

"In his day, Edward G. Robinson has been one of the screen's greatest criminals. There was a time in fact, during the height of the vogue, when he was said to be widely imitated in the underworld. What a sad thing it is, then, to see this distinguished inhabitant of the Rogues' Gallery, this Napoleon of crime, this indominably amoral spirit who belongs with the Borgias, feebly trying to go straight in *Blackmail*."

Robert W. Dana, *New York Herald-Tribune*, September 15, 1939

"The greater part of the film paints the villainy and inhuman treatment that exists in chain-gangs. It is not a pretty picture: it becomes a fairly real one, though, as Mr. Robinson and his unfortunate comrades conduct it, but even with an exciting escape and the ultimate atonement of justice, *Blackmail* proves little more than the fact that Mr. Robinson is a sturdy villain."

DR. EHRLICH'S MAGIC BULLET (Warner Bros., 1940) 103 M.

Producer, Jack L. Warner and Hal B. Wallis; associate producer, Wolfgang Reinhardt; Director, William Dieterle; story, Norman Burnside; screenplay, John Huston, Heinz Herald and Burnside; music, Max Steiner; art director, Carl Jules Weyl; sound, Robert E. Lee; camera, James Wong Howe; editor, Warren Low; special microscopic effects, Robert Burks.

DR. PAUL EHRLICH	Edward G. Robinson
HEIDI EHRLICH	Ruth Gordon
DR. EMIL VON BEHRING	Otto Kruger
MINISTER ALTHOFF	Donald Crisp
DR. HANS WOLFERT	Sig Rumann
FRANZISKA SPEVER	Maria Ouspenskaya
DR. LANTZ	Henry O'Neill
DR. MORGENROTH	Edward Morris
JUDGE	Harry Davenport
PROFESSOR HARTMAN	Montagu Love
DR. ROBERT KOCH	Albert Basserman
DR. KUNZE	Louis Jean Heydt
MITTELMEYER	Donald Meek
SPEIDLER	Douglas Wood
BECKER	Irving Bacon
SENSENBRENNER	Charles Halton
MISS MARQUARDT	Hermine Sterler
BROCKDORF	Louis Calhern
HIRSCH	John Hamilton
DEFENSE ATTORNEY	Paul Harvey
OLD DOCTOR	Frank Reicher
KADEREIT	Torben Meyer
DR. KRAUS	Theodore Von Eltz
DR. BERTHEIM	Louis Arco
DR. HATA	Wilfred Hari
DR. BUCHER	John Henrick
MARIANNE	Ann Todd
STEFFI	Polly Stewart
HANS WEISGART	Ernst Hausman
MALE NURSE	Stuart Holmes
ARAB MAN	Frank Lackteen
ARAB WOMAN	Elaine Renshaw
ASSISTANT	Herbert Anderson
MARTL	Egon Brecher
KOERNER	Robert Strange
HAUPT	Cliff Clark

Synopsis

Paul Ehrlich does not fit in as a doctor in the staid Berlin Hospital. He breaks the rules by telling patients the truth and spends most of his time working on seemingly dubious experiments.

When Dr. Emil Von Behring, an assistant of the great Robert Koch, sees Ehrlich's experiments, the young doctor is on his way with the backing of Koch. The job which Koch gives Ehrlich as a reward for his development of the chemical staining process at first provides his family security. However, Ehrlich contracts tuberculosis and must go with his wife to Egypt for a rest cure. There he works on the perfection of antitosis.

With a government subsidy, Ehrlich has almost carte blanche to carry on apparently pointless research. Then an impatient government committee, seeing no tangible results to his efforts, cuts off his funds.

Although his children have grown up and he and his wife could survive on his much reduced stipend, his research is too important to be stopped. His wife goes to Frau Ziska Speizer, a philanthropist, who agrees to furnish money to allow Ehrlich to continue his work.

With Ann Todd, Rolla Stewart and Ruth Gordon in
Dr. Ehrlich's Magic Bullet.

With Maria Ouspenskaya in Dr. Ehrlich's Magic
Bullet.

With Otto Kruger in **Dr. Ehrlich's Magic Bullet.**

Finally formula 606 works out in the laboratory as a cure for syphilis. Beseiged with requests Ehrlich is persuaded to release the compound. A few deaths, however, occur among the thousands of cures and Ehrlich must defend himself against the criminal charges. His cause is nearly lost until Dr. Emil Von Behring comes forward to testify, supporting Ehrlich. Ehrlich's works go on. He dies with a final plea for the maintenance of truth and justice.

Reviews

Frank Nugent, *The New York Times*, February 24, 1940

"We have to go . . . [to] *The Story of Louis Pasteur* to match it in its line, combing out new synonyms for 'great' to classify Edward G. Robinson's performance of a famous microbe hunter. . . . There is a perfect delineation of the man by Mr. Robinson. It is a rounded gem of a portraiture, completely free from the devastating self-consciousness that plagues so many actors when they are forced to wear a beard, almost electric in its attractiveness, astonishingly apart from the manneristic screen behavior of *Little Caesar*."

Howard Barnes, *New York Herald-Tribune*, February 24, 1940

"The most dramatic and moving medical film I have ever seen . . . due in no small degree to the brilliant portrayal of Dr. Ehrlich by Edward G. Robinson. Aided by superb make-up, the erstwhile player of gangster roles gives a modulated and understanding performance which is in the first rank of biographical portraits."

Variety, February 7, 1940

"Edward G. Robinson's portrayal of the famed Dr. Ehrlich is one of the most distinguished performances in the star's lengthy screen career."

BROTHER ORCHID (Warner Bros., 1940) 91 M.

Executive producer, Hal B. Wallis; associate producer, Mark Hellinger; director, Lloyd Bacon; story, Richard Connell; screenplay, Earl Baldwin; assistant director, Dick Mayberry; art director, Max Parker; special effects, Byron Haskin and Willard Van Enger; music, Heinz Roemheld; camera, Tony Gaudio; editor, William Holmes.

LITTLE JOHN SARTO	Edward G. Robinson
FLO ADDAMS	Ann Sothern
JACK BUCK	Humphrey Bogart
CLARENCE FLETCHER	Ralph Bellamy
BROTHER SUPERIOR	Donald Crisp
WILLIE (THE KNIFE) CORSON	Allen Jenkins
BROTHER WREN	Charles D. Brown
BROTHER GOODWIN	Cecil Kellaway
BROTHER MacEWEN	Joseph Crehan
BROTHER MacDONALD	Wilfred Lucas
PHILADELPHIA POWELL	Morgan Conway
MUGSY O'DAY	Richard Lane
TEXAS PEARSON	John Ridgely
BUFFALO BURNS	Dick Wessel
CURLEY MATTHEWS	Tom Tyler
FRENCH FRANK	Paul Phillips
AL MULLER	Don Rowan
PATTONSVILLE SUPT.	Granville Bates
FIFI	Nanette Vallon
RED MARTIN	Paul Guilfoyle
TURKEY MALONE	Tim Ryan
HANDSOME HARRY EDWARDS	Joe Caites
DOPEY PERKINS	Pat Gleason
JOSEPH	Tommy Baker
TIM O'HARA	G. Pat Collins
MR. PIGEON	John Qualen
ENGLISHMAN	Leonard Mudie
ENGLISHMAN	Charles Coleman
MEADOWS	Edgar Norton
FRENCHMAN	Jean Del Val
FRENCHMAN	Armand Kaliz
STABLE BOY	Charles de Ravenne
ARTIST	Gino Corrado
WAREHOUSE MANAGER	Paul Porcasi
CASINO ATTENDANT	George Sorel
CABLE OFFICE CLERK	Georges Renavent
1st REPORTER	De Wolfe Hopper
2nd REPORTER	George Haywood
3rd REPORTER	Creighton Hale
MRS. SWEENEY	Mary Gordon
SUPT. OF SERVICE	Frank Faylen
POLICEMAN	Lee Phelps
JANITOR	Sam McDaniel
PARKING ATTENDANT	James Flavin

Synopsis

Deciding to chuck the rackets and seek some cultural refinement, "Little John" Sarto sets up his girlfriend Flo Addams as a hatcheck girl in a local nightclub and sails for Europe.

Several years pass and "Little John," broke comes back to the States. Instead of welcoming him back, the boys, headed by Jack Buck, take him for a ride. Wounded, "Little John" manages to escape and reach a monastery.

At first cynical of the brothers' goodly nature, he thinks the "joint" would make a good hideout. Soon he realizes by the selfless goodness around

With Humphrey Bogart and Paul Guilfoyle in Brother Orchid.

him that life has more to offer than an easy buck. When he begins growing flowers at the monastery, he is named Brother Orchid.

His idyll is temporarily disturbed when the Brothers inform him that they cannot sell their flowers in town at the market because of a gangland protection racket, headed by Jack Buck. Sarto calls upon Flo's rancher fiancee, Clarence Fletcher, and his country friends to break up the racketeer monopoly, and to destroy Buck's gang.

After giving Flo and Clarence his blessings to marry, Brother Orchid returns to the monastery, happy in his new found home, which has true class.

Reviews

Bosley Crowther, *The New York Times*, June 8, 1940

"A funnier piece of hardboiled impudence hasn't been enjoyed hereabouts since Mr. Robinson's Remy Marco found his new house cluttered up with certain parties, not so tastefully composed, in *A Slight Case of Murder.* . . . Obviously, this is a story which was destined for no one but Mr. Robinson, and he plays it with all the egotistical

With Ann Sothern in Brother Orchid.

In **A Dispatch from Reuters.**

but vaguely cautious push that one would expect from a gangster who found himself in such a spot. [He] can't help but swagger, even down to putting a feather in his monk's hat, but he is also awkwardly aware of a feeling of humbleness."

Howard Barnes, *New York Herald-Tribune*, June 8, 1940

"The gayest variation of the gangster film since *A Slight Case of Murder*. Midway between straight melodrama and outright burlesque, it shows one what happens when a king-pin of the rackets lands in a monastery and discovers that life can be lived without playing all the angles. The story is funnier than the treatment given it, I would say, but even so, the production keeps to a high level of entertaining nonsense and is frequently hilarious. Ed-

ward G. Robinson . . . plays with vigor and humor the gangster-turned-monk."

A DISPATCH FROM REUTERS (Warner Bros., 1940) 89 M.

Producer, Hal B. Wallis; associate producer, Henry Blanke; Director, William Dieterle; story, Valentine Williams and Wolfgang Wilhelm; screenplay, Milton Krims; music director, Leo F. Forbstein; sound, C.A. Riggs; art director, Anton Grot; special effects, Byron Haskin; camera, James Wong Howe, editor, Warren Low.

JULIUS REUTER .... Edward G. Robinson
IDA REUTER .... Edna Best
MAX STARGARDT .... Eddie Albert
FRANZ GELLER .... Albert Bassermann
SIR RANDOLPH PERSHAM .... Nigel Bruce
HERR BAUER .... Gene Lockhart

DELANE .... Montagu Love
MAGNUS .... Otto Kruger
CAREW .... James Stephenson
NAPOLEON III .... Walter Kingsford
BRUCE .... David Bruce
GEANT .... Alec Craig
JULIUS REUTER (BOY) .... Dickie Moore
MAX STARGARDT (BOY) .... Billy Dawson
HERBERT .... Richard Nichols
CHAIRMAN OF THE ANGLO-IRISH TEL. CO ....
                                    Lumsden Hare
AMERICAN AMBASSADOR .... Hugh Sothern
REINGOLD .... Egon Brecher
STEIN .... Frank Jaquet
VON DANSTADT .... Walter O. Stahl
JOSEPHAT BENFEY .... Paul Irving
CHEMIST .... Edward McWade
LORD PALMERSTON .... Gilbert Emery
OPPOSITION SPEAKER .... Robert Warwick
SPEAKER .... Ellis Irving
OTTO .... Henry Roquemore
GAUSS .... Paul Weigel
ASSISTANT .... Joseph Stefani
BIT GIRL .... Mary Anderson
POST OFFICE CLERK .... Wolfgang Zilzer
MAN .... Frederic Mellinger
ATTENDANT .... Stuart Holmes
COMPANION .... Sunny Boyne
HEINRICH .... Ernst Hansman
YOUNG WOMAN .... Grace Stafford
ACTOR .... Theodore Von Eltz
MEMBERS OF PARLIAMENT ..... Kenneth Hunter
                                    Holmes Herbert
                                    Leonard Mudie
                                    Lawrence Grant
WORKMAN .... Pat O'Malley
NEWS VENDORS .... Cyril Delevanti
                                    Norman Ainsley
                                    Bobby Hale

Synopsis

In 1833 Paul Julius, Baron Reuter, is trying to establish his "pigeon post" as an agency for the fast transmission of news between European centers not yet linked by the new telegraph system. As that system expands, the use of carrier pigeons becomes virtually obsolete, and Reuter turns to the transmission of news by wire. Soon after leasing the wires linking stations he has set up in Paris with his London office, he comes up with his first scoop—the transmission of Louis Napoleon's speech. This coup establishes his future, based on his credo of speed, truth and accuracy on which he built the great English news-gathering agency in 1858.

An invaluable aid to Reuter in his work is his wife, Ida, who shows him early in his career that, above all else, his moral obligations to the public must be the prime guide to a news man.

As his wire service grows, competition develops in the Anglo-Irish Telegraph Co. Reuter successfully meets the challenge with his own cable from Cork to Crookshaven by again scooping the world with news of Abraham Lincoln's assassination, flashing the information before the American ambassador has even learned of it.

In **A Dispatch from Reuters.**

Reviews

Thomas M. Pryor, *The New York Times*, December 12, 1940

"Edward G. Robinson gives a sincere though not always convincing performance in the leading role."

Robert W. Dana, *New York Herald-Tribune*, December 12, 1940

"The Warners have given Edward G. Robinson a fat and rewarding role in Reuter, and his performance justifies their good judgement. . . . Robinson, with the aid of William Dieterle's thoughtful

With Alexander Knox in **The Sea Wolf.**

direction, makes Reuter a compelling figure, one that the Fourth Estate should be happy to extol. . . . [The picture] isn't a great picture by any means, but it shows that screen biography has its own proper role to play in motion picture education."

Walt., *Variety,* September 25, 1940

"Robinson provides an excellent characterization of the resourceful Reuter who, time after time, stakes everything on his aim to 'make the world smaller by quicker transmission of the news.'"

THE SEA WOLF (Warner Bros., 1941) 100 M.

Producer, Jack L. Warner and Hal B. Wallis; associate producer, Henry Blanke; director, Michael Curtiz; based on the novel by Jack London; screenplay, Robert Rossen; art director, Anton Grot; special effects, Byron Haskin and H. F. Koenekamp; music, Erich Wolfgang Korngold; camera, Sol Polito; editor, George Amy.

WOLF LARSEN .... Edward G. Robinson
GEORGE LEACH .... John Garfield
RUTH WEBSTER .... Ida Lupino
HUMPHREY VAN WEYDEN ...... Alexander Knox
DR. LOUIE PRESCOTT .... Gene Lockhart
COOKY .... Barry Fitzgerald
JOHNSON .... Stanley Ridges
SVENSON .... Francis McDonald
YOUNG SAILOR .... David Bruce
HARRISON .... Howard da Silva
SMOKE .... Frank Lackteen
AGENT .... Ralf Harolde
MEMBER OF CREW .... Louis Mason
MEMBER OF CREW .... Dutch Hendrian
1st DETECTIVE .... Cliff Clark

With John Garfield in **The Sea Wolf.**

2nd DETECTIVE . . . . William Gould
1st MATE . . . . Charles Sullivan
PICKPOCKET . . . . Ernie Adams
SINGER . . . . Jeane Cowan
HELMSMAN . . . . Wilfred Lucas

Synopsis

Humphrey Van Weyden, a writer, and Ruth Webster, a fugitive from justice, survive a ferry sinking and are taken aboard the *Ghost,* a mystery ship commanded by a brutal, heartless captain named Wolf Larsen, who believes that mercy is a sign of weakness.

Also on board is cabin boy George Leach whom Larsen takes delight in tormenting. One day, the crew mutinies and there is an unsuccessful attempt to kill Larsen. Humphrey, Leach and Ruth decide to get off the ship at any cost and put to sea in a small open boat.

After days of drifting, they sight the *Ghost* apparently sinking. Leach climbs abroad looking for water, but when he fails to return Ruth and Humphrey follow. Humphrey finds Larsen sitting in his cabin slowly going blind and learns that Leach is locked up in the galley where he will soon be trapped by the rising water. When Humphrey turns to leave, Larsen levels a gun at him and demands that he remain in the cabin.

Promising to stay aboard and go down with the captain, Humphrey is given the key which he passes under the door to Ruth. Ruth then frees Leach and they row away toward an island refuge.

With (from left) John Garfield, Stanley Ridges, Francis McDonald, Ethan Laidlaw and Charles Sullivan (lying on deck) in The Sea Wolf.

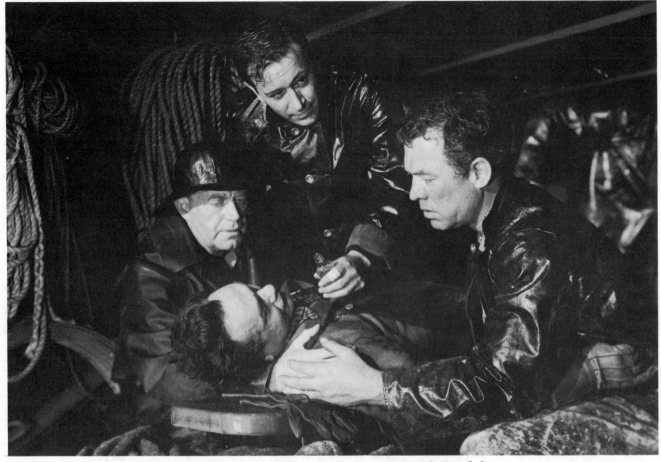

With Cliff Clark, George Raft and Ward Bond in
Manpower.

Reviews

Bosley Crowther, *The New York Times,* March 22,
   1941

"We don't recall that he [Larsen] has ever been
presented with such scrupulous psychological respect as he is in [this] version of *The Sea Wolf.* . . .
This time his monstrous sadism is explored, and
the mind of the Wolf is exposed as just a bundle
of psychoses. With Edward G. Robinson playing
him, the expose is vivid indeed. . . . Some of *The
Sea Wolf* is too heavily drenched with theatrical
villainy, and Mr. Robinson occasionally overacts
the part. But on the whole, the slapping and cuffing
are done with impressive virility and in a manner
distinctive to Warner films."

A.S.G., *New York Herald-Tribune,* March 22, 1941

"On the whole, the cast is first rate. Robinson gives

to a few moments of overacting as the tyrannical
captain of the Ghost, but he is generally helpful to
the melodramatic scheme of things."

Walt., *Variety,* March 26, 1941

"*The Sea Wolf* is strong adventure drama that will
sail a profitable course through theatre boxoffices,
with the fair weather aided considerably by the
marquee voltage of Edward G. Robinson, John
Garfield and Ida Lupino. . . . Robinson provides
plenty of vigor and two-fisted energy to the actor-
proof role of Wolf Larsen and at times is over-
directed."

MANPOWER (Warner Bros., 1941) 105 M.

Executive producer, Hal B. Wallis; producer, Mark
Hellinger; director, Raoul Walsh; screenplay, Richard
Macaulay and Jerry Wald; music, Adolph Deutsch; art
director, Max Parker; sound, Dolph Thomas; special effects,

With George Raft and Marlene Dietrich in **Manpower.**

Byron Haskin and H. F. Koenekamp; camera, Ernest
Haller; editor, Ralph Dawson.

HANK McHENRY	Edward G. Robinson
FAY DUVAL	Marlene Dietrich
JOHNNY MARSHALL	George Raft
JUMBO WELLS	Alan Hale
OMAHA	Frank McHugh
DOLLY	Eve Arden
SMILEY QUINN	Barton MacLane
SIDNEY WHIPPLE	Walter Catlett
SCARLETT	Joyce Compton
FLO	Lucia Carroll
EDDIE ADAMS	Ward Bond
POP DUVAL	Egon Brecher
CULLY	Cliff Clark
SWEENEY	Joseph Crehan
AL HURST	Ben Welden
NOISY NASH	Carl Harbaugh
MARILYN	Barbara Land
POLLY	Barbara Pepper
WILMA	Dorothy Appleby
MAN	Roland Drew
1st MAN	Eddie Fetherston
2nd MAN	Charles Sherlock
3rd MAN	Jeffrey Sayre
4th MAN	De Wolfe Hopper
5th MAN	Al Herman
MAN AT PHONE	Ralph Dunn
FOREMAN	Harry Strang
WAITER	Nat Carr
BOUNCER	John Kelly
NURSE	Joan Winfield
FLOOR NURSE	Isabel Withers
NURSE	Faye Emerson

With Alan Hale, George Raft and Frank McHugh in
Manpower.

ORDERLY .... James Flavin
CLERK .... Chester Clute
FLOORLADY .... Nella Walker
JUSTICE OF THE PEACE .... Harry Holman
MRS. BOYLE .... Dorothy Vaughan
LINEMEN .... Murray Alper
                                  Dick Wessel
CHINESE SINGER .... Beal Wong
HAT CHECK GIRL .... Jane Randolph
1st DETECTIVE .... Eddy Chandler
2nd DETECTIVE .... Lee Phelps
BONDSMAN .... Robert Strange

Synopsis

Hank McHenry and Johnny Marshall, power company linesmen, are called on to repair some

With Alan Hale, Frank McHugh and George Raft in **Manpower.**

storm-damaged lines, and Hank saves Johnny from electrocution on the high voltage wires. Hank, however, suffers an electric shock in one leg, crippling him for life. Hank and Johnny, who room together, become closely involved with Fay Duval, a hostess in a dingy nightclub, when they come to inform her of her father's death on a repair assignment. Johnny had previously met Fay, who had been in prison, when he and Pop went to meet her on her release. While Johnny has no use for Fay, Hank idealistically becomes attached to her, thinking that fate had dealt her a bad deal.

As time passes, Hank and Johnny find themselves fighting over Fay, with Johnny still thinking the girl is out to make a chump of his pal. Fay is impressed by the unassuming Hank and intrigued by his devotion to her. When Hank proposes to her, Fay accepts, although she does not love him.

When Johnny is injured on the job, the newlyweds insist he come to their place to recuperate. Finally Fay admits to Johnny that she loves him. Johnny, however, feels too loyal to his pal to cheat on him. Fay cannot bear to hurt Hank nor to be without Johnny, so she decides to leave town, but is nabbed in a raid when she visits the Club for the last time. Johnny learns of her arrest and bails her out, hoping to keep the news from Hank. When she professes her love again, Johnny slugs her, reminding her that Hank is her husband. Fay seeks out Hank at the company workshack and tells him the truth. He flies into a rage and rushes out into the storm to find Johnny, who is on a repair assignment. In a bitter fight on the high poles, Hank falls to his death, leaving Fay and Johnny to start a new life together.

Reviews

Bosley Crowther, *The New York Times*, July 5, 1941

"The Warner Brothers, like vulcan, know the pat way to forge a thunderbolt. They simply pick a profession in which the men are notoriously tough and the mortality rate is high, write a story about it in which both features are persistently stressed, choose a couple of aces from their pack of hard-boiled actors, and, with these assorted ingredients, whip together a cinematic depth charge.... To say that Mr. Raft and Mr. Robinson make excellent 'squirrels' is like saying two and two make four. ... Take it from us, *Manpower* is a tough picture, awfully tough."

Howard Barnes, *New York Herald-Tribune*, July 5, 1941

"The trouble is that *Manpower* has a really bad script. The story itself wanders vaguely around in circles until it settles for that old gag about two pals being estranged by a siren. The wrong guy gets killed, of course, living only long enough to give his blessing to the real lovers. ... Robinson, Raft and Dietrich are no novices at handling conventional screen situations and infusing in them a bit of vitality, but they are stopped in their tracks by the inanities of *Manpower*. ... The human drama which finds [them] forming a romantic triangle is never credible. The stars work

With Broderick Crawford and Ed Brophy in Larceny,
Inc.

hard to make you care whether or not Robinson
marries Dietrich or Raft finally wins her."

UNHOLY PARTNERS (MGM, 1941) 94 M.

Producer, Samuel Marx; director, Mervyn LeRoy; screenplay, Earl Baldwin, Bartlett Cormack and Lesser Samuels;
music, David Snell; art director, Cedric Gibbons; sound,
Douglas Shearer; camera, George Barnes; editor, Harold
F. Kress.

BRUCE COREY	Edward G. Robinson
MISS CRONIN	Laraine Day
MERRILL LAMBERT	Edward Arnold
GAIL FENTON	Marsha Hunt
TOMMY JARVIS	William T. Orr
MIKE REYNOLDS	Don Beddoe
CLYDE FENTON	Charles Dingle
INSPECTOR BRODY	Charles Cane
MANAGING EDITOR	Walter Kingsford
KAPER	Charles Halton
JASON GRANT	Clyde Fillmore
MOLYNEAUX	Marcel Dalio
ROGER ORDWAY	Frank Faylen
JERRY	Joseph Downing
BOY	William Benedict
COPY BOY	Charles B. Smith
OLD MAN	Frank Dawson
REPORTER	Tom Seidel
YOUNG MAN	Tom O'Rourke
OLD TIMER	George Ovey
COLONEL MASON	Emory Parnell
RECTOR	Al Hill
STICK MAN	Jay Novello
CIRCULATION MAN	John Lilson
BARBER	Billy Mann

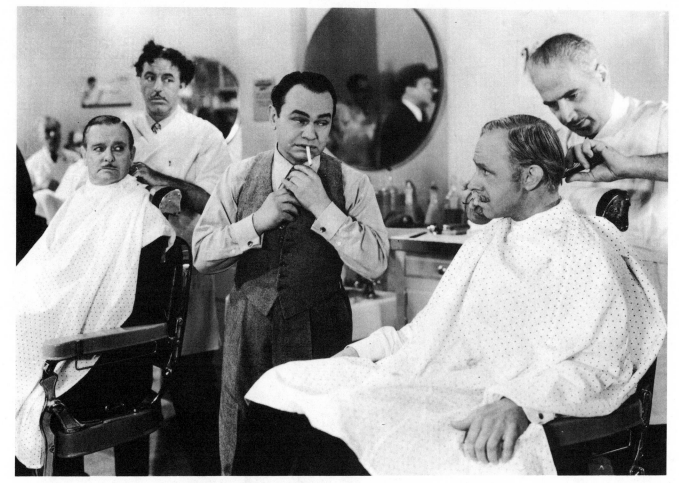

With Creighton Hale, Fortunio Bonanova and John Qualen in Larceny, Inc.

HAZEL	Ann Morrison
TONY	Lester Scharff
GLAMOR GIRL	June MacCloy
PELOTTI	Don Costello
GIRL AT PARTY	Larraine Krueger
GIRL AT PARTY	Natalie Thompson
MARY	Florine McKinney
GORILLA	Charles Jordan
OPERATOR	Ann Pennington
MECHANIC	Lee Phelps
CIRCULATION MANAGER	Lester Dorr
NEWSPAPER WOMEN	Gertrude Bennett
	Estelle Etterre
DRUNK	Milton Kibbee

Synopsis

Back from World War I, where he covered the action as a reporter, Bruce Corey decides to publish his own tabloid. In order to finance it, he is forced to accept gangster Merrill Lambert as his partner. With the aid of Tommy Jarvis, Corey sets up his paper in direct opposition to the many Lambert interests. Tommy and Lambert both fall in love with Gail Fenton, a beautiful singer, and, knowing that she loves him, Tommy is bewildered when she is seen constantly with Lambert whom she professes to hate. After some investigation Tommy discovers that Gail's father is the victim of one of Lambert's many rackets, forcing those who owe him gambling debts to take out insurance from his company.

Before the tabloid can expose the racket, Lambert kidnaps Tommy and tries to ransom the young reporter to Corey in exchange for complete control of the paper. Tensions lead to a bitter argument between the "partners" and Corey is forced to kill Lambert in self defense. He then dictates a confession to his devoted secretary, Miss Cronin, and takes off with a wild pilot on a suicidal trans-Atlantic flight, sponsored by the paper. When news comes back that the plane is lost at sea, Miss Cronin burns the confession, and the paper continues under her and Tommy's leadership—after Tommy and Gail return from their honeymoon.

Reviews

Theodore Strauss, *The New York Times*, December 29, 1941

"Mervyn LeRoy and three able-bodied scriptwriters have sketched out a hardbitten melodrama of a tabloid editor during the Twenties when 'death and emotions were cheap.' They have brought in Edward G. Robinson to play the editor, and he knows how to make a caustic line flip like the tip of a bull-whip. . . . Credit much of the film's intermittent excitement to Mr. Robinson, who still packs more drive than almost any six actors one could name."

Flin., *Variety*, October 15, 1941

"Both Robinson and Arnold play the leads with the snarling bravado reminiscent of the gangster style of films. In fact, it all seems like a reissue."

LARCENY, INC. (Warner Bros., 1942) 95 M.

Producer, Hal B. Wallis; associate producer, Jack Saper and Jerry Wald; director, Lloyd Bacon; based on the play *The Night Before Christmas* by Laura and S. J. Perelman; screenplay, Everett Freeman and Edwin Gilbert; camera, Tony Gaudio; editor, Ralph Dawson.

PRESSURE MAXWELL .... Edward G. Robinson
DENNY COSTELLO .... Jane Wyman
JUG MARTIN .... Broderick Crawford
JEFF RANDOLPH .... Jack Carson
LEO DEXTER .... Anthony Quinn
WEEPY DAVIS .... Edward Brophy
HOMER BIGELOW .... Harry Davenport
SAM BACHRACH .... John Qualen
MADEMOISELLE GLORIA .... Barbara Jo Allen
ASPINWALL .... Grant Mitchell
HOBART .... Jack C. (Jackie) Gleason
OSCAR ENGELHART .... Andrew Tombes

SMITTY .... Joseph Downing
MR. JACKSON .... George Meeker
ANTON COPOULOS .... Fortunio Bonanova
WARDEN .... Joseph Crehan
FLORENCE .... Jean Ames
McCARTHY .... William Davidson
BUCHANAN .... Chester Clute
MR. CARMICHAEL .... Creighton Hale
OFFICER O'CASEY .... Emory Parnell
UMPIRE .... Joe Devlin
CONVICT .... Jimmy O'Gatty
ANOTHER CONVICT .... Jack Kenney
BATTER .... John Kelly
GUARD .... Eddy Chandler
CHUCK .... Dutch Hendrian
MUGGSY .... Bill Phillips
PLAYER .... Hank Mann
PLAYER .... Eddie Foster
PLAYER .... Cliff Saum
PLAYER .... Charles Sullivan
GUARD .... James Flavin
AUTO DRIVER .... Charles Drake
WOMAN .... Vera Lewis
YOUNG MAN .... Ray Montgomery
CUSTOMER .... Lucien Littlefield
SECRETARY .... Grace Stafford
MAN .... Roland Drew
CUSTOMER .... De Wolfe Hopper
POLICEMAN .... Pat O'Malley

With Marcel Dalio in **Unholy Partners.**

Synopsis

On the eve of their parole from Sing Sing, small time hoods Pressure Maxwell and Jug Martin are asked by fellow inmate Leo Dexter to join him in a bank robbery when he gets out. They refuse, deciding to go straight on the outside.

***With Laraine Day and Edward Arnold in* Unholy Partners.**

But Maxwell's idea of making a living is to get rich quick, and soon he and Jug are making plans to knock over a bank. Maxwell purchases a small luggage shop adjoining the bank and plans to drill a tunnel from the store's basement into the vault. He has his adopted daughter, Denny Costello, run the shop. She soon falls for Jeff Randolph, a high-pressure luggage salesman, who finds the proprietress a pushover for his merchandise.

Meanwhile, Maxwell becomes a popular and respected member of the local community and, when the bank authorities offer him a large sum for the shop so they can enlarge their premises, he decides that honesty and the straight life might not be so bad—and he accepts.

Just as the deal is going through, Dexter turns up, learns of Maxwell's original scheme and attempts to carry through on the planned underground heist. However, too much dynamite is used; the shop is blown up and the police arrive to escort Dexter back to Sing Sing.

With nobody else aware that the robbery plan was theirs, Maxwell, Jug and their cronies are left to start life all over again—as upstanding citizens.

Reviews

Bosley Crowther, *The New York Times*, April 25, 1942

"You can't say that Edward G. Robinson doesn't try hard to go straight. In his past three or four pictures, he has played more or less 'legitimate' roles . . . [but] in *Larceny, Inc.* he is found on the shady side of the street. And considering the traffic is very hectic and amusing over there, it is a passing pleasure to see him back with the mob. . . . Mr. Robinson, as usual, is a beautifully hard-boiled yegg. The principal joy is to watch him. His 'Pressure' cooks with gas."

Howard Barnes, *New York Herald-Tribune*, April 25, 1942

"[It] has all sorts of pretentious trimmings. It has the ebullient Edward G. Robinson as star, a handsome production and a notable supporting cast . . . [but] it has lost much of the Perelman nonsense humor that gave a certain zest to the play. . . . Broderick Crawford plays a dumb safecracker with considerable comic effect. Jack Carson and Edward Brophy go all the way in mugging, and so does Mr. Robinson on more than one occasion."

TALES OF MANHATTAN (20th Century-Fox, 1942) 118 M.

Producer, Boris Morros and S. P. Eagle; director, Julien Duvivier; original stories-screenplay, Ben Hecht, Ferenc Molnar, Donald Ogden Stewart, Samuel Hoffenstein, Alan Campbell, Ladislas Fodor, Laslo Vadnay, Laszlo Gorog, Lamar Trotti and Henry Blankfort; assistant director, Robert Stillman; original music, Sol Kaplan; art director, Richard Day, Boris Leven; sound, W. D. Fleck, Roger Heman; camera, Joseph Walker; editor, Robert Bischoff.

SEQUENCE A

ORMAN	Charles Boyer
ETHEL	Rita Hayworth
HALLOWAY	Thomas Mitchell
LUTHER	Eugene Pallette
ACTRESS	Helene Reynolds

SEQUENCE B

DIANE	Ginger Rogers
GEORGE	Henry Fonda
HARRY	Cesar Romero
ELLEN	Gail Patrick
EDGAR, THE BUTLER	Roland Young

SEQUENCE C

CHARLES SMITH	Charles Laughton
MRS. SMITH	Elsa Lanchester
ARTURO BELLINI	Victor Francen
WILSON	Christian Rub
GRANDMOTHER	Adeline DeWalt Reynolds
PICCOLO PLAYER	Sig Arno

SKEPTIC .... Will Wright
PROPRIETOR .... Dewey Robinson
LATECOMER .... Tom O'Grady
DIGNIFIED MAN .... Forbes Murray

SEQUENCE D
BROWNE .... Edward G. Robinson
WILLIAM .... George Sanders

With George Sanders in Tales of Manhattan.

FATHER JOE .... James Gleason
HANK BRONSON .... Harry Davenport
DAVIS .... James Rennie
JUDGE .... Harry Hayden
HENDERSON .... Morris Ankrum
MOLLY .... Don Douglas
MARY .... Mae Marsh

SEQUENCE E
LUKE .... Paul Robeson
ESTHER .... Ethel Waters
LAZARUS .... Rochester (Eddie Anderson)
COSTELLO .... J. Carrol Naish
HALL JOHNSON CHOIR ...... Themselves (40 voices)
GRANDPA .... Clarence Muse
CHRISTOPHER .... George Reed
NICODEMUS .... Cordell Hickman
MONK .... John Kelly

Synopsis

Orman, a highly successful actor, purchases an evening tail coat, which, he is informed by the head tailor, is cursed. Wearing it one evening during a rendezvous with Ethel, Orman is shot by the woman's jealous husband, Halloway. At first it seems Orman is dying, and then it is revealed the shot missed him. Meanwhile, Orman has discovered Ethel's true selfish nature.

Orman's valet Luther sells the coat to Harry's butler Edgar for $10, since there is a bullet hole in it. When Harry's fiancee Diane discovers a passionate love note in the pocket, she becomes furious with Harry. To put her mind at ease, Harry gets his best friend George to say that the coat is his. This causes Diane, who always thought George too shy, to see him in a new light, and they run off together, leaving Harry with the coat.

It next turns up in a pawn shop where it is bought by the wife of Charles Smith, a barroom pianist who has composed a great symphony, which he has just been given the chance to conduct. That evening while he is introducing the work for the socialite audience, the much-too-small garment splits, interrupting the concert. Maestro Arturo Bellini, Smith's benefactor, takes over for the composer and the symphony is heard to completion.

The moth-eaten coat now has found its way to the Bowery, where, at the Mission, Father Joe insists that down-and-out attorney Browne wear it to attend a 25th anniversary college reunion dinner at the Waldorf Astoria. At the function, William wrongly accuses Browne of picking another man's pocket and Browne confesses his state of poverty and leaves the banquet hall. Three classmates follow him and offer him a new career opportunity.

The coat then falls into the possession of a thief, Costello, who wears it while committing a robbery. He stuffs the $40,000 into the coat and prepares to make his getaway in a plane. During the flight, the coat catches fire and Costello tosses it out, forgetting about the bulging pockets. The coat lands near a poverty stricken Negro village and is recovered by two sharecroppers, Luke and Esther. They take the money to the preacher Lazarus, who uses the funds to bolster the community economics.

Reviews

Bosley Crowther, *The New York Times,* September 25, 1942

"*Tales of Manhattan* is one of those rare films. . . . Neither profound nor very searching, it nevertheless manages to convey a gentle, detached comprehension of the irony and pity of life. . . . Edward

With Don Douglas and James Rennie in Tales of **Manhattan.**

G. Robinson gives a masterful performance as the bum who has seen better days."

Bosley Crowther, *The Sunday New York Times,* October 4, 1942

"Edward G. Robinson, a decidedly derelict in Chinatown, is dispatched in (the coat) to a dinner of his prosperous college classmates 'uptown.' The coat is his comeback ticket, but fate very cruelly

With James Gleason, Mae Marsh and Don Brodie in Tales of Manhattan.

intervenes. . . . Mr. Robinson fills the bill superbly, but the writers let him down in the end."

Howard Barnes, *New York Herald-Tribune,* September 25, 1942

"An impressive line-up of stars is to be found in *Tales of Manhattan.* High-ranking scenarists have spun the plot. The distinguished French director Julien Duvivier has staged the show. If it is big movie names you want, [it] is a prodigal offering. Obviously they lend an aura of glamor and fascination to the proceedings. What they fail to do is make *Tales of Manhattan* more than a disjointed and pretentious picture."

DESTROYER (Columbia, 1943) 99 M.

Producer, Louis F. Edelman; director, William A. Seiter; based on a story by Frank Wead; screenplay, Wead, Lewis Melzer and Borden Chase; art director, Lionel Banks; music, Anthony Collins; camera, Franz F. Planer; editor, Gene Havlick.

STEVE BOLESLAVSKI	Edward G. Robinson
MICKEY DONOHUE	Glenn Ford
MARY BOLESLAVSKI	Marguerite Chapman
KANSAS JACKSON	Edgar Buchanan
SAROCKY	Leo Gorcey
LT. COMM. CLARK	Regis Toomey
CASEY	Ed Brophy
LT. MORTON	Warren Ashe

With Marguerite Chapman in Destroyer.

BIGBEE	Craig Woods
YASHA	Curt Bois
ADMIRAL	Pierre Watkin
KNIFE EATING SAILOR	Al Hill
SOBBING SAILOR	Bobby Jordan
CHIEF ENGINEER	Roger Clark
FIREMAN MOORE	Dean Benton
FIREMAN THOMAS	David Alison
DOCTOR	Paul Perry
CHIEF QUARTER MASTER	John Merton
HELMSMAN	Don Peters
SPINSTER	Virginia Sale
SOROCKY'S GIRL	Eleanor Counts
SAILOR	Dale Van Sickel
GERGUSON	Addison Richards
1st SHIP FITTER	Lester Dorr
2nd SHIP FITTER	Bud Geary
SURVIVOR	Eddie Dew
DOCTOR NO. 1	Tristram Coffin
ENSIGN JOHNSON	Larry Parks
CHIEF GUNNER'S MATE	Eddie Chandler

With Glenn Ford in **Destroyer.**

2nd FIREMAN . . . . Lloyd Bridges
COMMUNICATIONS OFFICER . . . . Dennis Moore
1st WORKMAN . . . . Edmund Cobb
RIVETER . . . . Eddy Waller
ASST. CHIEF ENGINEER . . . . Charles McGraw

Synopsis

Steve Boleslavski, known as "Boley," is a welder working on a new destroyer that is to replace the old ship *John Paul Jones.* Much to the surprise of all who know him, Boley becomes a nuisance on the job—finding fault with his fellow workers, constantly prodding them for perfection.

At the launching of the *Jones,* the reason for Boley's intensity is revealed. He was in the Navy as Chief Boatswain's mate on the ship's predecessor.

Lt. Commander Clark, in charge of the new destroyer, looks upon Boley as his mentor: when Clark was just a seaman, Boley heckled him into taking the Annapolis exams.

With the ship properly launched, Boley goes back into the Navy, determined to make the new *Jones* a reincarnation of the old. He gets himself stationed on the destroyer as Chief Boatswain's Mate. Here he meets Mickey Donohue, a new Navy man who was Chief Boatswain's Mate till Boley arrived. Mickey is resentful, but tries to get along with Boley. The latter seeks absolute perfection and he nags the crew until the ship is practically a madhouse.

Clark is urged by his superiors to transfer Boley, but he sticks by his friend. A violent sea battle between the *Jones* and the Japanese brings Boley into his own and a hero among his mates.

Feeling that his mission is completed, Boley steps aside and Mickey takes over. Mickey also wins the hand of Boley's daughter, whom he had met on shore leave.

Boley meanwhile watches with almost paternal pride as the *Jones* steams out to join the Pacific Fleet.

Reviews

Bosley Crowther, *The New York Times*, September 2, 1943

"Another ripe old-timer in the Hollywood actor ranks has been mustered into service for the movies' own particular brand of war. This time it is Edward G. Robinson, complete with haunch, paunch and scowl, who has been given a petty officer's rating in Columbia's *Destroyer* and may now be seen heaving Navy spirit onto the screen. . . . As this indestructible hero, Mr. Robinson utilizes the same tough snarl, the same withering looks and mute sarcasm that made him the scourge of muggs in days gone by. . . . It is a leaky and top-heavy vessel on which Mr. Robinson serves."

Otis Guernsey Jr., *New York Herald-Tribune*, September 2, 1943

"The film catches the spirit of naval camaraderie in one scene in which Mr. Robinson relates the story of the Bon-homme Richard's last fight, but on the whole, the film contains none of the incisive character lines and sharp technique that made such a stirring film out of *In Which We Serve*.

Eileen Creelman, *New York Sun*, September 2, 1943

"Edward G. Robinson plays Boley with a skillful mixture of comedy and sentiment. This is the kind of role that might have had Wallace Beery afloat with tears. Mr. Robinson keeps his Boley within the bounds of reason, a likeable and believable fellow."

FLESH AND FANTASY (Universal, 1943) 93 M.

Producer, Charles Boyer and Julien Duvivier; director, Duvivier; based on the story "Lord Arthur Saville's Crime" by Oscar Wilde, and stories by Laslo Vadnay and Ellis St. Joseph; screenplay, Ernest Pascal, Samuel Hoffenstein and St. Joseph; art director, John B. Goodman, Richard Riedel and Robert Boyce; music, Alexander Tansman; camera, Paul Ivano, Stanley Cortez; editor, Arthur Hilton.

MARSHALL TYLER	Edward G. Robinson
PAUL GASPAR	Charles Boyer
JOAN STANLEY	Barbara Stanwyck
HENRIETTA	Betty Field
MICHAEL	Robert Cummings
SEPTIMUS PODGERS	Thomas Mitchell
KING LAMARR	Charles Winninger
ROWENA	Anna Lee
LADY PAMELA HARDWICK	Dame May Whitty
DEAN OF CHICHESTER	C. Aubrey Smith
DOAKES	Robert Benchley
STRANGER	Edgar Barrier
DAVIS	David Hoffman
LADY THOMAS	Mary Forbes
LIBRARIAN	Ian Wolfe
MRS. CAXTON	Doris Lloyd
ANGEL	June Lang
EQUESTRIENNE	Grace McDonald
ACROBAT	Joseph Crehan
DETECTIVES	Arthur Loft
	Lee Phelps
RADIO ANNOUNCER	James Craven
JUSTINE	Marjorie Lord
POLICEMAN	Eddie Acuff
PIERROT	Peter Lawford
SATAN	Lane Chandler
DEATH	Gil Patrick
HARLEQUINS	Paul Bryer
	George Lewis
OLD NEGRO	Clinton Rosemond
OLD MAN PROSPECTOR	Charles Halton
ANGEL	Jacqueline Dalya

Synopsis

At their club, members Doakes and Davis heatedly discuss the meaning of dreams, predictions and the supernatural. Doakes relates the strange dreams he recently had.

Episode #1: Henrietta, an embittered dressmaker, blames her romantic frustrations on her slovenly appearance and unattractive face. On Mardi Gras night in New Orleans she is handed a beautiful face-mask by a strange masked man and told that the face she hates will radiate beauty once she drives hatred and envy from her soul. She meets Michael, a disillusioned young lawyer, and finds renewed courage. A romance with Michael blossoms. He urges her to remove the mask, and she finally does, discovering truth in the moral.

Episode #2: Septimus Podgers is a palmist performing at a London social gathering. Attorney

In Flesh and Fantasy.

With Heather Thatcher, Thomas Mitchell, Edward Fielding and Dame May Whitty in Flesh and Fantasy.

Marshall Tyler scoffs at the predictions but nevertheless submits to a reading, and becomes intrigued when he is told he will commit murder. The prediction preys on his mind and he finally embarks on a plan to commit the predestined crime. After making unsuccessful attempts on two victims, he removes the hex by strangling Podgers. In trying to escape the police, he runs through a circus and dies as a result of an accident. The Great Gaspar witnesses the tragedy.

Episode #3: Paul Gaspar is upset by a dream which predicts he will meet disaster while performing as a circus high wire artist. The dream upsets him to the extent that he cannot perform his thrill stunt. On the boat to America with King Lamarr's circus he meets Joan Stanley, the girl clearly shown in his dream. They fall in love. While he tries to toss off the hex, she is concealing her identity as a member of a jewel theft mob. However, her

In Flesh and Fantasy.

capture by the police is also revealed to Gaspar in a dream. He overcomes the psychological consciousness of his fall during the performance, but the girl's arrest happens as he envisioned.

Reviews

Thomas M. Pryor, *The New York Times,* November 18, 1943

"Seldom has murder been contemplated on the screen with more diabolical delight (for the audience) than when Mr. Robinson of the flesh argues with Mr. Robinson of the Fantasy, or the failure, about who the victim should be or how the crime would be committed. . . . Julien Duvivier, the director, has underscored this sequence with mounting suspense, but unfortunately brings it to a disappointing climax by permitting Mr. Robinson to fulfill his destiny in a very routine manner. Yet this is still the best part of the picture."

Otis Guernsey Jr., *New York Herald Tribune,* November 18, 1943

"*Flesh and Fantasy* is an example of one-act play techniques adapted for motion pictures. . . . The second [act] is a melodrama with Edward G. Robinson playing a rich lawyer who has been told by a fortune teller, Thomas Mitchell, that he will commit a murder. Things pick up in this sequence as the fantasy becomes mixed with excitement and good performances by the two above-mentioned actors. But here again, the one-act form is marred by repetition of the same effect and long conversational pauses."

TAMPICO (20th Century-Fox, 1944) 75 M.

Producer, Robert Bassler; director Lothar Mendes; original story-adaptation, Ladislas Fodor; screenplay, Kenneth Gamet, Fred Niblo Jr. and Richard Macaulay; special effects, Fred Serson; art director, James Basevi and Albert Hogsett; set director, Thomas Little; camera, Charles Clarke, editor, Robert Fritch.

CAPT. BART MANSON	Edward G. Robinson
KATHIE BALL	Lynn Bari
FRED ADAMSON	Victor McLaglen
WATSON	Robert Bailey
VALDEZ	Marc Lawrence
SILHOUETTE MAN	E. J. Ballantine
DOLORES	Mona Maris
KRUGER	Tonio Selwart
MUELLER	Carl Ekberg
CRAWFORD	Roy Roberts
STRANGER	George Sorel
GUN CREW NAVAL OFFICER	Charles Lang
QUARTERMASTER O'BRIEN	Ralph Byrd
IMMIGRATION INSPECTOR	Daniel Ocko
BIT	Karen Palmer
NAVAL COMMANDER	Nester Paiva
MESSENGER BOY	David Cota
RODRIGUEZ	Muni Seroff
PHOTOGRAPHER	Juan Varro
JUSTICE OF PEACE	Antonio Moreno
DR. BROWN	Ben Erway
MRS. KELLY	Helen Brown
SERRA	Martin Garralaga
STEWARD	Martin Black
WAITER	Chris-Pin Martin
PROPRIETOR	Margaret Martin

WAITER .... Trevor Bardette
SEAMAN .... Virgil Johanson
NAVIGATOR .... Arno Frey
PILOT .... Jean Del Val

Synopsis

Bringing his tanker *Calhoun* into Tampico, Captain Bart Manson picks up an S.O.S. from a

With Victor McLaglen in Tampico.

ship torpedoed by a submarine, and against the advice of his first mate Fred Adamson he goes to the rescue.

Among the survivors picked up is Kathie Ball. None of the others rescued recall having seen her aboard the torpedoed ship and she has no identification papers. The port authorities in Tampico decide to hold her for investigation, but Manson obtains her release in his custody.

Manson is intrigued by Kathie, and despite Adamson's warning, they get married. Ordered back to sea, Manson refuses to tell Kathie the date, but she finds out and goes aboard to say goodbye. At sea, a submarine halts the *Calhoun*. Adamson argues that the ship should be turned over to the Nazis, but Manson decides to fight. The ship is sunk, and Adamson is lost in combat. En route back to port, Manson broods. He feels that only Kathie knew the ship's course. An investigation seems to point out that she is involved with the Axis spy ring. Manson denounces Kathie and leaves her, but he cannot force himself to turn her over to the authorities.

The next night, Manson makes the rounds of Tampico's bars, appearing very embittered, but actually setting a trap. He casually leaves his papers

on a bar and follows a mysterious man who picks them up, leading Manson straight to the headquarters of the ring preying on the tankers.

In a tense climax, Manson captures the plotters, including Adamson who was working for the Axis.

Manson sets out to find Kathie and they are reunited.

Reviews

P. P. Kennedy, *The New York Times,* June 2, 1944

"Mr. Robinson's role as a love-chastened ship's captain is carried off in his usual businesslike manner, although his admirers will likely feel that the chastening isn't particularly advantageous to his traditional characterization."

Bert McCord, *New York Herald-Tribune,* June 2, 1944

"If the film has any virtue at all, it is that of underplaying, but while this has proved to be the outstanding feature of many of our most exciting pictures, this quality in itself is not sufficient. . . .

With Margaret Martin and Lynn Bari in Tampico.

Wearing the four stripes of the merchant marine, Edward G. Robinson comes off with most of the acting honors."

MR. WINKLE GOES TO WAR (Columbia, 1944) 80 M.

Producer, Jack Moss; associate producer, Norman Dem-

With Robert Armstrong and Bob Haymes in **Mr. Winkle Goes to War.**

ing; director, Alfred E. Green; from the novel by Theodore Pratt; screenplay, Waldo Salt, George Corey and Louis Solomon; assistant director, Earl Bellamy; music score, Carmen Dragon and Paul Sawtell; art director, Lionel Banks and Rudolph Sternad; camera, Joseph Walker; editor, Richard Fanite.

WILBERT WINKLE	Edward G. Robinson
AMY WINKLE	Ruth Warrick
BARRY	Ted Donaldson
JACK PETTIGREW	Bob Haymes
SERGEANT "ALPHABET"	Richard Lane
JOE TINKER	Robert Armstrong
RALPH WESCOTT	Richard Gaines
PLUMMER	Walter Baldwin
McDAVID	Art Smith
MARTHA PETTIGREW	Ann Shoemaker
A. B. SIMKINS	Paul Stanton
JOHNSON	Buddy Yarus
CAPTAIN	William Forrest
GLADYS	Bernardine Hayes
HOSTESS #1	Jeff Donnell
MAYOR	Howard Freeman
GIRL BIT	Nancy Evans
GIRL BIT	Ann Loos
M.P.	Larry Thompson
GIRL BIT	Earl Cantrell
CAPTAIN	Warren Ashe
SERGEANT #1	James Flavin
CORPORAL	Bob Mitchum
DOCTOR	Herbert Hayes
SERGEANT #2	Fred Kohler Jr.
DRAFTEE #1	Fred Lord
DRAFTEE #2	Cecil Ballerino
DRAFTEE #3	Ted Holley
DOCTOR	Ben Taggart
DOCTOR	Sam Flint
DOCTOR	Nelson Leigh
DOCTOR	Forbest Murray
DOCTOR	Ernest Hilliard
DRAFTEE	Les Sketchley

DRAFTEE .... Ed Jenkins
DRAFTEE .... Paul Stupin
M.P. .... Terry Frost
RANGE OFFICER .... Hugh Beaumont
SERGEANT .... Dennis Moore
BARBER .... Emmett Vogan
4th KID .... Tommy Cook

Synopsis

In 1942, the United States is still drafting men up to age 45. Wilbert George Winkle has been a bank clerk for fourteen years and is sick of it. He

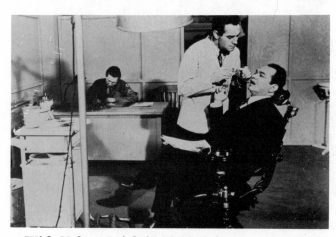

***With Nelson Leigh in* Mr. Winkle Goes to War.**

finally quits the bank and devotes himself full time to the fix-it business he has been running in a little shop he has built next to his home. His wife Amy gives Winkle an ultimatum: either return to the bank, or move into the fix-it shop. Winkle chooses the latter.

A notice from the draft board arrives. Winkle, 44, does not believe he will pass the physical. At the induction center is Jack Pettigrew, a neighbor's son. They both pass the examination. At the Ordnance Corps barracks, Winkle and Jack meet Tinker and Sgt. Alphabet. Basic training almost kills Winkle, but he perseveres and refuses to leave the Army when the draft age is lowered to 38.

Somewhere in the South Pacific, the four men are on the edge of action. A bulldozer has become disabled and Winkle is sent to repair it, as the Japanese attack. Winkle heads the bulldozer for a fox-hole in which enemy troops are hiding and plows them under.

Wounded, he is taken to the hospital, where he learns that Tinker and Alphabet were killed. Honorably discharged with national honors heaped on him, Winkle remains his own quiet, unassuming self. He is proud but humble and bypasses the home town celebration awaiting his arrival, going directly to his fix-it shop. There he is reconciled with Amy who forgives him his past eccentricities.

Reviews

Bosley Crowther, *The New York Times,* August 3, 1944

"If you can take Edward G. Robinson as a very mouse of a man, hen-pecked beyond endurance and virtually subsisting on a diet of pills, then you may find modest entertainment in [this picture]. . . . True, the erstwhile Little Caesar does everything within his power to give a comic situation of a Casper Milquetoast-turned-G.I. . . . But somehow, his granite chiseled visage and his plainly hard-boiled voice betray a contradiction which instantly muddles his act. It is hard to believe that Mr. Robinson would take what he does lying down."

Howard Thompson, *New York Herald-Tribune,* August 3, 1944

"Columbia has made the grave error of casting Edward G. Robinson in the Mr. Winkle part. He never succeeds in being either meekly amusing or properly courageous. Since the script has involved him with a small boy who is never completely identified, and a mean wife whose ultimate understanding of his true worth is quite incredible, it is not altogether Robinson's fault. The truth remains that he merely walks through his role in *Mr. Winkle Goes to War,* leaving a trail of tiny, tiresome situations behind him. . . . [He] swaggers through most of the sequences, not quite sure whether he is Little Caesar or a timid bookkeeper."

DOUBLE INDEMNITY (Paramount, 1944) 106 M.

Producer, Joseph Sistrom; director, Billy Wilder; based on the novel by James M. Cain;* screenplay, Wilder and Raymond Chandler; assistant director, C. C. Coleman, Jr.; set director, Betram Granger; sound, Stanley Cooley; music, Miklos Rozsa; art director, Hans Dreier and Hal Pereira; camera, John Seitz; editor, Doane Harrison.

* Based on the 1927 slaying of New Yorker Albert Snyder by his wife Ruth and her lover Judd Gray, for his insurance.

WALTER NEFF .... Fred MacMurray
PHYLLIS DIETRICHSON .... Barbara Stanwyck

With Fred MacMurray in **Double Indemnity.**

BARTON KEYES	Edward G. Robinson
JACKSON	Porter Hall
LOLA DIETRICHSON	Jean Heather
MR. DIETRICHSON	Tom Powers
NINO ZACHETTE	Byron Barr
MR. NORTON	Richard Gaines
SAM GORLOPIS	Fortunio Bonanova
JOE PETE	John Philliber
BIT	George Magrill
NORTON'S SECRETARY	Bess Flowers
CONDUCTOR	Kenan Cripps
RECAP	Harold Garrison
PULLMAN PORTER	Oscar Smith
NETTIE (MAID)	Betty Farrington
WOMAN	Constance Purdy
PULLMAN CONDUCTOR	Dick Rush
PULLMAN PORTER	Frank Billy Mitchel
TRAIN CONDUCTOR	Edmund Cobb
PULLMAN PORTER	Floyd Shackelford
PULLMAN PORTER	James Adamson
GARAGE ATTENDANT	Sam R. McDaniel
COLORED MAN	Clarence Muse
PACIFIC ALL-RISK TELE. OPERATOR	Judith Gibson
KEYES' SECRETARY	Miriam Franklin

Synopsis

Seriously wounded with a bullet in his shoulder, insurance agent Walter Neff slowly recites into a dictaphone a memo to the company's claims manager, Barton Keyes. It is the story leading up to his gun wound.

Some months before, Neff met Phyllis Dietrichson when he had stopped by her house to check her husband's automobile insurance. Although she expressed more than casual interest in accident insurance, Neff passed off the matter, but later became suspicious. The next night, Phyllis visited his apartment and again began pursuing the accident insurance angle with particular stress on the double indemnity clause.

A short time later, Dietrichson was preparing to leave for a class reunion at Stanford, but a few days before his departure, he fractured his leg. His wife now convinced him to go by train—recalling that accidental death from a train pays double. Neff and Phyllis, who had been meeting secretly, then began making their plans.

Neff had prepared an airtight alibi for the night of the crime. Wearing a suit similar to Dietrichson's, Neff walked to their house and hid in Dietrichson's car. The couple, along with the hidden insurance agent, backed out of the driveway, and Phyllis drove to a dark street where Neff reached up and broke Dietrichson's neck. Then Neff, on the crutches, boarded the train, posing as the murdered man. Hobbling back to the observation platform, Neff waited until the other passengers moved inside. Everything was covered, although Neff began feeling all would go wrong. He threw the crutches to the side of the railroad bed, just at the spot where Phyllis had dumped her husband's body.

Returning to the Dietrichson house, he and Phyllis engaged in a violent argument, when he discovered that she was also double-crossing him. She shot him. Grabbing her in his arms, he tried wrestling her gun from her. It went off and she fell dead.

Neff made his way back to the insurance office where he is now dictating the memo to Keyes, when Keyes walks in. They have been like father and son. But Neff must pay the penalty. Keyes calls the police.

Reviews

Bosley Crowther, *The New York Times*, September 7, 1944

"The performance of Mr. Robinson . . . as a smart

With Fred MacMurray (in gas chamber), Lee Shumway and Edward Hearn in scene cut from Double Indemnity.

With Fred MacMurray and Barbara Stanwyck in **Double Indemnity.**

adjustor of insurance claims is a fine bit of characterization within its allotment of space. With a bitter brand of humor and irritability, he creates a formidable guy. As a matter of fact, [he] is the only one you care two hoots for in the film. The rest are just neatly carved pieces in a variably intriguing crime game."

Howard Barnes, *New York Herald-Tribune,* September 7, 1944

"With perfectly coordinated acting by Fred MacMurray, Barbara Stanwyck and Edward G. Robinson and the lesser players, it hits clean and hard right between the eyes. . . . Robinson plays an insurance company sleuth with splendid authority."

THE WOMAN IN THE WINDOW (RKO, 1945) 99 M.

Producer, Nunnally Johnson; director, Fritz Lang; based on the novel *Once Off Guard* by J. H. Wallis; screenplay, Johnson; assistant director, Richard Harlan; art director, Duncan Cramer; music, Arthur Lang; special effects, Vernon Walker; camera, Milton Krasner; editor, Marjorie Johnson.

PROF. RICHARD WANLEY . . . . . Edward G. Robinson
FRANK LALOR . . . . Raymond Massey
ALICE REED . . . . Joan Bennett
DR. BARKSTONE . . . . Edmond Breon
HEIDT . . . . Dan Duryea
MRS. WANLEY . . . . Dorothy Peterson
BOY SCOUT . . . . Spanky MacFarland
CAPT. KENNEDY . . . . Arthur Space
BLONDE . . . . Claire Carleton
CLAUDE MAZARD . . . . Arthur Loft
STEWARD . . . . Frank Dawson
ELSIE . . . . Carol Cameron
INSPECTOR JACKSON . . . . Thomas E. Jackson
DICKIE . . . . Bobbie Blake

Synopsis

After seeing his family off on a summer vacation

With Thomas Jackson, Arthur Space and Raymond Massey in The Woman in the Window.

where he will join them after a lecture tour, psychology Professor Richard Wanley goes to his club. There he becomes involved in a discussion with several members about the probability of adventure happening to anyone and the typical man's reaction to strange events. Later that evening, the professor stops, as he often does, in front of an art gallery to gaze at the portrait of a woman in the window. This particular night he notices a woman standing nearby. She is the subject of the painting. Alice Reed, the artist's model, engages the professor in conversation and an acquaintanceship is struck up.

The professor innocently goes to visit Alice late one night, unaware that she is the mistress of a famous financier, Claude Mazard, who arrives unexpectedly, misunderstands the situation, and in a burst of rage makes a murderous assault on the professor. To save his own life, the professor is forced to kill the man with a pair of scissors handed to him by Alice. Suddenly, Wanley is in the very web of peril he had been earlier discussing with his club associates. To avoid disgrace and the ruin of his career, he disposes of the body instead of calling the police.

He is soon surprised to learn through his friend, District Attorney Frank Lalor, how much the police have learned about the killing and how close they are to the killer and his female accomplice.

Heidt, the financier's bodyguard, tries to blackmail Alice and Wanley, forcing the professor still further into a life of crime. Failing in his attempt to kill Heidt, Wanley decides to poison himself. Ironically, at that fatal moment, Alice is calling to tell him that the police have shot Heidt, convinced that he was the murderer.

Suddenly, the professor is shaken awake, only to learn that he had fallen asleep at the club after dinner. He hurries on home, refusing to stop and look at the "woman in the window" or to talk to a girl standing nearby.

Reviews

Thomas M. Pryor, *The New York Times,* January 26, 1945

"Let it be noted that *The Woman in the Window* is a humdinger of a mystery melodrama . . . superlatively directed by Fritz Lang, and we couldn't imagine a better set of performers than the cast this picture boasts. Each player, from Edward G. Robinson and Joan Bennett as the unwitting principals in a celebrated murder to Thomas Jackson as the police homicide bureau chief, is almost letter

perfect. . . . Mr. Robinson, who was so good as the insurance investigator of *Double Indemnity,* gives a masterly performance as the professor."

Howard Barnes, *New York Herald-Tribune,* January 26, 1945

"Edward G. Robinson has seldom, if ever, been better than he is as the professor whose logical and ultimately desperate attempts to cover up his act are foiled at every turn."

Walt., *Variety,* October 11, 1944

"Nunnally Johnson whips up a strong and decidedly suspenseful murder melodrama in *The Woman in the Window* . . . Robinson gives everything he has to the role as the reserved and reticent professor, scoring solidly."

With (from left) Agnes Moorehead, Margaret O'Brien, Morris Carnovsky, Greta Granstedt, Elizabeth Russell, Jackie (Butch) Jenkins, Sara Haden and George Lloyd in **Our Vines Have Tender Grapes.**

OUR VINES HAVE TENDER GRAPES (MGM, 1945) 105 M.

Producer, Robert Sisk; director, Roy Rowland; based on the novel *For Our Vines Have Tender Grapes* by George Victor Martin; screenplay, Dalton Trumbo; music, Bronislaw Kaper; art director, Cedric Gibbons and Edward Carfagno; sound, Douglas Shearer; camera, Robert Surtees; editor, Ralph E. Winters.

MARTINIUS JACOBSON	Edward G. Robinson
SELMA JACOBSON	Margaret O'Brien
NELS HALVERSON	James Craig
BRUNA JACOBSON	Agnes Moorehead
ARNOLD HANSON	Jackie "Butch" Jenkins
BJORN BJORNSON	Morris Carnovsky
VIOLA JOHNSON	Frances Gifford
MRS. BJORNSON	Sara Haden
MR. FARAASEN	Louis Jean Heydt
MINISTER	Francis Pierlot
MRS. FARAASEN	Greta Granstedt
MR. PETER HANSON	Arthur Space
KOLA HANSON	Elizabeth Russell
INGBORG JENSEN	Dorothy Morris
KURT JENSEN	Charles Middleton
DVAR SVENSON	Arthur Hohl
GIRL	Abigail Adams
DRIVER	Johnny Berkes
MARGUERITE LARSEN	Rhoda Williams

Synopsis

A slice of Americana, as viewed by a seven-year-old.

In a Norwegian farm community in southern Wisconsin, the Jacobsons, Martinius and Bruna

With Arthur Space, Morris Carnovsky and James Craig in Our Vines Have Tender Grapes.

and their young daughter Selma, are intimately concerned with the life of Benson Junction and neighboring farm families.

There is a childhood tragedy in Selma's accidental killing of a squirrel and excitement when Viola Johnson, a new school teacher from Milwaukee, comes to town.

Nels Halverson, Selma's older friend and editor of the town newspaper, takes a rather close interest in Viola. Their friendship turns to love, but the teacher has trouble adjusting to the stark simplicities of the tiny farming community, finding the town frankly dull.

Nels has been rejected by the Army, but following treatments for his back, he is accepted. Selma's idea of "peace on earth" is seriously threatened by the knowledge that a friend like Nels is in danger of being hurt in the war. Pa explains that freedom must be fought for.

Problems of Selma's life comprise Pa's punishment for her failing to share her new skates with her cousin Arnold, a dawn visit to town to watch the circus caravan pass and to ride on the elephant's trunk, the proud ownership of a New Jersey calf, and a near disaster when Selma and Arnold go rowing in the spring freshet in Pa's metal bath tub.

Death and disaster by fire affect the neighbors and trouble Selma. Sympathetically, she leads the way in offering her calf to Bjorn Bjornson, whose farm was struck by lightning.

Viola eventually accepts Nels's proposal, as she now understands the spirit of the whole town. Pa denies himself a much desired new barn.

Reviews

Thomas M. Pryor, *The New York Times*, September 7, 1945

"Edward G. Robinson is solid and loveable as Martinus and in this role gives one of the finest performances of his long and varied career."

Howard Barnes, *New York Herald-Tribune*, September 7, 1945

"Edward G. Robinson . . . has switched from tough roles to that of a benevolent farmer who has a rather inordinate affection for his daughter. He plays the part for all it is worth, but it does not always make for entertainment."

Brog., *Variety*, July 18, 1945

"Robinson gives a deft study of the farmer, an in-

With Joan Bennett in Scarlet Street.

articulate, soil-bound man whose greatest dream is for a new barn. His groping for answers to his daughter's questions and drawing on parallels from farm life for explanations make empathetic points to the script's philosophy of simplicity."

SCARLET STREET (Universal, 1946) 103 M.

Executive producer, Walter Wanger; producer-director, Fritz Lang; based on the novel and play *La Chienne* by Georges de la Fouchardière; assistant director, Melville Shyer; special photography, John Fulton; set director, Russel A. Gausman and Carl Lawrence; art director, Alexander Golitzer; music, H. J. Salter; camera, Milton Krasner; editor, Arthur Hilton; screenplay, Dudley Nichols.

CHRISTOPHER CROSS	Edward G. Robinson
KITTY MARCH	Joan Bennett
JOHNNY PRINCE	Dan Duryea
JANEWAY	Jess Barker
MILLIE	Margaret Lindsay
ADELE CROSS	Rosalind Ivan
CHARLES PRINGLE	Samuel S. Hinds
DELLAROWE	Arthur Loft
POP LEJON	Vladimir Sokoloff
PATCHEYE	Charles Kemper
HOGARTH	Russell Hicks
MRS. MICHAELS	Anita Bolster
NICK	Cyrus W. Kendall
MARCHETTI	Fred Essler
POLICEMAN	Edgar Dearing
POLICEMAN	Tom Dillon
CHAUFFEUR	Chuck Hamilton
EMPLOYEE	Gus Glassmire
EMPLOYEE	Ralph Littlefield
EMPLOYEE	Sherry Hall
EMPLOYEE	Howard Mitchell
EMPLOYEE	Jack Statham
BARNEY	Rodney Bell
WAITER	Henri de Soto
SAUNDERS	Milton Kibbee
PENNY	Tom Daly
HOLLIDAY	George Meader

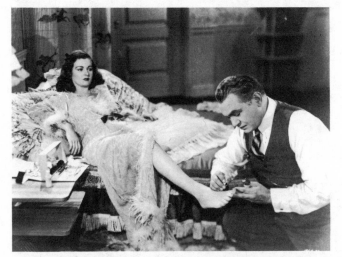

With Joan Bennett in Scarlet Street.

With Rosalind Ivan in Scarlet Street.

With Joan Bennett in Scarlet Street.

With Joe Devlin, George Lloyd and Syd Saylor in
Scarlet Street.

In Scarlet Street.

With Matt Willis, Lee Phelps and Russell Hicks in
Scarlet Street.

On the set of Journey Together *with Lt. John Boulting, the director (left), and Maj. Roy Boulting (right).*

TINY .... Lou Lubin
POLICEMAN .... Lee Phelps
POLICEMAN .... Matt Willis
BEN .... Clarence Muse
HURDY GURDY MAN .... John Barton
PROSECUTION ATTORNEY .... Emmett Vogan
POLICEMAN .... Robert Malcolm
MILKMAN .... Horace Murphy
LOAN OFFICE MANAGER .... Will Wright
CROCKER .... Syd Saylor
DERELICT .... Dewey Robinson
EVANGELIST .... Fritz Leiber
JONES .... Byron Foulger
2nd DETECTIVE .... Dick Wessel
3rd DETECTIVE .... Dick Curtis

Synopsis

At a banquet honoring his twenty years of faithful service, Christopher Cross, cashier for a New York clothing firm, becomes slightly drunk from the champagne, and on his way home, he finds a man beating a woman. He fights off her assailant with his umbrella and takes the girl, Kitty March, to a bar where he leads her to believe that he is a famous artist. Cross, unhappily married to a browbeating wife, easily becomes infatuated with Kitty, unaware of her attachment to punk Johnny Prince. Kitty and Johnny decide to capitalize on Cross's alleged genius, and Kitty persuades Cross to rent an apartment for her, as a combination studio and rendezvous. When Cross brings his paintings to the apartment, Johnny has them appraised. Discovering they are sensational, he forges Kitty's name to them. Cross finds out, but is elated to have his paintings recognized.

Soon, however, he is forced to embezzle his company's funds to maintain his apartment. Disgraced and discharged from his job, he comes to the apartment only to find Kitty in Johnny's arms. Unseen, Cross waits for Johnny to leave, then he denounces Kitty, and when she taunts him he kills her with an ice pick, arranging the evidence so it points to Johnny as the murderer.

On the night of Johnny's execution, Cross climbs a pole nearby, hoping to hear the high voltage rushing through to the electric chair; then he descends to face the future.

Now a derelict, he receives final retribution when he sees his portrait of Kitty sold for $10,000.

Reviews

Bosley Crowther, *The New York Times*, February 15, 1946

"In the role of the love-blighted cashier, Edward

G. Robinson performs monotonously and with little illumination of an adventurous spirit seeking air."

Howard Barnes, *New York Herald-Tribune*, February 15, 1946

"Robinson, who is no mean art connoisseur, must

In Journey Together.

have had a field day acting the part of the cashier who discovers that he has real talent in a thwarted love affair. He gives his all to the portrayal, sometimes a bit too much."

Brog., *Variety*, January 2, 1946

"Edward G. Robinson is the mild cashier and amateur painter whose love for Joan Bennett leads him to embezzlement, murder and disgrace. Two stars turn in top work to keep the interest high."

JOURNEY TOGETHER (English Films, 1946) 80 M.

Producer, Royal Air Force Film Unit; director, John Boulting; author, Terence Rattigan; screenplay, Boulting; music, Gordon Jacob; production designer, John Howell; special effects, Ray Morse; camera, Harry Waxman.

DAVID WILTON .... Sgt. Richard Attenborough
JOHN AYNESWORTH ...... Aircraftsman Jack Watling
SMITH .... Flying Officer David Tomlinson
A FITTER .... Warrant Officer Sid Rider
A FLIGHT SGT. FITTER ....
.... Squadron Leader Stuart Latham
AN ACTING LT. .... Squadron Leader Hugh Wakefield

With Jack Watling in **Journey Together.**

A.C. 2 JAY ..... Leading Aircraftsman Bromley Challenor
AN ANSON PILOT ...... Flying Officer Z. Peromowski
DEAN McWILLIAMS .... Edward G. Robinson
FLIGHT LT. MANDER .... Patrick Waddington
SQUADRON LEADER MARSHALL ....
.... Flight Lieutenant Sebastian Shaw
THE COMMANDING OFFICER ....
.... Wing Commander Ronald Adam
MARY McWILLIAMS .... Bessie Love
A DRIVER .... Sergeant Norvell Crutcher
and Personnel of the Royal Air Force, Royal Canadian Air
Force, United States Army

Synopsis

During World War II, David Wilton, a Cockney
lad, and John Aynesworth, a college graduate, both
enlisted in the R.A.F. at about the same time, seeking to become pilots.

Their vigorous training begins in England and
later shifts to the United States where American
Dean McWilliams becomes their tough but understanding instructor. McWilliams tries to impart
some sense of teamwork into Wilton, but without
much success. Wilton goes to the Canadian Naviga-
tion School, while Aynesworth gets his Wings and
returns to England. Wilton is depressed as he can
qualify only as an R.A.F. Navigator, and finds it
tough sledding under the Canadian training rigor.
The instructor, however, manages to impress on
him his vital contribution to the aircrew team.

Eventually, Wilton and Aynesworth find themselves on the same bomber, flying a mission over
Berlin. On their way back to England, they are
forced to ditch their ship in the North Sea. By the
time they are rescued, each has learned the importance of his job on a bomber.

Reviews

Bosley Crowther, *The New York Times*, March 4,
1946

"[It] is a dandy little picture about British airmen
during the war, solidly authentic and full of char-

With Richard Attenborough and Jack Watling in
Journey Together.

acter, action and suspense. . . . All of the cast—
with the exception of Edward G. Robinson, who
plays an instructor at the Arizona field, and Bessie
Love, who plays his wife—were recruited from
RAF personnel. It is no reflection on Mr. Robinson or Miss Love (and their roles are naturally
brief) to say that the actual airmen are much more
creditable in the film than they are."

Joe Pihodna, *New York Herald-Tribune,* March 4,
1946

"Edward G. Robinson has been dragged into the
picture as an American pilot-training officer. He
does his bit in a fatherly way."

THE STRANGER (RKO, 1946) 94 M.

Producer, S. P. Eagle; director, Orson Welles; based on
the story by Victor Trivas and Decia Dunning; screenplay,
Anthony Veiller; Adaptation and dialogue, Veiller, John
Huston and Orson Welles; assistant director, Jack Voglin;
music, Bronislaw Kaper; art director, Perry Ferguson; camera, Russell Metty; editor, Ernest Nims.

WILSON	Edward G. Robinson
MARY LONGSTREET	Loretta Young
PROF. CHARLES RANKIN	Orson Welles
JUDGE LONGSTREET	Philip Merivale
NOAH LONGSTREET	Richard Long
DR. JEFF LAWRENCE	Byron Keith
POTTER	Billy House
KONRAD MEINIKE	Konstantin Shayne

SARA .... Martha Wentworth
MRS. LAWRENCE .... Isabel O'Madigan
MR. PEABODY .... Pietro Sasso

Synopsis

Inspector Wilson of the Commission for War Crimes follows Konrad Meinike, an escaped Nazi official, to Harper, Connecticut, in the hope of finding the notorious German leader, Franz Kindler, who is posing now as Charles Rankin, professor in a boys' school. Pretending to be an antique collector, Wilson ingratiates himself to Rankin's fiance, Mary Longstreet, and to her father, the judge. Shortly after Rankin and Mary marry, Meinike seeks out Rankin, who murders him to protect his identity.

A chance anti-Semitic remark made by Rankin at dinner one night convinces Wilson that Rankin is his man. When Meinike's body is discovered, Wilson feels the time has come for Mary to know the true identity of her husband.

Only a timely intervention by Wilson interrupts Rankin's attempt to do away with Mary, who has confronted her husband with her knowledge of his past, and Rankin makes a hasty retreat. With Wilson in pursuit, Rankin attempts to hide out in the clock tower in the town's square, but falls to his

With Loretta Young and Orson Welles in **The Stranger.**

"It is true that Mr. Welles has directed his camera for some striking effects, with lighting and interesting angles much relied on in his technique. The fellow knows how to make a camera dynamic in telling a tale. And it is true, too, that Edward G. Robinson is well restrained as the unrelenting sleuth. . . . But the whole film comes off a bloodless, manufactured show."

Bosley Crowther, *The Sunday New York Times,* July 14, 1946

"Two very good performances in the picture, by Edward G. Robinson as the sleuth and by Billy House as a small-town meddler, are . . . partial tribute to Mr. Welles."

Howard Barnes, *New York Herald-Tribune,* July 11, 1946

"Edward G. Robinson matches staccato line for staccato line with Welles as his nemesis, charged with bringing Nazi criminals to justice."

THE RED HOUSE (United Artists, 1947) 100 M.

Producer, Sol Lesser; director, Delmer Daves; based on the novel by George Agnew Chamberlain; screenplay, Daves; music, Miklos Rozsa; art director, McClure Capps; camera, Bert Glennon; editor, Merrill White.

PETE MORGAN .... Edward G. Robinson
NATH STORM .... Lon McCallister
ELLEN MORGAN .... Judith Anderson

With Byron Keith, Richard Long and Philip Merivale in **The Stranger.**

death impaled on the sword of a warrior, one of the hands on the huge clock.

Reviews

Bosley Crowther, *The New York Times,* July 11, 1946

With Lon McCallister and Allene Roberts in **The Red House.**

MEG MORGAN .... Allene Roberts
TIBBY .... Julie London
TELLER .... Rory Calhoun
MRS. STORM .... Ona Munson
DR. BYRNE .... Harry Shannon
OFFICER .... Arthur Space
DON BRENT .... Walter Sande
COP .... Pat Flaherty

Synopsis

Pete Morgan, a moody farmer, lives a life of rigid seclusion with his sister, Ellen, and his adopted daughter, Meg, whose parents mysteriously disappeared fifteen years before. Crippled, Morgan has hired a young neighbor, Nath Storm, to help with the farm work, but he has warned Nath and all others away from Oxhead Woods—which borders on his farm—as well as "The Red House and the screams in the night." Nath becomes curious about Morgan's vague and erratic remarks about this Red House and its curse, and

he arranges with Meg to spend Sunday searching for it.

Morgan, learning of the youngsters' search, orders Teller, the caretaker he has hired, to use his gun on trespassers. Meg eventually locates the mysterious house, but breaks her leg as she flees from a fusillade of Teller's bullets.

As the weeks pass by, Ellen Morgan realizes that her brother's mental condition is deteriorating, and she decides to burn the Red House that harbored his secrets in the hope that it would aid him. She makes her way into the woods, but is shot by Teller. Before she dies, she confides to Meg and Nath the secret she has kept for years: her brother, because of his unrequited love for Meg's mother, had murdered both her parents in the Red House.

In the course of events, Morgan, now completely demented, lures Meg to the house, but Nath and the police have followed them and arrive in time to save her from a fate similar to her parents.

With Judith Anderson in **The Red House.**

With Allene Roberts in **The Red House.**

With Allene Roberts in **The Red House.**

*With Mady Christians, Howard Duff, Burt Lancaster
and Louisa Horton in* All My Sons.

Morgan cunningly evades his pursuers and commits suicide by driving his truck into the soggy mud adjoining the Red House, where he had sunk the bodies of Meg's parents fifteen years before.

Reviews

A. H. Weiler, *The New York Times,* March 17, 1947

"It's been a long time since the Hollywood artisans have turned out an adult horror number. *The Red House* is just such an edifying offering, which should supply horror-hungry audiences with the chills of the month. . . . Edward G. Robinson is excellent as crippled Peter, whose mind is cracking under the thrall of the horrible secret of *The Red*

House, and Judith Anderson gives a taut performance as his sister who has silently shared his mental burden."

Otis Guernsey Jr., *New York Herald-Tribune,* March 17, 1947

"An ordinary mystery story has received a booster charge of good direction in *The Red House,* and the result is a moody hair-raiser of a melodrama. . . . With veterans Edward G. Robinson and Judith Anderson pacing four talented young newcomers to a round of convincing performances, this Sol Lesser production is a taut and steady item of menacing make-believe. . . . Daves' direction has brought the scenery so much to life that it becomes the most important character of the piece, making the villainy of Edward G. Robinson as the farmer and Judith Anderson as his sister seem weak in comparison."

ALL MY SONS (Universal, 1948) 94 M.

Producer, Chester Erskine; director, Irving Reis; from the play by Arthur Miller; screenplay, Erskine; assistant director, Frank Shaw; music, Leith Stevens; set director, Russell A. Gausman, Al Felds; sound, Leslie Carey and Carson Jowett; art director, Bernard Herzbrun, Hilyard Brown; camera, Russell Metty; editor, Ralph Dawson.

JOE KELLER .... Edward G. Robinson
CHRIS KELLER .... Burt Lancaster
KATE KELLER .... Mady Christians
ANN DEEVER .... Louisa Horton
GEORGE DEEVER .... Howard Duff
HERBERT DEEVER .... Frank Conroy
JIM BAYLISS .... Lloyd Gough
SUE BAYLISS .... Arlene Francis
FRANK LUBEY .... Henry Morgan
LYDIA LUBEY .... Elisabeth Fraser
CHARLES .... Walter Soderling
MINNIE .... Therese Lyon
ELLSWORTH .... Charles Meredith
ATTORNEY .... William Johnstone
WERTHEIMER .... Hebert Vigran
JUDGE .... Harry Harvey
BARTENDER .... Pat Flaherty
HEADWAITER .... George Sorel
MRS. HAMILTON .... Helen Brown
McGRAW .... Herbert Haywood
NORTON .... Joseph Kerr
HALLIDAY .... Jerry Hausner
FOREMAN .... Frank Kreig
ED .... William Ruhl
TOM .... Al Murphy
JORGENSON .... Walter Boon
BILL .... Richard La Marr
WORKMAN .... Jack Gargan
ATTENDANTS .... Victor Zimmerman
George Slocum

With Burt Lancaster in All My Sons.

Synopsis

Joe Keller owns a prosperous stove factory in a small city where people are already forgetting that during World War II he was tried, but acquitted, for selling defective airplane parts to the government. Twenty-one flyers died because of the resulting faulty motors.

Joe's partner, Herbert Deever, is still in prison for the wartime crime, but Ann, his daughter, returns to the town where she grew up. She goes to visit the Kellers, invited there by Chris, Joe's son, who is in love with her.

Before the war, Ann was engaged to Chris's brother Larry, a pilot missing in action. The boys' mother, Kate, still believes Larry may be alive and opposes the marriage of Chris and Ann.

Ann's brother George has been insisting that Joe is also guilty in the defective parts scandal and urges his sister not to marry Chris and become part of the "blood-stained" Keller household. Chris worships Joe but is compelled by conscience to learn the truth. He calls on Deever in prison and discovers that Joe escaped conviction through a legal technicality.

With Mady Christians in All My Sons.

Uncovering the whole story, Chris confronts his father. He shows Joe a letter sent to Ann by Larry, stating that the pilot intended to fly to his death in shame over his father's unpatriotic and criminal deed.

Joe commits suicide. Ann and Chris go away together.

With Burt Lancaster and Mady Christians in All My Sons.

Reviews

Bosley Crowther, *The New York Times*, March 29, 1948

"Through a fine performance by Edward G. Robinson, it certainly reveals a character. . . . [He] does a superior job of showing the shades of a personality in a little tough guy who has a softer side. . . . Clearly he reveals the blank bewilderment of a man who can't conceive in the abstract the basic moral obligation of the individual to society."

Howard Barnes, *New York Herald-Tribune*, March 29, 1948

"While there are scenes of fine indignation in the motion picture, realized to the full by Edward G. Robinson, Burt Lancaster, Mady Christians and Frank Conroy, they do not off-set fabricated situations and blurred characterizations."

Brog., *Variety*, February 25, 1948

"Edward G. Robinson gives an effective performance as the small-town manufacturer who sends defective parts to the Army Air Forces. It's a humanized study that rates among his best and lends the thought behind the film much strength."

KEY LARGO (Warner Bros., 1948) 101 M.

Producer, Jerry Wald; director, John Huston; based on

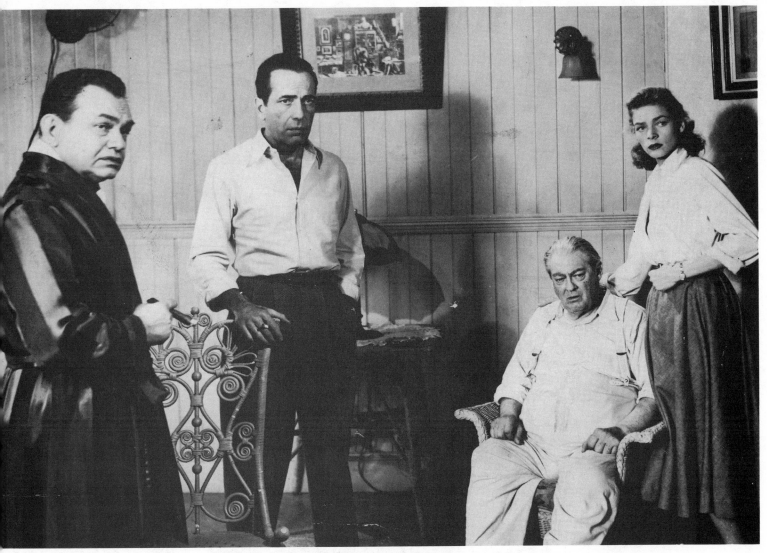

With Humphrey Bogart, Lionel Barrymore and Lauren Bacall in Key Largo.

the play by Maxwell Anderson; screenplay, Richard Brooks and Huston; assistant director, Art Lueker; music, Max Steiner; art director, Leo K. Kuter; set director, Fred M. MacLean; sound, Dolph Thomas; special effects, William McGann and Robert Burks; camera, Karl Freund; editor, Rudi Fehr.

FRANK McCLOUD . . . . Humphrey Bogart
JOHNNY ROCCO . . . . Edward G. Robinson
NORA TEMPLE . . . . Lauren Bacall
JAMES TEMPLE . . . . Lionel Barrymore
GAYE DAWN . . . . Claire Trevor
CURLEY HOFF . . . . Thomas Gomez
TOOTS BASS . . . . Harry Lewis
DEPUTY CLYDE SAWYER . . . . John Rodney
ZIGGY . . . . Marc Lawrence
ANGEL GARCIA . . . . Dan Seymour
SHERIFF BEN WADE . . . . Monte Blue
RALPH FEENEY . . . . William Haade

TOM OSCEOLA . . . . Jay Silverheels
JOHN OSCEOLA . . . . Rodric Redwing
BUS DRIVER . . . . Joe P. Smith
SKIPPER . . . . Albert Marin
MAN . . . . Pat Flaherty
ZIGGY'S HENCHMEN . . . . Jerry Jerome
John Phillips
Lute Crockett
OLD INDIAN WOMAN . . . . Felipa Gomez

Synopsis

Frank McCloud, an ex-army officer, comes to lonely Key Largo and ends up at a run-down hotel operated by James Temple, a cripple, and Nora, his daughter-in-law, whose late husband had been a wartime buddy of Frank.

With (from left) Claire Trevor, Dan Seymour, Thom-
as Gomez, John Rodney, Humphrey Bogart and Lau-
ren Bacall in Key Largo.

With Harry Lewis, Dan Seymour, William Haade
and Thomas Gomez in Key Largo.

Frank finds the hotel taken over by gangster Johnny Rocco and his henchmen. When he has a chance to kill the Rocco, however, he passes the opportunity by, too concerned about saving his own life, and too disillusioned by humanity to really care.

When a fierce storm rakes the Florida island, Rocco loses his cool, and Frank finds new strength. He comes to the aid of Gaye Dawn, Rocco's aging alcoholic mistress, and receives a beating for his efforts. Nora is attracted to Frank and Temple realizes that maybe a new man of the house has finally arrived.

When Sheriff Ben Wade comes searching for his deputy and finds him dead, Rocco thrusts the blame on a pair of local Indians. The sheriff kills

With Harry Lewis, Humphrey Bogart, Dan Seymour, Thomas Gomez, Lauren Bacall and Lionel Barrymore in Key Largo.

them when they try to escape. This makes Frank realize the dangerousness of Rocco, a destroyer of innocent people.

Frank agrees to pilot a boat for Rocco, who is heading for Cuba. With a gun smuggled to him by Gaye, who is left behind, he plans to get rid of the mob once out at sea. One by one Frank picks off the boys, with Rocco killing the last henchman who is cowering below in the cabin. After a cat-and-mouse chase on the small cruiser, Frank shoots Rocco and heads back to Key Largo and to Nora.

Reviews

Bosley Crowther, *The New York Times*, July 17, 1948

"With remarkable filming and cutting, [John]

Huston has notably achieved a great deal of interest and tension in some rather static scenes—and scenes, too, that give the bald appearances of having been written for the stage. . . . He has also got stinging performances out of most of his cast—notably out of Mr. Robinson, who plays the last of the red-hot gangsters in top-notch style. Indeed, [his] performance is an expertly timed and timbered scan of the vulgarity, corruption and egoism of a criminal mind."

Otis Guernsey, Jr., *New York Herald-Tribune*, July 17, 1948

"Although not as honest and thoughtful a portrayal of human beings as its predecessor [*The Treasure of Sierra Madre*], it is a bowstring-tight humdinger of movie make-believe. . . . Robinson is Little Caesar all over again, terrorizing both his henchmen and the bystanders trapped with him in a lonely seaside hotel. In a story of modern crime, his acting might seem extreme, but here its touch of the Twenties is exactly what is required of a brutish has-been who hopes that 'prohibition will come back in a couple of years.' "

NIGHT HAS A THOUSAND EYES (Paramount, 1948) 80 M.

Producer, Endre Bohem; director, John Farrow; based on the novel by Cornell Woolrich; screenplay, Barre Lyndon and Jonathan Latimer; music, Victor Young; art director, Hans Dreier and Franz Bachelin; camera, John F. Seitz; editor, Eda Warren.

JOHN TRITON	Edward G. Robinson
JEAN COURTLAND	Gail Russell
ELLIOTT CARSON	John Lund
JENNY	Virginia Bruce
LIEUT. SHAWN	William Demarest
PETER VINSON	Richard Webb
WHITNEY COURTLAND	Jerome Cowan
DR. WALTERS	Onslow Stevenson
MR. GILMAN	John Alexander
MELVILLE WESTON	Roman Bohnen
MR. MYERS	Luis Van Rooten
BUTLER	Henry Guttman
MISS HENDRICKS	Mary Adams
CHAUFFEUR	Philip Van Zandt
DR. RAMSDELL	Douglas Spencer
EDNA (maid)	Jean King
2nd MAID	Dorothy Abbott
GOWAN	Bob Stephenson
BERTELLI	William Haade
3rd SCIENTIST	Stuart Holmes
YOUNG CHINESE WOMAN	Jean Wong
YOUNG CHINESE WOMAN	Anna Tom
YOUNG CHINESE MAN	Weaver Levy

With Jerome Cowan and Virginia Bruce in **Night Has a Thousand Eyes.**

CHINESE WAITER .... Artarne Wong
NEWSTAND WOMAN .... Jane Crowley
RADIO ANNOUNCER .... Joey Ray
SCRUBWOMAN .... Eleanore Vogel
BIT WOMAN (ITALIAN) .... Minerva Urecal
1st SECRETARY .... Renee Randall
2nd SECRETARY .... Marilyn Gray
MR. BYERS .... Lester Dorr
HUSBAND OF FRANTIC MOTHER .. Harland Tucker
DEB'S MOTHER .... Violet Goulet
BIT MAN .... Edward Earle
2nd COMPANION .... Julia Faye
AGNES .... Margaret Field
DEB'S FATHER .... Major Sam Harris
ELDERLY DOORMAN .... John Sheehan
SECRETARY .... Betty Hannon
JAILER .... James Davies

Synopsis

John Triton is a vaudeville mentalist who finds himself with the power to perceive forthcoming tragic events. His inability to prevent their occurrence disturbs him, and he retires from the stage when he foresees the death of his friend, Jenny, in childbirth following her marriage to his partner, Whitney Courtland.

Years later, Triton hears on the radio that Courtland, now a wealthy industrialist, is attempting to set a new coast-to-coast speed record in his private plane. Triton receives a premonition of the man's impending death, and in an effort to save him, he visits his daughter Jean and pleads with her to stop the flight. Her fiance, Elliott Carson, thinks that Triton is a crackpot, but she agrees to communicate with her father. She is unable to reach him, and shortly thereafter word comes of his death in a crash.

Triton, heartbroken over the tragedy, becomes even more dejected when he foresees the girl's death in an accident. Jean agrees to let him help her avoid the accident, but Elliott gets suspicious and contacts the police. The police, having learned that Courtland's plane had been tampered with, suspect that Triton may have been involved in the murder and that he might be planning to do away with the girl too, so they take him into custody.

As the hour of Jean's impending death draws near, Triton, by predicting the suicide of a convict before it happens, convinces the police of his strange powers; they release him and he rushes to Jean's home. There, despite the fact that she was closely guarded by the police, Triton bursts in just as one of her father's associates is preparing to kill her to cover up a crooked stock deal. Triton rushes to her defense and saves her, but the police on the scene mistake his motives and shoot him down. In his pocket they find a note predicting his own death that night.

Reviews

Bosley Crowther, *The New York Times,* October 14, 1948

"[It] is such unadulterated hokum that it almost ingratiates itself . . . [except that] it tries to put over the pretense that it is serious, solemn stuff. . . . From the very beginning to the very end of the film, we are asked to believe that a fellow really might have supernatural sight. . . . Now, this sort of thing might be charming—or funny at least—if done in a spirit of thinly veiled fooling or out-and-

With Virginia Bruce and Jerome Cowan in **Night Has a Thousand Eyes.**

out fantasy. But here it is done in sombre fashion with Edward G. Robinson playing the gent as a figure of tragic proportions."

Howard Barnes, *New York Herald-Tribune*, October 14, 1948

"Robinson labors diligently and sometimes effectively in the part of the crystal-ball gazer who is doomed to unhappiness and extinction by his supernatural powers."

HOUSE OF STRANGERS (20th Century-Fox, 1949) 101 M.

Producer, Sol C. Siegel; director, Joseph L. Mankiewicz; from the novel by Jerome Weidman; screenplay, Philip Yordan; music, Daniele Amfitheatrof; special effects, Fred Sersen; art director, Lyle Wheeler, George W. Davis; set director, Thomas Little and Walter M. Scott; camera, Milton Kramer; editor, Harmon Le Maire.

GINO MONETTI	Edward G. Robinson
IRENE BENNETT	Susan Hayward
MAX MONETTI	Richard Conte
JOE MONETTI	Luther Adler
PIETRO MONETTI	Paul Valentine
TONY MONETTI	Efrem Zimbalist Jr.
MARIA DOMENICO	Debra Paget
HELENA DOMENICO	Hope Emerson
THERESA MONETTI	Esther Minciotti
ELAINE MONETTI	Diane Douglas
LUCCA	Tito Vuolo
VICTORO	Albert Morin
WAITER	Sid Tomack
JUDGE	Thomas Browne Henry
PROSECUTOR	David Wolfe
DANNY	John Kellogg
WOMAN JUROR	Ann Morrison
NIGHT CLUB SINGER	Dolores Parker
BIT MAN	Mario Siletti
PIETRO'S OPPONENT	Tommy Garland
GUARD	Charles J. Blynn
BAT BOY	Joseph Mazzuca
COP	John Pedrini
3rd APPLICANT	Argentina Brunetti

With Richard Conte in House of Strangers.

*With Richard Conte and Charles J. Flynn (as guard)
in* House of Strangers.

BIT MAN	Maurice Samuels
COPS	George Magrill
NEIGHBORS	Mike Stark
	Herbert Vigran
REFEREE	Mushy Callahan
PRELIMINARY FIGHTERS	Bob Cantro
	Eddie Saenz
DOORMAN	George Spaulding
TAXI DRIVER	John "Red" Kullers
DETECTIVES	Scott Landers
	Fred Hillebrand

Synopsis

After serving seven years in Sing Sing, Max Monetti returns to New York's Little Italy and goes straight to the Monetti Trust Company to settle an old score with his brothers, Joe, Tony and Pietro. The brothers are solicitous to him, but he spurns their money offer and leaves them in fear of his one-man vendetta. Max then goes to the apartment of his old girl friend, Irene Bennett, who tries to get him to leave with her. He refuses until he has avenged his father's betrayal. Irene's pleas only anger Max and he leaves for the

With Tito Vuolo in House of Strangers.

With (from left) Efrem Zimbalist Jr., Luther Adler, Diana Douglas, Esther Minciotti, Hope Emerson, Debra Paget and Richard Conte in House of Strangers.

Monetti mansion where old memories come back.

Seven years earlier, in 1932, Gino Monetti reigned supreme in his loan office, handing out money eagerly, but at high interest rates. At home, the Monetti family lived in hate and distrust: Joe was married to Elaine; Max was engaged to Maria Domenico; Tony was the family Beau Brummell; Pietro, the dumbhead, was an amateur prize fighter.

One day, Irene came into Max's law office to seek legal advice and a torrid love affair developed, much to the chagrin of Maria's mother.

Gino's banking methods eventually led to an indictment. Joe, Tony and Pietro deserted their father, but Max defended him. The trial went bad and Max attempted to fix a juror. Joe tipped off the police and Max was arrested and convicted. The three brothers then took over the loan business, with Gino going free on a mistrial.

Tony married Maria, and the brothers were living in luxury. Shortly before Gino died he visited Max in prison and demanded that he (Max) make his brothers pay for stealing the company from him.

As Max now stands before his father's portrait in the deserted house, all the memories return. The brothers arrive, ready for the vendetta, but they begin to fight among themselves, leaving Max free. He staggers out of the house to Irene and they go off together.

With Pat Flaherty, Jack Carson and Doris Day in
It's a Great Feeling.

Reviews

Bosley Crowther, *The New York Times*, July 2, 1949

"Edward G. Robinson, as usual, does a brisk and colorful job of making Papa Monetti a brassy despot with a Sicilian accent."

Howard Barnes, *New York Herald-Tribune*, July 2, 1949

"It has solid characterizations by Edward G. Robinson, Richard Conte, Luther Adler, Susan Hayward and their assistants. . . . Robinson gives [Monetti] ominous quality, but he lingers too fondly over reminiscences of his youth as a barber on Mulberry Street and makes far too much of an Italian accent."

Wear., *Variety,* June 15, 1949

"Despite a rather weak title, *House of Strangers* is a strong picture. . . . The stars, Edward G. Robinson, Susan Hayward and Richard Conte, contribute some of their finest work in this film. . . . Robinson is especially vivid when he realized that the three sons have turned against him and when he seeks revenge through his fourth."

IT'S A GREAT FEELING (Warner Bros. 1949) 84 M. Color.

Producer, Alex Gottlieb; director, David Butler; story, I. A. L. Diamond; screenplay, Jack Rose and Melville Shavelson; art director, Stanley Fleischer; set director, Lyle B. Reifsnider; sound, Dolph Thomas and Charles David Frost; special effects, William McGann, H. F. Koenekamp; assistant director, Phil Quinn; music numbers staged-directed, LeRoy Prinz; music, Ray Heindorf; camera, Wilfrid M. Cline; editor, Irene Morra.

HIMSELF .... Dennis Morgan
JUDY ADAMS .... Doris Day
HIMSELF .... Jack Carson
ARTHUR TRENT .... Bill Goodwin
INFORMATION CLERK .... Irving Bacon
GRACE .... Claire Carleton
PUBLICITY MAN .... Harlan Warde
TRENT'S SECRETARY .... Jacqueline de Witt
AND: (as themselves) David Butler, Michael Curtiz, King Vidor, Raoul Walsh, Gary Cooper, Joan Crawford, Errol Flynn, Sydney Greenstreet, Danny Kaye, Patricia Neal, Eleanor Parker, Ronald Reagan, Edward G. Robinson, Jane Wyman.

Synopsis

Because of Jack Carson's unbounding ego and overexaggerated acting techniques, he and co-star Dennis Morgan are having great difficulties in finding any director on the Warner Brothers lot to work with them on their upcoming picture. Michael Curtiz, King Vidor, Raoul Walsh, David Butler—the top names at the studio—all have turned thumbs down at working with Carson.

The producer decides, against his better judgment, to let Carson direct the film himself, but the Carson-Morgan team has almost as much trouble finding a leading lady who will put up with Carson's hamming as they had getting someone to set in the director's chair. They soon discover that Judy Adams, a star-struck waitress in the studio commissary, has been making the rounds hoping to break into films. They decide, for lack of anyone else, to give her a break and pull out all stops by giving her the big buildup as an important future star.

In the course of making the film, many of the top stars on the Warner Brothers lot unwittingly become involved with Carson and Morgan or try to give an acting tip or two to the boys' ingenue. Gary Cooper, Ronald Reagan, Eleanor Parker and Patricia Neal are among the stars who become involved. Edward G. Robinson does a takeoff on his famed hard-boiled gangster character, Joan Crawford is encountered in a dress shop, and Danny Kaye is spotted in a railroad station and is "on."

Soon, though, Judy Adams becomes disenchanted with her newfound fame, and with coping with Carson and Morgan, and heads back to Wisconsin to marry her old boy friend, Jeffrey Bushdinkel.

Reviews

A. H. Weiler, *The New York Times*, August 13, 1949

"Edward G. Robinson contributes a travesty on his hard-boiled gangster characterization."

Brog., *Variety*, July 27, 1949

"A broad take-off on Broadway and picture making. It has a gay, light air, color and a lineup of surprise guest stars that greatly enhance word-of-mouth values. . . . Edward G. Robinson gives a swell take-off on his stock hard-boiled gangster character in a sequence played for loud chuckles."

MY DAUGHTER JOY (U.S. title: *Operation X*) (Columbia, 1950) 79 M.

Producer-director, Gregory Ratoff; associate producer, Phil Brandon; based on the novel *David Golder* by Irene

With Nora Swinburne and director Gregory Ratoff on set of Operation X.

Nemirowsky; screenplay, Robert Thoeren and William Rose; set director, Andre Andrejew; sound, Jack Drake; assistant director, Cliff Brandon; camera, Georges Perinal; editor, Raymond Poulton.

GEORGE CONSTANTIN .... Edward G. Robinson
AVA CONSTANTIN .... Nora Swinburne
GEORGETTE .... Peggy Cummins
LARRY BOYD .... Richard Greene
SIR THOMAS MacTAVISH .... Finlay Currie
MARCOS .... Gregory Ratoff
COLONEL FOGARTY .... Ronald Adam
ANDREAS .... Walter Rilla

With Ronald Adam in Operation **X.**

With Peggy Cummins, Nora Swinburne and Richard Greene in Operation **X.**

PROFESSOR KAROL .... James Robertson Justice
ENNIX .... David Hutcheson
POLATO .... Dod Nehan
SULTAN .... Peter Illing
DR. SCHINDLER .... Ronald Ward
PRINCE ALZAR .... Roberto Villa
BARBOZA .... Harry Lane

Synopsis

George Constantin is a brilliant, ruthless businessman, and he lets neither himself nor anyone else forget it. His days as a youngster in Constantinople, where he earned his pennies as a bootblack, have long since been seared into his mind. His consuming passion then, and now, is to rule the world. Next to this driving force, Constantin has room for only one other thing in his life, his beloved, beautiful daughter, Georgette.

Constantin has supposedly found the key to supreme power, a project he calls Operation X. The one ingredient missing, though, is a vital material which is controlled by the Sultan of a certain mideast country. To obtain the missing link, Constantin plans to give his daughter in marriage to the potentate's son.

With Peggy Cummins in Operation X.

Georgette, meanwhile, has become engaged to Larry Boyd, a resourceful young journalist, who has been doing a bit of investigation and has stumbled upon Operation X. Enraged, Constantin forces Larry to leave.

Constantin's wife intercedes, pleading with her husband to give Georgette the happiness he has been promising her for so long by letting her go with Larry. When he refuses, she confesses that Georgette is not his daughter.

The shock of the news dooms both Operation X and its brilliant backer, who almost ruled the world.

Reviews

A. H. Weiler, *The New York Times,* December 11, 1950

"Edward G. Robinson gives the film's solitary rounded performance. He is a restrained schemer whose dreams of 'mastery of the world' seem ominously real."

Otis Guernsey Jr., *New York Herald-Tribune,* December 11, 1950

"Edward G. Robinson strides through the leading role in a suitable imitation of megalomania. . . . [His] version of a power-hungry millionaire is one who strides into a room, comforts three resentful graybeards, and announces: 'Gentlemen, whether you like it or not, you are going to loan me two million dollars!' "

ACTORS AND SIN (United Artists, 1952) 85 M.

Producer-director-screenplay, Ben Hecht; co-director-camera, Lee Garmes; set director, Howard Bristol; music, George Antheil; editor, Otto Ludwig.

ACTOR'S BLOOD
MAURICE TILLAYOU .... Edward G. Robinson
MARCIA TILLAYOU .... Marsha Hunt
ALFRED O'SHEA .... Dan O'Herlihy
OTTO LACHSLEY .... Rudolph Anders
TOMMY .... Alice Key
CLYDE VEERING .... Rick Roman

WOMAN OF SIN
ORLANDO HIGGENS .... Eddie Albert
J. B. COBB .... Alan Reed
MISS FLANNIGAN .... Tracey Roberts
MR. BLUE .... Paul Guilfoyle
MR. DEVLIN .... Doug Evans
DAISY MARCHER .... Jenny Hecht
MRS. EGELHOFER .... Jody Gilbert
MOVIE HERO .... John Crawford

Synopsis

ACTOR'S BLOOD: Maurice Tillayou, a fading Shakespearian actor from the old school, devotes his old age to his daughter Marcia, a glamorous

With Marsha Hunt in **Actors and Sin.**

actress of enormous ability and a savage temper. Success goes to her head. She alienates her friends, drives her husband from her and leads a most wasteful existence. Bad luck comes in the form of a series of stage flops and she realizes her career is finished.

Marcia poisons herself, but rather than admit her failure to the world, Maurice makes his daughter's death look like murder. At a party of those suspected by the police of committing the crime, the lights suddenly go out and Maurice is found dying from a dagger wound, unable to put his hand on the man he thinks is the murderer. His ruse is discovered: he stabbed himself, and the assembled guests salute his melodramatic flair.

WOMAN OF SIN: In 1930s Hollywood, a fast talking, unprincipled talent agent, Orlando Higgens, sells a lush romantic story to a big film studio. He is shocked to discover that the author is Daisy Marcher, a horrid girl of nine. The story is filmed and when the studio discovers the truth the agent is able to blackmail it into offering the kid a five-year contract as a script writer.

With Bob Carson in **Actors and Sin.**

Reviews

Howard Thompson, *The New York Times,* May 30, 1952

"*Actors' Blood* is a stiff, glum and narcissistic tale of a retired actor's devotion to his daughter, a neurotic, dimming Broadway star who commits suicide. . . . Edward G. Robinson and Marsha Hunt, the leads, bleakly intone some of Mr. Hecht's most sonorous dialogue."

Otis Guernsey Jr., *New York Herald-Tribune,* May 30, 1952

"The characters are pretty familiar, including the star's doting father, played by Edward G. Robinson in a combination of pride and anxiety."

VICE SQUAD (United Artists, 1953) 88 M.

Producer, Jules Levy and Arthur Gardner; director, Arnold Laven; based on the novel *Harness Bull* by Leslie T. White; screenplay, Lawrence Roman; art director, Carroll Clark; music, Herschel Burke Gilbert; camera, Joseph C. Biroc; editor, Arthur H. Nadel.

CAPTAIN BARNABY	Edward G. Robinson
MONA	Paulette Goddard
GINNY	K. T. Stevens
JACK HARTRAMPF	Porter Hall
MARTY KUSALICH	Adam Williams
AL BARKIS	Edward Binns
PETE	Lee Van Cleef
FRANKIE	Jay Adler
VICKIE	Joan Vohs
LIEUTENANT IMLAY	Dan Riss
CAROL	Mary Ellen Kay

Synopsis

Attempting to steal a car for a bank robbery, two hoods, Al Barkis and Pete, are interrupted in the darkened parking lot by a policeman. Barkis shoots and kills the policeman but Jack Hartrampf, who had been visiting the girl in Room 17 at a nearby hotel, stumbles onto the scene just in time to witness the crime. He is picked up by the police, but refuses to give evidence for fear of implicating the girl and damaging his reputation.

Taking personal charge of the case, Police Captain Barnaby holds Hartrampf in custody, hoping that he will eventually identify the killers. He also enlists the help of Mona, who runs an escort bureau and has an extraordinarily wide range of underworld connections. She gives him a lead on a man named Marty Kusalich. Barnaby learns that Barkis is planning a bank robbery, and the gang arrives at the bank to find the police waiting for

With Paulette Goddard in Vice Squad.

them. Barkis and Pete, however, escape again, using a young girl teller as a shield.

Meanwhile, under Barnaby's pressure, Hartrampf wrongly identifies Kusalich as one of the killers. Proclaiming his innocence he reveals Barkis's hideout to the police and Barnaby and a squad surround the place, rescuing the girl hostage after killing Barkis and capturing Pete.

This is another "routine" day for the Captain of Detectives and he prepares for another day of attempting to stop rich old ladies from being bilked, attending the morning lineups for petty thieves, questioning material witnesses, and other normal duties.

Reviews

A. H. Weiler, *The New York Times,* August 26, 1953

"Edward G. Robinson, who hasn't been around lately to glower at movie audiences, is back in harness, this time as a captain of detectives plagued by a variety of cons, stoolies, gunmen and molls, and the problems of running down a cop-killing gang of bank robbers."

Paul V. Beckley, *New York Herald-Tribune,* August 26, 1953

With Edgar Dearing (at desk) in **Vice Squad.**

"Edward G. Robinson plays the tired captain with conviction and sour patience."

Monthly Film Bulletin, October 1953

"There are competent performances from the supporting cast, but it is surprising to find Edward G. Robinson wasting his talent in the unrewarding role of Captain Barnaby."

BIG LEAGUER (MGM, 1953) 73 M.

Producer, Matthew Rapf; director, Robert Aldrich, story, John McNulty and Louis Morheim; screenplay, Herbert Baker; art director, Cedric Gibbons, Eddie Imazu; sound, Douglas Shearer; music director, Alberto Colombo; camera, William Mellor; editor, Ben Lewis.

JOHN B. "HANS" LOBERT	Edward G. Robinson
CHRISTY	Vera-Ellen
ADAM POLACHUK	Jeff Richards
BOBBY BRONSON	Richard Jaeckel
JULIE DAVIS	William Campbell
CARL HUBBELL	Himself
BRIAN McLENNAN	Paul Langton
CHUY AGUILAR	Lalo Rios
TIPPY MITCHELL	Bill Crandall
WALLY MITCHELL	Frank Ferguson
DALE ALEXANDER	John McKee
MR. POLACHUK	Mario Siletti
POMFRET	Robert Caldwell
LITTLE JOE	Donald "Chippie" Hastings
AL CAMPANIS	Himself
BOB TROCOLOR	Himself
TONY RAVISH	Himself

Synopsis

John Lobert, an aging baseball player, is given

Lobby card for Big Leaguer.

In Big Leaguer.

With Jeff Richards and William Campbell (center)
in Big Leaguer.

the job of heading the Florida training camp of the New York Giants.

Among the new rookies Lobert must whip into shape are, Adam Polachuk, son of a Polish miner who wants the boy to become a lawyer; a famous player's son who would rather be an architect than a first baseman; Julie Davis, a New York Ninth Avenue know-it-all; and Bobby Bronson, a show-off pitcher from Ohio.

Lobert's niece, Christy, falls in love with Polachuk and is dismayed to learn that his father believes he is studying in college.

On the day of the big exhibition game, Polachuk's father arrives and is so impressed with Adam's prowess on the field that he agrees to letting him pursue a baseball career.

Reviews

Brog., *Variety,* July 15, 1953

"A human interest story on the training of baseball-minded youth, [and] the presence of Edward G. Robinson helps bolster this presentation. . . . [He] is good as the camp founder and believable in the hokum that has been mixed in with fact."

Monthly Film Bulletin, February 1956

"The film treats its subject with an almost hushed reverence and its appeal is restricted almost entirely to baseball enthusiasts. Edward G. Robinson's reliable performance and some effectively shot match scenes barely compensate for the trite story and conventional characterization."

THE GLASS WEB (Universal, 1953) 81 M.

Producer, Albert J. Cohen; director, Jack Arnold; based on the novel by Max S. Ehrlich; screenplay, Robert Blees and Leonard Lee; art director, Bernard Herzbrun, Eric Orbom; music director, Joseph Gershenson; camera, Maury Gertsman; editor, Ted J. Kent. Filmed in 3-D.

HENRY HAYES	Edward G. Robinson
DON NEWELL	John Forsythe
LOUISE NEWELL	Marcia Henderson
PAULA RANIER	Kathleen Hughes
DAVE MARKSON	Richard Denning
LT. STEVENS	Hugh Sanders
SONIA	Jean Willes
JAKE	Harry O. Tyler
BOB WARREN	Clark Howat
OTHER MAN	Paul Dubov
ANNOUNCER	John Hiestand
PLAINCLOTHESMAN	Bob Nelson
EVERETT	Dick Stewart
BARBARA NEWELL	Jeri Lou James
JIMMY NEWELL	Duncan Richardson
FIRST ENGINEER	Jack Kelly
WAITRESS	Alice Kelly
AD LIB	Lance Fuller
LEW	Brett Halsey
MRS. O'HALLORAN	Kathleen Freeman
VIV	Eve McVeagh
SALLY	Beverly Garland
CLIFFIE	Jack Lomas
MRS. DOYLE	Helen Wallace
WEAVER	Howard Wright
GILBERT (Lawyer)	Herbert C. Lytton
MR. WEATHERBY	James Stone
FRED ABBOTT	John Verros
TRAMP COMIC	Benny Rubin
TOURIST	Eddie Parker
DISTRICT ATTORNEY	Tom Greenway
PAPER MAN	Donald Kerr

Synopsis

Don Newell, a television script writer, is being

With Kathleen Hughes in The Glass Web.

blackmailed by Paula Ranier, an ambitious young actress who stars in his *Crime of the Week* video show. The two had previously had an affair which he wishes to keep from his wife. Newell arrives at Paula's apartment with the last of the blackmail payments and finds her murdered. Apparently, Paula also had been blackmailing Henry Hayes, research director for the show, who too had been contributing to her luxury, and who had quarreled with her estranged husband.

The police fail to solve the case, which is selected for enactment on the *Crime of the Week* show. Hayes procures evidence against Newell, who is

With John Forsythe and Richard Denning in **The Glass Web.**

forced to include it in his script. However, in his plan to prove Newell's guilt, Hayes gives himself away by one mistake.

Realizing that Newell knows he is the murderer, Hayes traps him in an empty studio, but the police arrive and shoot him before he can kill Newell.

Reviews

Bosley Crowther, *The New York Times,* November 12, 1953

"The reintroduction of the traffic ('the rats and the hoods and the killers') was provided with Universal's *The Glass Web,* a minor criminal excursion with Edward G. Robinson and John Forsythe as its stars."

Joe Pihodna, *New York Herald-Tribune,* November 12, 1953

"Edward G. Robinson meanders through the part of a studio technician who is in love with Kathleen Hughes, the TV actress out to get all she can."

BLACK TUESDAY (United Artists, 1954) 80 M.

Producer, Robert Goldstein; director, Hugo Fregonese; story-screenplay, Sydney Boehm; assistant director, Sam Wurtzel; art director, Hilyard Brown; set director, Al Spencer; music, Paul Dunlap; sound, Tom Lambert; camera, Stanley Cortez; editor, Robert Golden.

VINCENT CANELLI .... Edward G. Robinson
PETER MANNING .... Peter Graves
HATTI COMBEST .... Jean Parker

With Hal Baylor (left), Ken Christy and James Bell in Black Tuesday.

FATHER SLOCUM .... Milburn Stone
JOEY STEWART .... Warren Stevens
FRANK CARSON .... Jack Kelly
ELLEN NORRIS .... Sylvia Findley
JOHN NORRIS .... James Bell
DR. HART .... Victor Perrin

Synopsis

Although death-row resident Vincent Canelli's days are numbered, he displays his usual arrogance, spending his time formulating a daring scheme to beat Black Tuesday (the official execution day in New Jersey). Next Tuesday is the day he is to die along with Peter Manning, another killer, who hid $200,000 from a big bank robbery before he was captured.

The night before Canelli's scheduled execution, his girlfriend, Hatti Combest, goes to the home of John Norris, the death-house guard, and coldly announces that his daughter Ellen has been kidnapped, and that the price of ransom is his help.

Among the reporters gathered at the death house is Joey Stewart, one of Canelli's henchmen. In the midst of the ensuing breakout Joey kills Norris and another guard. Canelli makes a bloody escape in a waiting hearse and goes to a deserted warehouse, where a group of captives is being held: Ellen Norris; Frank Carson, a reporter; Dr. Hart;

a priest; and a watch guard. Manning was wounded in the escape, and Canelli orders Dr. Hart to operate. Next day, Manning retrieves the stolen money from a bank safety deposit box. However, his blood-dripping wounds give him away, and the police trail him back to the warehouse.

When they arrive, Canelli threatens to kill all five hostages unless he and Manning are given safe passage out. When Carson protests Canelli's actions, the latter shoots and wounds him.

The police refuse Canelli's deal and the gangster sends out the first dead hostage, the guard. When Canelli prepares to shoot the priest, Manning rebels and kills Canelli. Then Manning heads downstairs, knowing he will probably be shot by the police.

Reviews

Howard Thompson, *The New York Times*, January 1, 1955

"Edward G. Robinson plays his old, snarling, sav-

With Jean Parker in Black Tuesday.

age self. . . . In contrast to [his] wholesale sputtering, the supporting cast of comparatively unfamiliar faces are brought, one by one, into personal but perceptive focus. . . . It's a pleasure to see Mr. Robinson shedding his good citizenship in such a colorful, lively show."

Paul V. Beckley, *New York Herald-Tribune*, January 1, 1955

"Mr. Robinson is still the old pro in this kind of

With Peter Graves in Black Tuesday.

With Warren Stevens, Ken Christy and Milburn Stone (right) in Black Tuesday.

With Barbara Stanwyck, Brian Keith and Glenn Ford
in The Violent Men.

thing and at no point in this film imitates his own past portrayals but gives a fresh and convincing portrait of an egomaniacal killer."

Brog., *Variety*, December 22, 1954

"Edward G. Robinson makes a return to gang czar roles in this story and has lost none of his menacing qualities."

THE VIOLENT MEN (Columbia, 1955) 96 M. Color.

Producer, Lewis J. Rackmil; director, Rudolph Mate; based on the novel by Donald Hamilton; screenplay, Harry Kleiner; music, Max Steiner; camera, Burnett Guffey and W. Howard Greene; editor, Jerome Thoms.

JOHN PARRISH	Glenn Ford
MARTHA WILKISON	Barbara Stanwyck
LEW WILKISON	Edward G. Robinson
JUDITH WILKISON	Dianne Foster
COLE WILKISON	Brian Keith
CAROLINE VAIL	May Wynn
JIM McCLOUD	Warner Anderson
TEX HINKLEMAN	Basil Ruysdael
ELENA	Lita Milan
WADE MATLOCK	Richard Jaeckel
MAGRUDER	James Westerfield
DEROSA	Jack Kelly
SHERIFF MARTIN KENNER	Willis Bouchey
PURDUE	Harry Shannon
GEORGE MENEFEE	Peter Hanson
JACKSON	Don C. Harvey
TONY	Robo Bechi
DRYER	Carl Andre
HANK PURDUE	James Anderson
MRS. VAIL	Katharine Warren
MR. VAIL	Tom Browne Henry

Synopsis

Egged on by his grasping wife, Martha, crippled cattle baron Lew Wilkison has been driving the small ranchers and farmers from his valley. Martha all the while has been carrying on an affair with Wilkison's younger brother, Cole, much to the disgust of Lew's daughter Judith.

Wilkison's empire-building plans are slowed when his henchmen push around John Parrish too much. Parrish, a pacifist disillusioned by his war-time experiences, wants no more fighting, but his pacifism causes his fiance, Caroline, to walk out on him. Soon, though, he is forced to turn to guerilla tactics to put down Wilkison's gunslingers.

When Wilkison's chief henchman, Wade Mattock, kills one of Parrish's hands, Parrish stalks the murderer and guns him down.

Before long, two big ranch fires, a horse stampede and an ambush see the violent end of Martha and Cole. Parrish wins Judith's hand in marriage and Wilkison is left with his home, family and empire smashed.

With Dianne Foster and Glenn Ford in **The Violent Men.**

BUD HINKLEMAN .... Bill Phipps
ANCHOR RIDER .... Edmund Cobb
MAHONEY .... Frank Ferguson
DR. HENRY CROWELL .... Raymond Greenleaf

With Brian Keith and Ginger Rogers in **Tight Spot.**

Reviews

Bosley Crowther, *The New York Times*, January 27, 1955

"Mr. Robinson is spared destruction, possibly because his performance is the best. . . . [He] and Miss Stanwyck have been twisted by cupidity into villains of more than routine blackness."

William Zinsser, *New York Herald-Tribune*, January 27, 1955

"Robinson plays 'Little Caesar' in buckskin. He has moved from urban vice dens to the wide open spaces, but henchmen still jump to do his bidding. Where once the command was 'Put the body in cement and drop it in the East River!', now it's 'Clean out the valley! I don't care if you have to burn every ranch and string up all the ranchers!' "

TIGHT SPOT (Columbia, 1955) 97 M.

Producer, Lewis J. Rackmil; director, Phil Karlson; based on the novel *Dead Pigeon* by Lenard Kantor; screenplay, William Bowers; art director, Carl Anderson; music director, Morris Stoloff; camera, Burnett Guffey; editor, Vila Lawrence.

SHERRY CONLEY . . . . Ginger Rogers
LLOYD HALLETT . . . . Edward G. Robinson
VINCE STRIKER . . . . Brian Keith
PRISON GIRL . . . . Lucy Marlow
BENJAMIN COSTAIN . . . . Lorne Greene
MRS. WILLOUGHBY . . . . Katherine Anderson
MARVIN RICKLES . . . . Allen Nourse
FRED PACKER . . . . Peter Leeds
MISSISSIPPI MAC . . . . Doye O'Dell
CLARA MORAN . . . . Eve McVeagh
WARDEN . . . . Helen Wallace
JIM HORNSBY . . . . Frank Gerstle
MISS MASTERS . . . . Gloria Ann Simpson
CARLYLE . . . . Robert Shield
ARNY . . . . Norman Keats
BIT GIRL HONEYMOONER . . . . Kathryn Grant
HARRIS . . . . Ed "Skipper" McNally

*With Lorne Greene, Ginger Rogers, Allen Nourse and
Peter Leeds in* Tight Spot.

BIT MAN .... Erik Paige
DETECTIVE .... John Marshall
PLAINCLOTHESMAN .... Will J. White
DOCTOR .... Tom de Graffenried
BIT MAN .... Kevin Enright
JUDGE .... Joseph Hamilton
BAILIFF .... Alan Reynolds
BIT MAN .... Tom Greenway
TONELLI .... Alfred Linder
1st DETECTIVE .... John Larch
2nd DETECTIVE .... Ed Hinton
TV SALESMAN .... Bob Hopkins

Synopsis

Sherry Conley, a model unjustly serving a prison term, is released in the custody of Lloyd Hallett, a U.S. attorney, as a material witness in the pending trial of big time gangster, Benjamin Costain. Although no witness to the gangster's activities has yet survived to testify in court, Hallett hopes to break down Sherry's resistance in the plusher hotel setting.

Sherry remains staunchly uncooperative with Hallett, until Mrs. Willoughby, the police matron on duty at the hotel, is killed while protecting her from the sniper shot of Costain's henchman. It also turns out that Vince Striker, the police detective assigned to guard her, and with whom she has a tentative romance, is in Costain's pay. At the last minute, he tries to save Sherry from Costain's thugs, but is killed in the melee.

Sherry goes to court to testify. When asked in the courtroom what her profession is, she replies, "gang buster."

Reviews

Howard Thompson, *The New York Times,* March 19, 1955

"*Tight Spot* is a pretty good little melodrama, the kind you keep rooting for as generally happened when Lenard Kantor's *Dead Pigeon* appeared on Broadway a while back. . . . Mr. Keith and Mr. Robinson are altogether excellent."

Brog., *Variety,* April 26, 1955

"Robinson is very good as the Fed down to his last witness."

A BULLET FOR JOEY (United Artists, 1955) 85 M.

Producer, Samuel Bischoff and David Diamond; director, Lewis Allen; story, James Benson Nablo; screenplay, Geoffrey Homes and A. I. Bezzerides; music, Harry Sukman; camera, Harry Neumann; editor, Leon Barsha.

INSPECTOR RAOUL LEDUC .... Edward G. Robinson
JOE VICTOR .... George Raft
JOYCE GEARY .... Audrey Totter
CARL MACKLIN .... George Dolenz
FRED .... Peter Hanson
ERIC HARTMAN .... Peter Van Eyck
MRS. HARTMAN .... Karen Verne
PAOLA .... Ralph Smiley
DUBOIS .... Henri Letondal
MORRIE .... John Cliff
NICK .... Joseph Vitale
JACK ALLEN .... Bill Bryant
PAUL .... Stan Malotte
YVONNE TEMBLAY .... Toni Gerry
MARIE .... Sally Blane
GARCIA .... Steven Geray
PERCY .... John Alvin
ARTIST .... Bill Henry

Synopsis

Three murders, all seemingly connected with atomic physicist Carl Macklin in Canada, has Inspector Raoul Leduc puzzled. He decides to trace the backgrounds of the victims and the person(s) who would be interested in doing away with Macklin.

With George Raft in Bullet for Joey.

That person is Eric Hartman, who happens to head a spy ring and who sends for an exiled gangster, Joe Victor, living in Lisbon. Following his illegal entry to Canada, Victor gets from Hartman a plan for the Macklin's abduction, and calls in

*With Tina Carver, Frank Hagney and Peter Hanson
in* Bullet for Joey.

With Sally Blane and Peter Hanson in Bullet for
Joey.

some former henchmen—Jack Allen and his old girlfriend, Joyce Geary.

Victor's scheme is for Joyce to seduce Macklin and for Jack to make a play for Macklin's secretary, Yvonne Temblay. Yvonne becomes too serious, and Jack kills her. Meanwhile, Joyce has fallen for Macklin.

During this time, while tracing Yvonne's killer,

With Bill Henry and Barry Regan in Bullet for Joey.

Leduc trails Hartman and pals to a ship ready to said. On board lies Macklin, drugged. A gun battle ensues and Joe Victor is killed and Leduc sets off a flare which alerts the River Patrol. The spy ring is soon rounded up.

Reviews

Bosley Crowther, *The New York Times*, April 16, 1955

"Age cannot wither nor custom stale the infinite uniformity of Edward G. Robinson and George Raft. . . . We need only scan the details of Mr. Raft's laying out the job and Mr. Robinson's patient checking on him every step of the way. These are the things Mr. Raft and Mr. Robinson can act with their eyes shut—and sometimes do."

Joe Pihodna, *New York Herald-Tribune*, April 16, 1955

"The veterans of make-believe mayhem, murder and other sordid crimes are Edward G. Robinson—in this case, a right guy—and George Raft, a fugitive called in to pull the big job."

Brog., *Variety*, April 6, 1955

"Performances follow generally acceptable patterns, but are not outstanding."

ILLEGAL (Warner Bros., 1955) 88 M.

Producer, Frank P. Rosenberg; director, Lewis Allen; based on the play *The Mouthpiece* by Frank J. Collins; screenplay, W. R. Burnett and James R. Webb; art director, Stanley Fleischer; music, Max Steiner; sound, Stanley Jones; camera, Peverell Marley; editor, Thomas Reilly.

VICTOR SCOTT	Edward G. Robinson
ELLEN MILES	Nina Foch
RAY BORDEN	Hugh Marlowe
JOE KNIGHT	Robert Ellenstein
EDWARD CLARY	De Forrest Kelley
JOSEPH CARTER	Jay Adler
ALLEN PARKER	James McCallion
RALPH FORD	Edward Platt
FRANK GARLAND	Albert Dekker
ANDY GARTH	Jan Merlin
MISS HINKEL	Ellen Corby
ANGEL O'HARA	Jayne Mansfield
GEORGE GRAVES	Clark Howatt
TAYLOR	Henry Kulky
STEVE HARPER	Addison Richards
E. A. SMITH	Howard St. John
AL CAROL	Lawrence Dobkin
POLICEMAN	George Ross
DETECTIVES	John McKee
	Barry Hudson
BLONDE GIRL	Kathy Marlowe
BAILIFF	Ted Stanhope
JUDGE	Charles Evans
DOCTOR	Jonathan Hale
NIGHT ORDERLY	Marjorie Stapp
THIRD GUARD	Fred Coby
BARTENDER	Max Wagner
BARFLY	John Cliff
JAILER	Henry Rowland
MISS WORTH	Julie Bennett
WOMAN	Pauline Drake
MISS HATHAWAY	Roxanne Arlen
MR. MANNING	Archie Twitchell
PHILLIPS	Stewart Nedd
1st POLICEMAN	Herb Vigran
2nd POLICEMAN	Chris Alcaide

Synopsis

Learning that he has sent an innocent man to the electric chair, District Attorney Victor Scott resigns and starts drinking heavily. His assistant, Ellen Miles, and his ex-investigator, Ray Borden, who later marry, try to help Scott. They convince him to put his legalistic knowledge to work in a new area—as a defense lawyer.

One of his first clients is racketeer Frank Garland. The gangster has had free reign for sometime through inside help in the District Attorney's office. Ray Borden is on the take, and on Garland's payroll. Ellen discovers this and is forced to shoot her husband in self-defense, when he makes an attempt on her life.

The District Attorney, believing Ellen to be the informer, puts her on trial for murder, and Scott antagonizes Garland by insisting on undertaking her defense. On Garland's orders, his men shoot Scott, who, though wounded, enters the courtroom with his star witness, Angel O'Hara, Garland's ex-mistress. Her testimony clears Ellen and incriminates Garland.

Reviews

Bosley Crowther, *The New York Times,* October 29, 1955

"We'd be willing to bet a nickel that the people who wrote and made Warner Brothers' *Illegal* had *The Asphalt Jungle* in mind and were doing their best to imitate it, difficult though that would be. . . . [It] invades the higher echelons of crime, with a fast-thinking, double-dealing lawyer as its principal character. . . . The fact that this hard-bitten lawyer is played by Edward G. Robinson in his old vein of stinging sarcasm is a clue to what you may expect."

Joe Pihodna, *New York Herald-Tribune,* October 29, 1955

"Edward G. Robinson plays the swivel-hipped lawyer, who swings from the right side to the wrong side of the law and then reverses the field again to the right side."

With Jayne Mansfield, Ellen Corby and Nina Foch in Illegal.

In Illegal.

HELL ON FRISCO BAY (Warner Bros., 1956) 98 M. Color.

Associate producer, George Bertholon; director, Frank Tuttle, based on a novel by William P. McGivern; screenplay, Sydney Boehm and Martin Rackin; art director, John Beckman; music, Max Steiner; sound, Charles B. Lang; camera, John Seitz; editor, Folmar Blangsted.

STEVE ROLLINS	Alan Ladd
VICTOR AMATO	Edward G. Robinson
MARCIA ROLLINS	Joanne Dru
BAN BIANCO	William Demarest
JOE LYE	Paul Stewart
KAY STANLEY	Fay Wray
MARIO AMATO	Perry Lopez
ANNA AMATO	Renata Vanni
LOU FIASCHETTI	Nestor Paiva
HAMMY	Stanley Adams
LT. NEVILLE	Willis Bouchey
DETECTIVE CONNORS	Peter Hanson
BESSIE	Tina Carver
BRODY EVANS	Rodney Taylor
SEBASTION PASMONICK	Anthony Caruso
GEORGE PASMONICK	Peter Votrain
FATHER LAROCCA	George J. Lewis
BLONDE	Jayne Mansfield

Synopsis

Embittered ex-cop Steve Rollins, framed for manslaughter, is released from prison after serving five years and begins the long hunt for the man who put him there. Spurning the aid of his unfaithful wife Marcia and his friend Lt. Dan Bianco, Rollins pays a visit to an old waterfront boss, Lou Fiaschetti. From him, Rollins learns that the frame was made by Victor Amato, the influential crime overlord of the Frisco docks. At his hotel, Rollins is approached with an offer to join Amato's gang and is told that Fiaschetti has "prematurely died" and so has the material witness in the killing that sent Rollins to prison. With Dan Bianco, Rollins goes to Amato to personally turn down the offer,

On boat in Hell on Frisco Bay. *Alan Ladd is the man seated, farthest right.*

and Amato signals one of his boys to ambush the pair as they leave. Instead, the henchman ends up dead, and Rollins collars Amato's nephew, Mario, and works him over until he reveals the hideout of the man responsible for eliminating the material witness, the one man who could have cleared Rollins. Learning that Mario has informed, Amato has his assistant, Joe Lye, take care of Mario, and then plans to eliminate Joe himself. Kay Stanley, Lye's girl friend, finds Rollins and tells him she heard Amato order Mario's death and that she knows enough about the earlier murders to clear him (Rollins). Rollins goes after Amato, who is about to escape aboard a speedboat, and after a wild battle on board the boat crashes into a bridge piling. The police pull the pair from the water, Amato is arrested and Rollins decides to make another go of it with Marcia.

Reviews

Bosley Crowther, *The New York Times*, January 7, 1956

"Thanks to Edward G. Robinson, who wears his role snugly as he wears his shoes, and to some

sardonic dialogue written for him by Martin Rackin and Sydney Boehm . . . *Hell on Frisco Bay* is two or three cuts above the quality of the run of pictures in this hackneyed genre. . . . Cut to Mr. Robinson (in his role as Mr. Big), the ruthless killer of the San Francisco wharfs, and slowly this routine, senseless fable takes on a little flash and style. . . . Every time Mr. Robinson slouches upon the scene, gnawing cigars and slobbering cynicisms, it is amusing, interesting—and good."

William K. Zinsser, *New York Herald-Tribune*, January 7, 1956

" (In it) it is Robinson who reigns supreme. Even after all these years he is a fascinating boss, in his pearl gray homburg and gray silk vest, glaring out of settled eyes at a man he is soon to kill, flicking the ashes of an expensive cigar nonchalantly on the rug. His commands are edged with a sardonic wit, and he is quick to give a girl the back of his hand if she spurns his silky advance. This is the old meanie at the top of his form, relishing every black minute of his role."

New York Post, January 7, 1956

"Edward G. Robinson is tops as a ruthless gangster."

Time Magazine, February 6, 1956

"The resident devil is Edward G. Robinson, a sort of menace emeritus who is invited by Alan Ladd, a cop he once framed, to retire from the daily grind to a peaceful chair at San Quentin. Eddie replies at some length: 'Oh y-a-a-a-a-a?' "

NIGHTMARE (United Artists, 1956) 89 M.

Producer, William Thomas, Howard Pine; director, Maxwell Shane; based on the novel by Cornell Woolrich; screenplay, Shane; art director, Frank Sylos; sound, Jack Solomon, Paul Wolff; camera, Joseph Biroc; editor, George Gittens.

RENE	Edward G. Robinson
STAN GRAYSON	Kevin McCarthy
GINA	Connie Russell
SUE	Virginia Christine
TORRENCE	Rhys Williams
BELNAP	Gage Clarke
WARNER	Barry Atwater
MADGE	Marian Carr
LOUIE SIMES	Billy May

With Alan Ladd and Paul Stewart in **Hell on Frisco Bay.**

Synopsis

Stan Grayson, a New Orleans jazz musician, finds himself unable to account for the strange feeling that he has killed a man with an awl and stuffed the body behind a mirrored door. He has a dream that is so vivid that he is certain the murder actually took place, especially when he finds blood on his wrist and thumb prints on his throat and discovers a mysterious key and a strange button in his hotel room.

He seeks help from his detective brother-in-law Rene to unravel the truth. Rene is inclined to pass it off as a bad dream of a man with shattered nerves. To get Stan's mind off his problems, Rene and his wife Sue prepare a picnic for Stan and his girlfriend vocalist, Gina. Caught in a rainstorm the quartet take refuge in what appears to be a vacant home. When Stan shows evidence of knowing the house and leads the group to the room where he dreamed the murder had been committed, Rene becomes intrigued with the case.

Later, when a body is found in the vacant house, Rene tells Stan to leave town before he reports the discovery to the police. When Stan tries suicide, Rene saves him, determining to prove his innocence.

Matching clues and information, Rene discovers that Stan's next door neighbor, Belnap, hypnotized him and used him to murder selected victims.

Deciding that the only way to trap Belnap is to repeat the events, Rene and Stan stage a scene in the murder house and Belnap finally confesses. In the process, Belnap puts Stan under hypnosis and almost drowns him, but Rene saves him. Stan is

With Kevin McCarthy in **Nightmare.**

eventually cleared of all charges following his brother-in-law's clever ruse in unmasking Belnap.

Reviews

Milton Esterow, *The New York Times,* May 12, 1956

"Nightmares are sometimes induced by (a) mistakes in diet, (b) nervous disorders, (c) imperfect ventilation, or (d) cramped sleeping positions. But that's not the simple case with jazz musician Stan Grayson's *Nightmare.* . . . And what a nightmare it was! It was enough to mix up even a Freud. . . . This Pine-Thomas-Shane production is a modest melodrama with some crooked but neat performances by Messrs. Robinson and McCarthy, Connie Russell and Virginia Christine."

Paul V. Beckley, *New York Herald-Tribune,* May 12, 1956

"Mr. Robinson does the best he can, as usual, with his lean material, but the fact is good acting does little more than remind one of the waste."

THE TEN COMMANDMENTS (Paramount, 1956) 221 M. Color.

Producer-director Cecil B. DeMille; based on the novels: *Prince of Egypt* by Dorothy Clarke Wilson, *Pillar of Fire*

In **Nightmare.**

On set of The Ten Commandments.

With Debra Paget in **The Ten Commandments.**

by Rev. J. H. Ingraham, *On Eagle's Wings* by Rev. G. E. Southon, in accordance with The Holy Scripture, the ancient texts of Josephus, Eusebius, Philo, The Midrash; screenplay, Aeneas MacKenzie, Jesse L. Lasky Jr., Jack Gariss and Fredric M. Frank; music, Elmer Bernstein; camera, Loyal Griggs; editor, Anne Bauchens.

MOSES	Charlton Heston
RAMESES	Yul Brynner
NEFRETIRI	Anne Baxter
DATHAN	Edward G. Robinson
SEPHORA	Yvonne De Carlo
LILIA	Debra Paget
JOSHUA	John Derek
SETHI	Sir Cedric Hardwicke
BITHIAH	Nina Foch
YOCHABEL	Martha Scott
MEMMET	Judith Anderson
BAKA	Vincent Price
AARON	John Carradine
JETHRO	Eduard Franz
MIRIAM	Olive Deering
MERED	Donald Curtis
JANNES	Douglas Dumbrille
HUR BEN CALEB	Lawrence Dobkin
ABIRAM	Frank DeKova
AMMINADAB	H. B. Warner
PENTAUR	Henry Wilcoxon
ELISHEBA	Julia Faye
JETHRO'S DAUGHTER	Lisa Mitchell
KORAH'S WIFE	Joan Woodbury
SIMON	Francis J. McDonald
THE BLIND ONE	Ian Keith
RAMESES I	John Miljan
KING OF ETHIOPIA	Woodrow Strode
SLAVE WOMAN	Dorothy Adams
COMMANDER OF THE HOSTS	Henry Brandon
AMALEKITE HERDER	Touch Connors
PRETTY SLAVE GIRL	Gail Kobe
FOREMAN	Fred Kohler Jr.
SLAVE	Kenneth MacDonald
FANBEARER	Addison Richards
LUGAL	Onslow Stevens
SARDINIAN CAPTAIN	Clint Walker
WAZIR	Frank Wilcox
OLD HEBREW—MOSES' HOUSE	Luis Alberni
1st TASKMASTER	Michael Ansara
HEBREW AT GOLDEN CALF	Zeev Bufman
SLAVE	Frankie Daro
HIGH OFFICIAL	Franklin Farnum
CHILD SLAVE	Kathy Garver
HERALD	Walter Woolf King

OLD MAN PRAYING .... Frank Lacteen
SLAVE .... Carl Switzer
HEBREW AT GOLDEN CALF .... Robert Vaughn
CRETAN AMBASSADOR .... John Hart

Synopsis

Moses, the future Hebrew Deliverer who was discovered as a baby in a tiny ark in the River Nile bulrushes by Princess Bithiah, Pharaoh's daughter, and raised by her, has become a general in the army of the new Pharaoh, Sethi I, and has conquered Ethiopia. Sethi's own son, the ambitious Prince Rameses, sees Moses as his rival for the Throne and has his father set a test of strength between the two. The winner will also win the hand of Princess Nefretiri. Sethi commands Moses to build a great city with Hebrew slaves, while Rameses is sent to learn of the Deliverer whom the slaves still talk about.

Under the Egyptian lash, the slaves labor on the massive construction, but it is Moses who orders rest for them and rations from the Pharaoh's own

With Kem Dibbs in The Ten Commandments.

grain storehouses. Rameses sees this as a plot to use the slaves against the Throne, but Sethi, who has come to check on his son's treason charges, is awed by the city's glory and announces that Moses, its creator, shall succeed him as Pharaoh.

With Frank De Kova in The Ten Commandments.

In **The Ten Commandments.**

Meanwhile, Nefretiri, preparing to marry Moses, has learned the secret of his lowly birth from Memnet, who had witnessed the child's discovery, and the princess tells Moses the truth about his background.

Moses leaves to find his real mother and joins his fellow Israelites in slavery in the mudpits of Goshen, where he saves the life of Joshua by slaying the Egyptian architect Baka. Moses is hailed as the Deliverer, but is betrayed by Dathan, the traitorous Hebrew overseer, and is exiled to the desert by Rameses. There he finds shelter with Jethro, Sheik of Midian, and eventually marries one of his host's seven daughters.

When Joshua appears and urges him to return to Egypt, now ruled by Rameses, and free his people, Moses becomes convinced of his Divine Mission and confronts the new Pharaoh. Rebuffed in his request to let the Hebrews depart Egypt, Moses calls forth the Plagues, each worse than the preceding one. When Rameses finally relents, Moses has Joshua assemble the hordes of slaves for the Exodus. Rameses, however, reneges and sends his army to pursue the Israelites, trapping them with their backs to the Red Sea. Moses then stretches out his hand and the sea divides, while Joshua leads the people through the dry corridor. Rameses' chariots speed after them as the towering sea canyons close with a roar.

In the Sinai Desert, Moses leaves his people under the leadership of his brother Aaron, and, with Joshua, ascends the mountain to receive God's law. During their forty-day absence, Dathan plots a return to Egypt and whips the multitude into a frenzy of fear, forcing Aaron to make them a Golden Calf to worship.

When Moses returns, carrying the Ten Commandments, he finds the people in a pagan revel, and, in a terrible rage, hurls the stone tablets to the ground. God's anger is now kindled against the Israelites and He makes them wander in the wilderness for forty years, until reaching the slopes of Mount Nebo. There, Moses gives his cloak and staff to Joshua, and turns over his leadership before ascending Mount Nebo alone to face his God as his people move toward the River Jordan and the Land of Promise.

Reviews

Bosley Crowther, *The New York Times*, November 9, 1956

"Mr. DeMille has worked photographic wonders. And his large cast of characters is very good, from Sir Cedric Hardwicke as a droll and urbane Pharaoh to Edward G. Robinson as a treacherous overlord."

Gene., *Variety*, October 10, 1956

"This new version of DeMille's silent (1927) saga, *The Ten Commandments*, overwhelms its audience, it's that big. Pictorially it is greatly impressive, dwarfing all cinematic things that have gone before it. It is unlikely that any other producer than DeMille would have attempted such a mammoth production and it's to be doubted that many others could have held the extraordinary project under control. . . . Competent work is done by Edward G. Robinson, as the evil Hebrew."

A HOLE IN THE HEAD (United Artists, 1959) 120 M. Color.

Producer-director, Frank Capra; co-producer, Frank Sinatra; based on the play by Arnold Schulman; screenplay, Schulman; assistant director, Arthur Black Jr.; art director, Edward Imazu; Jack R. Berne; sound, Fred Lau; music, Nelson Riddle; camera, William H. Daniels; editor, William Hornbeck.

With Jimmy Komack and Thelma Ritter in A Hole in the Head.

With Frank Sinatra, Eleanor Parker and Thelma Ritter in A Hole in the Head.

TONY MANETTA .... Frank Sinatra
MARIO MANETTA .... Edward G. Robinson
ALLY MANETTA .... Eddie Hodges
MRS. ROGERS .... Eleanor Parker
SHIRL .... Carolyn Jones
SOPHIE MANETTA .... Thelma Ritter
JERRY MARKS .... Keenan Wynn
DORINE .... Joi Lansing
MENDY .... George DeWitt
JULIUS MANETTA .... Jimmy Komack
FRED .... Dub Taylor
MISS WEXLER .... Connie Sawyer
MR. DIAMOND .... Benny Rubin
SALLY .... Ruby Dandridge
HOOD .... B. S. Pully
ALICE .... Joyce Nizzari
MASTER OF CEREMONIES .... Pupi Campo

Synopsis

Tony Manetta, an improvident 40 year old widower with a young son Ally, owns a run-down Miami Beach hotel. Tony dreams of becoming a big promoter. He runs around with a crazy bongo enthusiast named Shirl.

When a foreclosure on the hotel is threatened, Tony calls his older brother Mario, a New York clothing manufacturer. He asks for money, claiming Ally is quite sick.

Leaving his garment business in the inept hands of his son, Mario flies to Miami with his wife Sophie, learns the truth, and turns down Tony's request for money. However, Mario does offer to assist him, if Tony will give up the hotel, start a practical business in the Bronx, and consider marrying a widow, Mrs. Rogers.

Although interested in Mrs. Rogers, Tony refuses Mario's offer. Instead, he contacts his old crony Jerry who has hit the big time, but Jerry turns him down cold.

Tony decides to send Ally off with Mario and Sophie, telling the boy that he no longer wants him. But on the way to the airport, Ally comes back to his dad. Mario and Sophie return, and there is a happy reconciliation.

Reviews

Bosley Crowther, *The New York Times*, July 16, 1959

"As the brother, a narrow-minded dullard, Edward G. Robinson is superb; funny while being most officious and withering while saying the drollest things."

Paul V. Beckley, *New York Herald-Tribune*, July 16, 1959

"[It] does have two yeasty performances by Thelma Ritter and Edward G. Robinson as the brother and sister-in-law who bail Frank Sinatra out of his

With Thelma Ritter in A Hole in the Head.

financial difficulties in Florida. . . . As entertainment, it owes most of its success to Miss Ritter and Robinson, whose sense of timing in dialogue is fascinating to watch."

With Thelma Ritter, Eddie Hodges, Eleanor Parker and Dub Taylor in A Hole in the Head.

SEVEN THIEVES (20th Century-Fox, 1960) 102 M.

Producer, Sydney Boehm; director, Henry Hathaway; based on the novel *Lions at the Kill* by Max Catto; screenplay, Boehm; art director, Lyle R. Wheeler, John De Cuir; sound, Harry M. Leonard; music, Domini Frontiere; camera, Sam Leavitt; editor, Dorothy Spencer.

PAUL MASON	Rod Steiger
THEO WILKINS	Edward G. Robinson
MELANIE	Joan Collins
PONCHO	Eli Wallach
LOUIS	Michael Dante
RAYMOND LE MAY	Alexander Scourby
HUGO BAUMER	Berry Kroeger

***With Rod Steiger in* Seven Thieves.**

DIRECTOR OF CASINO	Sebastian Cabot
DUC DI SALINS	Marcel Hillaire
CHIEF OF DETECTIVES	John Berardino
GOVERNOR	Alphonse Martell
SEYMOUR	Jonathan Kidd
GOVERNOR'S WIFE	Marga Ann Deighton

Synopsis

An aging American gangster, Theo Wilkins, hoping to pull off one last grand coup before he dies, masterminds a sensational plot to rob the Monte Carlo gambling casino of $4 million. He enlists the aid of six others.

Accordingly Melanie, a stripper, inveigles Raymond Le May, the Casino Director's secretary, into arranging for the others' admittance on the night of the Governor's Ball. While Paul Mason, Wilkins's "right arm" and Louis, a safe cracker, break into the vaults, Theo poses as the personal physician of an eccentric crippled millionaire in a wheelchair, impersonated by Melanie's partner, Poncho.

The Baron apparently has a heart attack at the tables, is pronounced dead by his doctor, and is taken to the Director's office, where Paul and Louis are waiting with the stolen money. The loot is stuffed into the "corpse's" wheelchair, and despite several setbacks, the thieves make a successful getaway in an ambulance driven by their colleague Hugo Baumer.

On the way Poncho revives, only to discover that Theo, for whom the excitement has proven too much, has suffered a fatal heart attack. Melanie, who has fallen in love with Paul, suddenly realizes that he is Theo's son. Paul discovers that the money is in large, new, serialized bills, and useless to them, and forces the others, already fighting amongst themselves, to return the boodle to the Casino.

After leaving the valise with the money in the checkroom, Paul and Melanie stop briefly at the roulette table, make a small bet and win $3,000.

Reviews

Bosley Crowther, *The New York Times,* March 12, 1960

"Simply as entertainment, it is altogether good—well-conceived for suspense and excitement, well directed by Henry Hathaway, and well played. . . . Edward G. Robinson and Rod Steiger do have the most elaborate roles, but Mr. Wallach, Miss Collins and Mr. Scourby support them manfully and womanly."

Paul V. Beckley, *New York Herald-Tribune,* March 12, 1960

"[It] does not come up to the expectations one would reasonably have of a crime suspense movie aided by Edward G. Robinson, Rod Steiger and Eli Wallach."

PEPE (Columbia, 1960) 195 M. Color.

Producer-director, George Sidney; associate producer, Jacques Gelman; based on a play by Ladislas Besh-Fekete; story, Leonard Spigelgass and Sonya Levien; screenplay, Dorothy Kingsley; assistant director, David Silver; sound, Charles J. Rice, James Z. Flaster; art director, Ted Haworth; music, Sammy Cahn, Andre Previn and Johnny Green; set director, William Kiernan; camera, Joe MacDonald; editor, Viola Lawrence and Al Clark.

PEPE	Cantinflas
TED HOLT	Dan Dailey

*With Berry Kroeger, Rod Steiger, Eli Wallach and
Michael Dante in Seven Thieves.*

With Joan Collins in Seven Thieves.

With Alexander Scourby and Sebastian Cabot in
Seven Thieves.

SUZIE MURPHY .... Shirley Jones
RODRUGUEZ .... Carlos Montalban
LUPITA .... Vicki Trickett
DANCER .... Matt Mattox
MANAGER .... Hank Henry
CARMEN .... Suzanne Lloyd
JEWELRY SALESMAN .... Stephen Bekassy
WAITRESS .... Carol Douglas
PRIEST .... Francisco Reguerra
CHARRO .... Joe Hyams
IMMIGRATION INSPECTOR .... Ernie Kovacs
STUDIO GATEMAN .... William Demarest
And (as themselves): Maurice Chevalier, Bing Crosby,
Michael Callan, Tony Curtis, Richard Conte, Bobby Darin,
Sammy Davis Jr., Jimmy Durante, Zsa Zsa Gabor, voice of
Judy Garland, Greer Garson, Hedda Hopper, Joey Bishop,
Peter Lawford, Janet Leigh, Jack Lemmon, Dean Martin,
Jay North, Kim Novak, Andre Previn, Donna Reed, Deb-
bie Reynolds, Edward G. Robinson, Cesar Romero, Frank
Sinatra, Billie Burke, Ann B. 'Schultz' Davis, Jack Entrat-
ter, Col. E. E. Fogelson, Jane Robinson, Bunny Waters,
Charles Coburn.

Synopsis

Pepe, a poor Mexican ranchhand, is heartbroken
when Don Juan, a magnificent white stallion, is
sold to a desolute film director, Ted Holt. Following Holt and the horse to Hollywood, Pepe persuades the director to let him remain on as Don
Juan's groom.

In the film capital Pepe meets and falls in love
with Suzie Murphy, a waitress who wants a film
career.

To help Holt finance a new film project, Pepe
takes his small savings and goes to Las Vegas, where
he wins some big money. Holt makes Pepe co-
producer on the film and gives Suzie a leading role.
When Holt runs out of funds, he is forced to sell
Don Juan to Edward G. Robinson, a film producer.

Though Pepe is again heartbroken, he consoles

With Greer Garson in Pepe.

himself with the thought of marrying Suzie, unaware that she loves Holt.

With the film successfully completed, Pepe realizes it is only friendship Suzie feels for him, and he bows out of the scene.

Holt refuses to sell Robinson control of the picture unless he returns Pepe's horse. Thus Robinson gets the film, Suzie gets Holt and Pepe retrieves Don Juan.

Reviews

Bosley Crowther, *The New York Times*, December 22, 1960

"The rare and wonderful talents of Mexican comedian Cantinflas . . . are pitifully spent and dissipated amid a great mass of Hollywooden dross in the over-sized, over-peopled *Pepe.* . . . What we mean, simply, is you won't 'find' the spirited comedian in these scenes. You will merely see a patient shadow of the real Cantinflas. Nor will you see him in the lengthy stretches of 'plot,' wherein Dan Dailey as the booze-bogged film director spars with

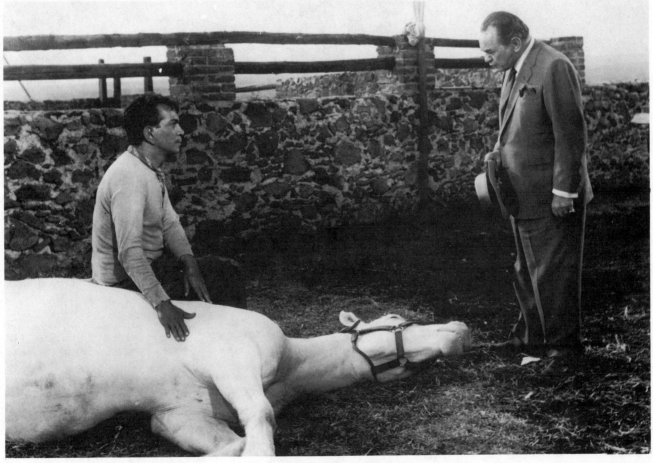

With Cantinflas in Pepe.

With Yves Montand and Bob Cummings in My Geisha.

Edward G. Robinson as a producer and jousts with a Hollywood hopeful, Shirley Jones."

Paul V. Beckley, *New York Herald-Tribune*, December 22, 1960

"When Robinson sees the completed film (within a film), he assures Dailey: 'Nothing to worry about. Pure entertainment.' Which may hint at the credos of screen writers Dorothy Kingsley and Claude Binyon and of producer-director George Sidney."

MY GEISHA (Paramount, 1961) 120 M. Color.

Producer, Steve Parker; director, Jack Cardiff; screenplay, Norman Krasna; art director, Hal Pereira, Arthur Lonergan, Makoto Kikuchi; music, Franz Waxman; sound. Harold Lewis and Charles Grenzbach; camera, Shunichiro Nakao; second unit camera, Stanley Sayer; editor, Archie Marshek.

LUCY DELL (Alias YOKO MORI) ... Shirley MacLaine
PAUL ROBAIX . . . . Yves Montand
SAM LEWIS . . . . Edward G. Robinson
BOB MOORE . . . . Bob Cummings
KAZUMI ITO . . . . Yoko Tani
KENICHI TAKATA . . . . Tatsuo Saito
AMATSU HISAKO . . . . Tamae Kyokawa
KAIDA . . . . Ichi Hayakawa
LEONARD LEWIS . . . . Alex Gerry
SHIGA . . . . Taugundo Maki
MAID . . . . Satoko Kuni
GEISHA . . . . Kazue Kaneko
GEISHA . . . . Junko Aoki
HEAD WAITRESS . . . . Nariko Muramatsu
GEISHA . . . . Akemi Shimomura
GEISHA . . . . Mayumi Momose

GEISHA .... Kyoko Takeuchi
HEAD WAITRESS .... Akiko Tsuda
BOBI'S GIRL FRIEND .... Marion Furness
BUTLER (GEORGE) .... George Furness

Synopsis

Tired of being known merely as the director of

With Shirley MacLaine, Tatsuo Saito and Ichiro Hayakawa in My Geisha.

his wife Lucy's films, Paul Robaix decides to film a new version of *Madame Butterfly* in Japan, starring an unknown Japanese girl.

Lucy, accompanied by her producer Sam Lewis, follows Paul to Japan, where at a swank party she dresses up as a geisha. When her husband fails to recognize her, she determines to get the leading role in his film.

Assuming the name of Yoko Mori, she takes geisha lessons, passes her screen test and becomes Paul's new discovery. Problems arise when her leading man Bob Moore falls in love with her, and asks Paul to help him win her in marriage.

While watching some of the films "rushes" Paul eventually realizes that Yoko is his wife, but does not let her know. He begins to make advances to her, which, if anything, improves her dramatic acting in the film.

The studio has decided to reveal Yoko's true identity at the Japanese premiere of the film, garnering more publicity for Lucy. Rather than have her husband lose his sole victory, Lucy announces at the premiere that Yoko has entered a convent and will never be seen again. Now contented, Paul tells Lucy that he knew of her deception for some time.

Reviews

A. H. Weiler, *The New York Times,* June 14, 1962

"(It is) a visually beautiful if only temporarily convincing romantic comedy drama . . . amiable and easy on the eyes and ears, but unfortunately it does not have too much to say that hasn't been said before this troupe made its trek to Japan. . . . [It deals with] a Hollywood director whose success is largely due to the efforts of his star-wife, attempting to make a film version in Japan of *Madama Butterfly* without the services of his talented helpmate to prove his own capabilities. . . . Edward G. Robinson takes the role of their understanding producer-mentor in casual but effective stride."

Paul V. Beckley, *New York Herald-Tribune,* June 14, 1962

"Much of it reminds you of television situation comedy, which is endurable only to those fascinated by the personalities of the players."

Monthly Film Bulletin, February, 1962

"It is perhaps a tribute to the cast that the film often appears less crass and vulgar than it might have been: Edward G. Robinson gives his customary relaxed and beautifully timed performance."

TWO WEEKS IN ANOTHER TOWN (MGM, 1962) 107 M. Color.

Producer, John Houseman; associate producer, Ethel

With Kirk Douglas and George Hamilton in Two Weeks in Another Town.

With Rosanna Schiaffino and Alberto Morin in **Two Weeks in Another Town.**

Winant; director, Vincente Minnelli; based on the novel by Irwin Shaw; screenplay, Charles Schnee; assistant director, Erich von Stroheim Jr.; art director, George W. Davis and Urie McCleary; set director, Keogh Gleason and Henry Grace; visual effects, Robert R. Hoag; music, David Raskin; sound, Franklin Milton; camera, Milton Krasner; editor, Adrienne Fazan, Robert J. Kern Jr.

JACK ANDRUS	Kirk Douglas
MAURICE KRUGER	Edward G. Robinson
CARLOTTA	Cyd Charisse
DAVIE DREW	George Hamilton
VERONICA	Dahlia Lavi
CLARA KRUGER	Claire Trevor
BRAD BYRD	James Gregory
BARZELLI	Rosanna Schiaffino
JANET BARK	Joanna Roos
LEW JORDAN	George Macready
TUCINO	Mino Doro
ZENO	Stefan Schanbel
ASSISTANT DIRECTOR	Vito Scotti
DR. COLD EYES	Tom Palmer
RAVINSKI	Erich Von Stroheim Jr.
CHANTEUSE	Leslie Uggams
NOEL O'NEILL	Janet Lake
SIGNORA TUCINO	Joan Courtenay
LIZ	Margie Liszt
1st HENCHMAN	Franco Corsaro
2nd HENCHMAN	Edward Comans
GERMAN TOURIST	Edit Angold
SOUNDMAN	Don Orlando
GEORGE JARRETT	Red Perkins
ELECTRICIAN	Albert Carrier
SOUND ENGINEER	James Garde
CAMERAMAN	Alberto Morin
CHINESE SISTER	Beulah Quo
LADY GODIVA	Cilly Feindt
1st BAR GIRL	Lilyan Chauvin
2nd BAR GIRL	Ann Molinari
BOUNCERS	Charles Horvath
	John Indrisano
AD LIBS IN LOUNGE	Benito Prezie
	Tony Randall
	Joe Dante

Synopsis

Following three-year stay in a New England sanatorium, former film star Jack Andrus heads for Rome in hopes of resurrecting his career. Scarred by divorce, alcoholism, a waning career, and a climactic car crash, he is hoping to make a comeback in a small role in Maurice Kruger's new spectacular. Andrus had had some of his biggest successes in Kruger's films.

Andrus arrives at the Cinecitta Studio in Rome and finds Kruger no less of a megalomaniac than before. However, the aging director is in difficulties with his producer, Tucino, and his two stars Barzelli and Davie Drew. The entire soundtrack has to be dubbed because Barzelli speaks little English and Tucino is threatening to take the film out of Kruger's hands if it runs over budget and time; and Davie Drew is refusing to work seriously, too busy battling with his girl friend, Veronica.

Kruger persuades Andrus to supervise the dubbing. Helped by the friendly Veronica, Andrus strives to control his own instability and to resist the destructive forces of his ex-wife Carlotta, drawn to Rome to prove to herself that she can still dominate him.

One night, at an anniversary party Kruger is giving for his possessive wife Clara, she accuses him of having an affair with Barzelli. He has a heart attack. Andrus is again prevailed upon, this time to finish directing the film. Rising to the occasion, Andrus saves both the film and Davie's career. Kruger turns against Andrus, but he survives the professional and emotional attack. Free of Kruger and Carlotta, having reconciled Davie and Veronica, Andrus leaves for Hollywood and a new career as a film director.

Reviews

Bosley Crowther, *The New York Times*, August 18, 1962

"When a group of top American filmmakers goes all the way to Rome to make a picture about the sort of Hollywood rejects who sometimes get involved in this sort of trash and then make it as trashy as the worst stuff, it is time for a loud and pained complaint. Such a cause for indignation is *Two Weeks in Another Town*, a drippy drama on a theme of degradation. . . . As the expatriate American director. . . . Edward G. Robinson snarls familiarly and gives but the barest impression of a human being in genuine distress."

Joseph Morganstern, *New York Herald-Tribune*, August 18, 1962

"Edward G. Robinson is the once great director, and his performance makes it hard to believe that the man ever directed a pedestrian successfully across a street."

Saturday Review, September 8, 1962

"The 'other town' is Rome, where an Italo-American co-production is under way—a penny-pinching, coldly calculated affair that is being ineptly directed by a frightened has-been . . . tellingly played by Edward G. Robinson [who] grinds out footage to the best of his dwindling ability, [and] knows that his work can be taken away from him at any time and completed by other, unsympathetic hands."

Tube., *Variety*, August 8, 1962

"Only remotely life-like characters in the story are Robinson and Claire Trevor as an ambiguous married couple whose personalities transform under the secretive cover of night. But the characters are

With Diane Baker in **The Prize.**

With Paul Newman, Diane Baker, Elke Sommer, Virginia Christine and Leo G. Carroll in **The Prize.**

as despicable as they are complex, and the film is desperately in need of simpler, nicer people. Robinson and Miss Trevor, two reliable performers, do all they can with the roles."

THE PRIZE (MGM, 1964) 136 M. Color.

Producer, Pandro S. Berman; associate producer, Kathryn Hereford; director, Mark Robson; based on the novel by Irving Wallace; screenplay, Ernest Lehman; assistant director, Hank Moonjean; art director, George W. Davis and Urie McCleary; set director, Henry Grace and Dick Pefferie; special effects, J. McMillan Johnson, A. Arnold Gillespie and Robert R. Hoag; music, Jerry Goldsmith; camera, William H. Daniels; editor, Adrienne Fazan.

ANDREW CRAIG	Paul Newman
DR. MAX STRATMAN	Edward G. Robinson
INGER LISA ANDERSEN	Elke Sommer
EMILY STRATMAN	Diane Baker
DR. DENIS MARCEAU	Micheline Presle
DR. CLAUDE MARCEAU	Gerard Oury
DR. CARLO FARELLI	Sergio Fantoni
DR. JOHN GARRETT	Kevin McCarthy
COUNT BERTIL JACOBSSON	Leo G. Carroll
DARANYI	Sacha Pitoeff
MONIQUE SOUVIR	Jacqueline Beer
HANS ECKART	John Wengraf
IVAR CRAMER	Don Dubbins
MRS. BERGH	Virginia Christine
MR. BERGH	Rudolph Anders
SARALEE GARRETT	Martine Bartlett
HILDING	Karl Swenson
OSCAR	John Qualen
CLARK WILSON	Ned Wever
STEEN EKBERG	Martin Brandt
HOTEL PORTER	Ivan Triesault
MRS. FARELLI	Grazia Narciso
DAVIS GARRETT	Larry Adare
AMY GARRETT	Robin Adare
BBC NEWS CORRESPONDENT	Lester Mathews

GERMAN CORRESPONDENT .... John Banner
TOKYO CORRESPONDENT .... Teru Shimada
AMERICAN TV NEWS CORRESPONDENT ....
.... Jerry Dunphy
FRENCH CORRESPONDENT ...... Michael Panaieff
MRS. AHLQUIST .... Edith Evanson
MISS FAWLEY .... Queenie Leonard
BRITISH REPORTER .... Ben Wright
PHOTOGRAPHER .... Erik Holland
SWEDISH WOMAN .... Alice Frost
BURLY SWEDES .... Carl Rydin
Ronald Nyman
SWEDISH BELLBOY .... Sven Peterson
OFFICER .... Peter Coe

Synopsis

In Stockholm to receive their Nobel Prize awards are Andrew Craig (literature), Dr. Max Stratman (physics), Dr. John Garrett and Dr. Carlo Farelli (medicine), and Drs. Claude and Denise Marceau (chemistry).

Stratman, who is accompanied by his niece Emily, is kidnapped with Emily's assistance, and his evil twin brother, Emily's father, takes his place. The plan is for the substitute Stratman to make an anti-American acceptance speech, while the real Stratman is shipped behind the Iron Curtain.

Craig, who has met the real Stratman, makes some casual remarks at a press conference, and is suspected by the Communists of knowing the facts behind the Stratman kidnapping plot. He soon finds himself the center of intrigue, involved in murder and, in escaping his persuers, at a nudist camp.

With the aid of Inger Lisa Anderson of the Swedish Foreign office, Craig rescues the real Stratman from a cargo ship about to embark for Russia and rushes him back to the ceremonies at the last minute to accept his Award. The substitute flees, only to be killed in error by the kidnappers. As he lies dying he pulls off his mask, showing that he is an actor masquerading as Stratman's brother.

Emily is reconciled with Stratman, Garrett and Farelli collaborate on an emergency treatment of a heart attack suffered by Stratman after his rescue and forget their jeolousy over sharing the Award for their simultaneous research discoveries; Dr. Marceau and his wife discover they are still in love; and Craig and Inger Lisa start their romance.

Reviews

Bosley Crowther, *The New York Times,* January 24, 1964

"This florrid farrago of fiction . . . plays fast and loose not only with the prestige of the Nobel affair but also with simple conventions of melodrama and with the intelligence of the customers. . . . It gathers together as recipients of Nobel awards about as lurid a lot of performers as might walk up to receive Oscars at one of those Academy Award nights in Hollywood. . . . [However] Mr. Robinson in both of his roles is good."

Judith Crist, *New York Herald-Tribune,* January 24, 1964

"You and I already know this: good old Edward G. Robinson, playing an umlaut-accented physicist, has had a meeting with a queer Iron Curtain type ('So we meet again, Eckart!') and has been kidnapped after he refuses to defect to the East—and good old Edward G. Robinson, with a slightly lighter umlaut-accent, is busy impersonating himself in order to make un-American remarks at the Nobel ceremonies while the real Edward G. Robinson is being shanghaied to Leningrad aboard a freighter."

Wanda Hale, *Daily News,* January 24, 1964

"The able old pro, Edward G. Robinson, seen briefly as Dr. Max Stratman, gives a performance of strength and dignity, the best in the film."

GOOD NEIGHBOR SAM (Columbia, 1964) 130 M. Color.

Producer-director, David Swift; associate producer, Marvin Miller; based on the novel by Jack Finney; screenplay, James Fritzell, Everett Greenbaun and Swift; assistant director, R. Robert Rosenbaum; set director, Ray Moyer; music, DeVol; production designer, Dale Hennesy; camera, Burnett Guffey; editor, Charles Nelson.

SAM BISSELL .... Jack Lemmon
JANET LAGERLOF .... Romy Schneider
MINERVA BISSELL .... Dorothy Provine
SIMON NURDLINGER .... Edward G. Robinson
HOWARD EBBETS .... Michael Connors
MR. BURKE .... Edward Andrews
REINHOLD SHIFFNER .... Louis Nye
EARL .... Robert Q. Lewis
GIRL .... Joyce Jameson
IRENE .... Anne Seymour
JACK BAILEY .... Charles Lane
EDNA .... Linda Watkins
PHIL REISNER .... Peter Hobbs
SONNY BLATCHFORD .... Tris Coffin

With Edward Andrews in Good Neighbor Sam.

With Romy Schneider in **Good Neighbor Sam.**

LARRY BOLING .... Neil Hamilton
MISS HALVERSON .... Riza Royce
MILLARD MELLNER .... William Forrest
THE HI-LOS .... Themselves
TARAGON .... Bernie Kopell
WYETH .... Patrick Waltz
HAUSNER .... William Bryant
JENNA .... Vickie Cos
ARDIS .... Kym Karath
MARSHA .... Quinn O'Hara
McVALE .... Hal Taggart
GLORIA .... Jan Brooks
FRENCH WAITER .... Peter Camlin
ASSISTANT DIRECTOR .... Tom Anthony
MRS. BURKE .... Bess Flowers
HERTZ COMMERCIAL MAN .... Dave Ketchum

Synopsis

Advertising man Sam Bissell is put in charge of his agency's most important account, the dairy of Simon Nurdlinger. Sam and his wife, Min, celebrate the promotion with her friend and neighbor, Janet, who is about to inherit $15 million—provided that she is living happily with her husband, Howard (a condition of her grandfather's will).

Janet, however, has just separated from Howard. To win the inheritance, she offers her good neighbor Sam a million dollars if he will pose as her husband. Two cousins, who will inherit the money if Janet is not living with her husband, employ a private investigator to snoop around. Complications arise when Howard comes home, but he is persuaded to continue the masquerade by moving into Sam's house for the night.

Nurdlinger, meanwhile, has come to believe Sam and Janet not only are husband and wife, but that they also are the perfect couple to endorse his products. He puts their pictures up on billboards around the city as part of his "wholesomeness" campaign, but Sam and Janet spend a hectic night defacing the posters and repainting the faces as unrecognizable clowns.

With (from left) Sammy Davis Jr., Joseph Ruskin,
Harry Wilson, Robert Carricart, Frank Sinatra, Peter
Falk, Robert Foulk and Allen Jenkins in Robin and
the Seven Hoods.

And, next day, Janet and Howard are back together again, and fighting. And Sam and Min are
back together again, still in love, and wealthier by
one of the inherited millions—a gift from Janet.

Reviews

A. H. Weiler, *The New York Times*, July 23, 1964

"*Good Neighbor Sam,* who is none other than Jack
Lemmon, the screen's perenially confused and har-
ried young-man-about-town, is hardly a changed
citizen in this swiftly-paced, pleasingly wacky but
loosely assembled farce. . . . Aiding in these manufactured frolics [is] Edward G. Robinson, as the
rich, Bible-spouting client."

ROBIN AND THE SEVEN HOODS (Warner Bros.,
1964) 103 M. Color.

Executive producer, Howard W. Koch; Producer, Frank
Sinatra; associate producer, William H. Daniels; director,
Gordon Douglas; screenplay, David R. Schwartz; art director, LeRoy Deane; set director, Ralph Bretton; assistant
director, David Salven and Lee White; music, Nelson Riddle; sound, Everett Hughes, Vinton Vernon; camera, Daniels; editor, Sam O'Steen.

ROBBO .... Frank Sinatra
JOHN .... Dean Martin
WILL .... Sammy Davis, Jr.
ALLEN A. DALE .... Bing Crosby
GUY GISBORNE .... Peter Falk
MARIAN .... Barbara Rush
SHERIFF POTTS .... Victor Buono
SIX SECONDS .... Hank Henry
BLUE JAW .... Robert Carricart

VERMIN	Allen Jenkins
TOMATOES	Jack LaRue
ROBBO'S HOODS	Sonny King
	Phil Crosby
	Richard Bakalyan
SHERIFF GLICK	Robert Foulk
GIMP	Phil Arnold
SOUP MEAT	Harry Swoger
TICK	Joseph Ruskin
LIVER JACKSON	Bernard Fein
GISBORNE'S HOODS	Harry Wilson
	Joe Brooks
	Richard Sinatra
	Roger Creed
COCKTAIL WAITRESS	Caryl Lee Hill
HOUSE GIRL	Carolyn Morin
GUARD	Al Silvani
HOODS	Joe Gray
	John Delgado
	Boyd "Red" Morgan
	John Pedrini
	Al Wyatt
	Tony Randall
PROSECUTING ATTORNEY	Bill Zuckert
JUDGE	Milton Rudin
LAWYERS	Ed Ness
	Frank Scannell
MR. RICKS	Hans Conried
BUTLER	Thom Conroy
2nd BUTLER	Joey Jackson
WOMAN DERELICT	Linda Brent
BOYS	Jerry Davis
	Manuel Padilla
	Mark Sherwood
*BIG JIM	Edward G. Robinson
HAMMACHER	Sig Ruman

* Unbilled.

Synopsis

In Chicago in 1928 the No. 1 hoodlum, Big Jim, is being honored at a lavish birthday party by gangland's finest. After the guests sing "happy birthday" to their friend, they shoot him dead.

Although Guy Gisborne declares himself the new No. 1, Robbo and his aides Will and Six Seconds warn him to stay out of the North Side.

Little John, a minor hood from Indiana, arrives in town and join's Robbo's gang. He partakes of the battle between Robbo and Gisborne for control of the illegal nightclub industry.

Big Jim's daughter, Marian, turns up at Robbo's office, offering him $50,000 to do away with her father's killers. Robbo refuses, but Marian, a tough dame, is persistent and sends him the money, which he has Will give away. The next day, Robbo is hailed as Chicago's "Robin Hood" and is visited by Allen A. Dale, an official of the orphanage. Dale suggests that this giveaway idea is good public relations and Robbo puts him in charge of his philanthropic enterprises.

Marian wants to take over the charitable racket herself and seeks to enlist the aid, successively, of

With Dean Martin in Robin and the Seven Hoods.

Robbo, Little John, crooked Sheriff Potts who is on Guy's payroll, and Guy himself.

While Robbo is combatting Gisborne's efforts to frame him for a murder, John falls for Marian and joins her in a counterfeiting scheme, using Robbo's charities as a front.

Marian tries to get Gisborne to get rid of Robbo and Little John, but when he fails, he is found dead. Then Marian organizes the women of Chicago to fight crime, and they wreck Robbo's operation.

Reduced to begging, Robbo and John find Marian with her latest boyfriend, Allen A. Dale.

Reviews

Bosley Crowther, *The New York Times,* August 6, 1964

"[It] is almost as strained and archaic in the fable it has to tell of Probibition-era gangsters in Chicago as the fable of Robin Hood it travesties. . . . For all those magnificent talents, it is an artless and obvious film. The brightest thing about it is its color photography."

Judith Crist, *New York Herald-Tribune,* August 6, 1964

"It's shades of *Little Caesar* and *Guys and Dolls* and every orphanage musical Crosby ever enhanced—but how wrong can it go when you start out with Edward G. Robinson as the top hood of 'em all?"

Whit., *Variety*, June 24, 1964

"The spirit of a hit is apparent and [the] picture stacks up nicely as mass entertainment. . . . [It] opens in 1928 with the gangster kingpin of the day —Edward G. Robinson doing a cameo bit here— guest of honor at a lush birthday party. After a sentimental rendition of 'For He's a Jolly Good Fellow' by the assembled company of hoods, they shoot Robinson dead."

THE OUTRAGE (MGM, 1964) 97 M.

Producer, A. Ronald Lubin; associate producer, Michael Kanin; director, Martin Ritt; based on the Japanese film *Rashomon;* from stories by Ryunosuke Akutagawa, and the play *Rashomon* by Fay and Michael Kanin; screenplay, Kanin; music, Alex North; art director, George W. Davis and Tambi Larsen; set director, Henry Grace and Robert

With William Shatner and Howard da Silva in **The Outrage.**

R. Benton; special effects, J. McMillan Johnson and Robert R. Hoag; assistant director, Daniel J. McCauley; camera, James Wong Howe; editor, Frank Santillo.

JUAN CARRASCO .... Paul Newman
HUSBAND .... Laurence Harvey
WIFE .... Claire Bloom
CON MAN .... Edward G. Robinson
PREACHER .... William Shatner
PROSPECTOR .... Howard Da Silva
SHERIFF .... Albert Salmi
JUDGE .... Thomas Chalmers
INDIAN   Paul Fix

Synopsis

Late in the nineteenth century, a preacher, a prospector, and a con man meet at a western railroad station. The con man is told by the other two of the recent trial of Juan Carrasco, the territory's most notorious outlaw, who was sentenced to death for the murder of a southern gentleman and the rape of his wife. The trial, however, was confusing because three witnesses each told different versions of what had occurred. Carrasco claimed that he had bound the husband, raped the wife as the man watched, and then killed him in a duel.

The wife claimed that the bandit had raped her and fled, and that, enraged, she had killed her husband when he accused her of encouraging Carrasco.

An old Indian, who happened to be in the woods at the time of the crime and had heard the husband's cries, testified that he came upon the man dying with the knife in the chest. He claims that the husband told him he had stabbed himself because of the humiliation he had suffered.

After the story about the events is finished, a cry is heard, and the three men discover an abandoned baby. The con man attempts to steal some gold that has been left for the child and the ensuing argument reveals the prospector not free from guilt. He had witnessed the crime, but did not testify because he had stolen the jeweled dagger from the dying man's chest.

His version is that the bandit was remorseful after the rape and had begged the wife to come away with him, but the wife had shamed the two men into a fight and the husband had fallen on the dagger.

When the prospector offers to raise the abandoned child, even though he has five others at home, the preacher's faith in humanity is somewhat restored. He feels he can return to his congregation and his work.

Reviews

A. H. Weiler, *The New York Times*, October 8, 1964

"Edward G. Robinson's portrayal of the bearded, seeded, cocky con artist is earthy and direct. 'You

With William Shatner and Howard da Silva in **The Outrage.**

tell people what they want to hear,' he says scornfully after a session of truthseeking. In focusing cynically on 'truths' that remain a mystery at the film's end, Martin Ritt and his willing company have done nobly by the original in their provocative and engrossing drama."

Judith Crist, *New York Herald-Tribune,* October 8, 1964

"Edward G. Robinson shows up as a Little Caesarized hobo-con man."

Wanda Hale, *Daily News,* October 8, 1964

"Edward G. Robinson is delightful as the cruddy old con man, a cynic who hears the various versions of the crimes and believes none."

CHEYENNE AUTUMN (Warner Bros., 1964) 149 M. Color.

Producer, Bernard Smith; director, John Ford; suggested by the novel *Cheyenne Autumn* by Mari Sandoz; screenplay, James R. Webb; associate director, Ray Kellogg; assistant director, Wingate Smith and Russ Saunders; art director, Richard Day; set director, Darryl Silvera; sound, Francis E. Stahl; music, Alex North; camera, William Clothier; editor, Otho Levering.

CAPTAIN THOMAS ARCHER ...... Richard Widmark
DEBORAH WRIGHT .... Carroll Baker
CAPTAIN OSCAR WESSELS .... Karl Malden
WYATT EARP .... James Stewart
CARL SCHURZ .... Edward G. Robinson
RED SHIRT .... Sal Mineo
SPANISH WOMAN .... Dolores Del Rio
LITTLE WOLF .... Ricardo Montalban
DULL KNIFE .... Gilbert Roland
DOC HOLLIDAY .... Arthur Kennedy
SECOND LIEUTENANT SCOTT ...... Patrick Wayne

With Richard Widmark in Cheyenne Autumn.

MISS GUINEVERE PLANTAGENET	Elizabeth Allen
MAJOR JEFF BLAIR	John Carradine
TALL TREE	Victor Jory
MAJOR DOG KELLY	Judson Pratt
FIRST SGT. STANISLAUS WICHOWSKY	
	Mike Mazurki
HOMER	Ken Curtis
MAJOR BRADEN	George O'Brien
TRAIL BOSS	Shug Fisher

PAWNEE WOMAN	Carmen D'Antonio
DEBORAH'S UNCLE	Walter Baldwin
LITTLE BIRD	Nancy Hseuh
TRAIL HAND	Chuck Roberson
RUNNING DEER	Moonbeam
MEDICINE MAN	Many Muleson
SVENSON	John Qualen
DR. O'CARBERRY	Sean McClory
LT. PETERSON	Walter Reed
SGT. OF THE GUARD	James Flavin
ENTERTAINERS	Stephanie Epper
	Mary Statler
	Jean Epper
	Donna Hall
TROOPER PLUMTREE	Ben Johnson
TROOPER SMITH	Harry Carey Jr.
TELEGRAPHER	Bing Russell
TOWNSMAN	Major Sam Harris
SENATOR HENRY	Denver Pyle
SECRETARY TO SCHURZ	Carleton Young
INFANTRY CAPTAIN	William Henry
WOMAN	Louise Montana

Synopsis

The few remaining Cheyenne on a wretched

In Cheyenne Autumn.

Oklahoma reservation in 1878 decide to return to their old homeland in Wyoming, and accompanied by Deborah Wright, the Quaker school teacher, and led by Chief Dull Knife, Chief Little Wolf, and elder Chief Tall Tree, the tribe begins its northward trek. Captain Thomas Archer and his cavalry pursue them, but, in battle, are mauled by Little Wolf and his braves. Obtaining reinforcements, Archer tries to arrange a capture without bloodshed, but one of his aides instigates another battle, bringing a second military defeat.

Archer finally negotiates a truce with one group of the Indians, led by Dull Knife. They are interned at Fort Robinson, where Captain Wessels is in charge. When Archer learns that Wessels plans to force the Indians back to Oklahoma, he goes to Washington to seek the help of Carl Schurz, U.S. Secretary of the Interior.

Because of poor living conditions at the Fort, Dull Knife's men escape, killing Wessels and rejoining Little Wolf's group. Schurz and Archer reach the area where the Cheyenne are cornered within range of Army artillery. Schurz suggests a truce that will let him get the Indians to their old homeland; Dull Knife and Little Wolf agree.

In the spring, after a 1500-mile trek, the Cheyenne are back at last in the Yellowstone country. Dull Knife's son Red Shirt and Little Wolf have a shootout over the latter's wife. Red Shirt dies, and Dull Knife goes into exile. Archer and Deborah are reunited and remain with the Indians.

Reviews

Bosley Crowther, *The New York Times,* December 24, 1964

"In *Cheyenne Autumn,* John Ford, that old master of the Western, has come up with an epic frontier film. . . . [But] the climax with Carl Schurz [Robinson] interceding on behalf of the Indians after a hurried trip to Washington is neither effective and convincing drama nor is it faithful to the novel of Mari Sandoz on which the script is based."

Judith Crist, *New York Herald-Tribune,* December 24, 1964

"The secretary [of the Interior] herein is Carl Schurz, as park loving New Yorkers may guess, and it's Edward G. Robinson in cameo."

Archer Winsten, *New York Post,* December 24, 1964

"Edward G. Robinson, playing Carl Schurz, Secretary of the Interior, seems extremely earnest, too earnest to shave all the time."

Life Magazine, November 27, 1965

"Edward G. Robinson plays Carl Schurz . . . who complains of his lumbago and eventually solves the problems of the Cheyenne in a confrontation scene that is just as hilarious (as the James Stewart–Arthur Kennedy interlude) but unintentionally."

Whit., *Variety,* October 7, 1964

"Edward G. Robinson does well by the Interior Secretary part."

A BOY TEN FEET TALL (Paramount, 1965) 88 M. Color.

Producer, Hal Mason; director, Alexander Mackendrick; based on the novel *Sammy Going South* by W. H. Canaway; screenplay, Denis Cannan; art director, Edward Tester; set director, Scott Slimon; camera, Erwin Hillier; editor, Jack Harris.

COCKY WAINWRIGHT	Edward G. Robinson
SAMMY HARTLAND	Fergus McClelland
GLORIA VAN IMHOFF	Constance Cummings
LEM	Harry H. Corbett
SPYROS DRACONDOPOLOUS	Paul Stassino
THE SYRIAN	Zia Mohyeddin
ABU LUBABA	Orlando Martins
HENEKER	John Turner
AUNT JANE	Zena Walker
DISTRICT COMMISSIONER	Jack Gwillim
CATHIE	Patricia Donahue
BOB	Jared Allen
DOCTOR	Guy Deghy
HASSAN	Marnie Maitland
EGYPTIAN POLICEMAN	Steven Scott
HEAD PORTER	Frederick Schiller

Synopsis

Ten-year-old Sammy Hartland, alone in Port Said after his parents have died in an air-raid during the Suez crisis, sets out to find his only relative, Aunt Jane in Durban, South Africa, 5000 miles away. In the desert, hungry and footsore, he meets an itinerant peddler and agrees to trek with him to Luxor. Halfway, an accident blinds the peddler who shackles himself to the boy's wrists. Next day, he is dead. Sammy frees himself, takes

With Fergus McClelland in A Boy Ten Feet Tall.

the peddler's money and heads on. A few days later, the boy is found feverish and delirious by Gloria van Imhoff, a rich tourist, who tries to help him.

Fearing, though, that he will be returned to Port Said, Sammy slips away and hits the back-trails to avoid any more well-meaning adults. In the bush, he meets Cocky Wainwright, an old diamond smuggler and big-game hunter. The two get along famously, with Cocky recounting his re-markable past.

Cocky's partner, Lem, flies in to collect the latest batch of diamonds, bringing the news that the police are searching for Sammy. For years, their patrols have been after Cocky, now they are clos-ing in.

Lem flies off, Cocky is captured and Sammy es-capes into the jungle. At police headquarters, Cocky wills his fortune to Sammy. When Aunt Jane arrives, Cocky insists that she must return

home and let Sammy finish the journey on his own.

Back in Durban, Aunt Jane is there to greet the boy-man, after his long, incredible trek.

Reviews

Howard Thompson, *The New York Times,* May 13, 1965

"Most fortunately, indeed, at about mid-point, that wonderful old actor, Edward G. Robinson saunters into view as a grizzled, warm-hearted diamond smuggler, and gives the picture its real substance."

Rich., *Variety,* March 27, 1963

"With the exception of Robinson, looking like a slightly junior Ernest Hemingway, and Paul Stas-sino, as a lib crook of a guide, the others are card-board."

With Fergus McClelland in **A Boy Ten Feet Tall.**

In **A Boy Ten Feet Tall.**

With Fergus McClelland and Harry H. Corbett in
A Boy Ten Feet Tall.

*With Steve McQueen, Ann-Margret, Karl Malden
and Joan Blondell in* The Cincinnati Kid.

THE CINCINNATI KID (MGM, 1965) 113 M. Color.

Producer, Martin Ransohoff; associate producer, John Calley; director, Norman Jewison; based on the novel by Richard Jessup; screenplay, Ring Lardner Jr. and Terry Southern; assistant director, Kurt Neumann; art director, George W. Davis and Edward Carfagno; set director, Henry Grace and Hugh Hunt; music, Lalo Schifrin; camera, Philip H. Lathrop; editor, Hal Ashby.

THE CINCINNATI KID	Steve McQueen
LANCEY HOWARD	Edward G. Robinson
MELBA	Ann-Margret
SHOOTER	Karl Malden
CHRISTIAN	Tuesday Weld
LADY FINGERS	Joan Blondell
SLADE	Rip Torn
PIG	Jack Weston
YELLER	Cab Calloway
HOBAN	Jeff Corey
FELIX	Theo Marcuse
SOKAL	Milton Selzer
MR. RUDD	Karl Swenson
CAJUN	Emile Genest
DANNY	Ron Soble
MRS. RUDD	Irene Tedrow
MRS. SLADE	Midge Ware
DEALER	Dub Taylor
HOBAN'S WIFE	Joyce Perry
GAMBLER	Claude Hall
DESK CLERK	Olan Soule
EDDIE	Barry O'Hara
1st PLAYER	Pat McCaffrie
POKER PLAYER	Bill Zuckert
2nd PLAYER	John Hart
3rd PLAYER (CHARLIE)	Howard Wendell
REFEREE	Andy Albin
BETTOR	Hal Taggart
PHILLY	Robert Do Qui
POKER PLAYER	Sandy Kevin

Synopsis

The Kid is a gambler who has built a reputation as a formidable studpoker player. Weary of hustling for nickel and dime stakes in New Orleans, he is thinking of moving on to Miami for big money, when an unexpected appearance of Lancey Howard, known as "The Man," keeps the Kid in the French Quarter a while longer to try to wrest the title from the old-timer who is the reigning champ.

The Man, in town for a private game, agrees to meet The Kid in a session, arranged by Shooter, another professional gambler, who will be the dealer. Slade, who has been gutted by The Man, is set on revenge and seeks to fix the game by calling in Shooter's unpaid debts. The Shooter's "assistance" is discovered by The Kid, who is determined to win the game his way.

Tension and suspense build up in the game, which takes place over a period of several days, until all their money is at stake. In the momentous final duel, in which Lady Fingers, a female card shark, is relief dealer, The Kid, holding a full house, is assured of his win, until the old pro turns up a straight flush to finish him.

Reviews

Howard Thompson, *The New York Times,* October 28, 1965

"In adapting Richard Jessup's novel, Ring Lardner Jr. and Terry Southern have told the story of a derelict card wizard, on the beatnik side, and his foot-loose personal relationships. The climax is his marathon duel of stud poker with Edward G. Robinson who is one of the film's two genuine bright

With Karl Malden, Joan Blondell and Cab Calloway (background) in The Cincinnati Kid.

*With Cab Calloway (back to camera), Steve Mc-
Queen, Karl Malden and Milton Selzer in* **The Cincinnati Kid.**

spots. The other is Joan Blondell, bless her.. . . .
Appearing briefly as a wily card king, Mr. Robinson is quiet, precise and deadly—all with his eyes.
And fortunately, for spectators bored by cards, into
that interminable climax, there breezes Joan Blondell, like a blowsy, good-natured gale."

Judith Crist, *New York Herald-Tribune,* October
   28, 1965

"Mr. Robinson proves himself The Man both as
an actor and as Lancey Howard, suave, weary and
unyielding in his tenure as the shrewdest gentleman gambler of all. . . . So skillfully is the contest
dramatized that non-card players are swept into the
suspenseful tale. Whether stud experts will agree
with The Man's ultimate verdict that 'making the

wrong move at the right time' is what the game
and the gamble are all about is a matter for post-
movie speculation."

Hollis Alpert, *Saturday Review,* November 6, 1965

"The elderly card shark [is] played consummately
by Edward G. Robinson."

Time Magazine, October 29, 1965

"McQueen v. Robinson put on a bristling good
show whenever they interrupt their marathon long
enough for a few words of subtly guarded small
talk—about health, luck, women trouble, anything
that might make an opponent's mind wander."

With Karl Malden in The Cincinnati Kid.

Whit., *Variety,* October 2, 1965

"Robinson is at his best in some years as the aging, ruthless Lancey Howard, champ of the poker tables for more than thirty years and determined now to defend his title against a cock-sure but dangerous opponent who believes he is ready for the big moment . . . [and] the final and deciding hand is played in what may well be the most suspenseful account of a poker game in film record."

LA BLONDE DE PEKIN (The Blonde from Peking)
(Paramount, 1968) 80 M. Color.

Director, Nicolas Gessner; based on the novel by James Hadley Chase; adaption, Jacques Vilfrid; screenplay, Gessner and Mark Behm; music, Francois de Roubaix; art director, Georges Petitot; camera, Claude Lecomte; editor, Jean-Michel Gauthier.

CHRISTINE .... Mireille Darc
GANDLER .... Claudio Brook
DOUGLAS .... Edward G. Robinson
SECRETARY .... Pascale Roberts
ERIKA .... Francoise Brion
DOCTOR .... Joe Warfield
and: Giorgia Moll, Karl Studer, Yves Elliot, Valery Inkjinoff, Joseph Warfield, Tiny Young, Aime de March, Jean-Jacques Delbo, Karl Studer.

Synopsis

Christine is found on a bench in Paris in a state of amnesia. She is hunted by agents from vari-

ous countries, including the American, Douglas, of the CIA. All are trying to determine if she is the real Erika Olsen, ex-mistress of a Chinese scientist, who has acquired important nuclear secrets.

Gandler, an actor, is recruited by Douglas to pose as Christine's husband. He learns that the "Blonde from Peking" is not a spy, but that she possesses The Blue Grape Pearl, which her sister had stolen from the Chinese. Gandler decides to get the pearl.

The Chinese, bent on killing Erika, murder her nurse by mistake, and the rumor is circulated among the foreign missions that the Blonde from Peking is dead. But Christine is alive and soon regains her memory. She informs Gandler that she is Erika's sister, and that Erika is now in Peking with the rare pearl in her possession.

Gandler and Christine go to Hong Kong to find Erika and locate her just as Russian and Chinese agents arrive on the scene. In the shootout, Erika is killed and the valued Blue Grape Pearl falls into the sea, leaving the Blonde from Peking and the erstwhile actor-turned CIA agent to pursue other employments.

Reviews

Mosk., *Variety,* January 29, 1968

"Spy shenanigans concern Chinese, Russian and Yank spies seeking errant Red Chinese missile data

With ? in The Blonde from Peking.

Holding photo of Mireille Darc in **The Blonde from Peking.**

plus a priceless jewel. But all this does not quite have the verve, ironic comic twists or sheer suspense and action flair to bring it off. It emerges possibly . . . on the color, scope and lure of the Edward G. Robinson name albeit he has a small role in the affair . . . [as] the shrewd CIA chief."

THE BIGGEST BUNDLE OF THEM ALL (MGM, 1968) 105 M. Color.

Producer, Joseph Shaftel; associate producer, Sy Stewart; director, Ken Annakin; story, Shaftel; screenplay, Sy Salkowitz; music, Riz Ortolani; assistant director, Victor Merenda; art director, Arrigo Equini; camera, Piero Portalupi; editor, Ralph Sheldon.

HARRY PRICE	Robert Wagner
JULIANA	Raquel Welch
BENJAMIN BROWNSTEAD	Godfrey Cambridge
CESARE CELLI	Vittorio De Sica
PROFESSOR SAMUELS	Edward G. Robinson
DAVY COLLINS	Davy Kaye
ANTONIO TOZZI	Francesco Mule
CAPTAIN GIGLIO	Victor Spinetti
TERESA	Yvonne Sanson
JOE WARE	Mickey Knox
UNCLE CARLO'S BRIDE	Femi Benussi
SIGNORA ROSA	Paola Bordoni
CARABINIERE	Andrea Aureli
CAPITANO DEL SIGNORE	Aldo Bufi Landi
FRANCO	Carlo Croccolo
UNCLE CARLO	Roberto De Simone
CAPTAIN CAPUANO	Piero Gerlini
LT. NALDI	Giulio Marchetti
EMMA	Ermelinda De Felice
SIGNORA CLARA	Gianna Dauro
MAITRE D'HOTEL	Carlo Rizzo
CHEF	Nino Musco
INSPECTOR BORDONI	Calisto Calisti

With Francesco Mule (?), Raquel Welch and Robert
Wagner in The Biggest Bundle of them All.

Synopsis

Harry Price and his inept crew of amateur criminals kidnap Cesar Celli, a deported American. gangster living in Italy, in order to collect a hefty ransom. When it turns out that none of Celli's friends will bail him out, Celli conceives the idea of a $5 million platinum robbery, both as a way of repaying Price and his gang for their kidnapping efforts and as a way of retaliating against a world that has passed him by.

Celli puts the novice criminals through rigorous physical training and brings in the renown Professor Samuels to blueprint the heist. The gang encounters a variety of difficulties in raising capital

With Vittorio De Sica in The Biggest Bundle of them All.

With Raquel Welch, Robert Wagner, Godfrey Cam-
bridge, Vittorio De Sica, Davy Kaye and Francesco
Mule in **The Biggest Bundle of them All.**

for the robbery (plans that backfire, holdups that don't pay off, etc.), but finally they are ready to put their scheme into action. They plan intercepting the train carrying the platinum ingots by blocking the tracks with a tank and loading the loot onto a hijacked B-25 Flying Fortress for transport to a fence in Morocco.

Despite consistent bumbling and threats by Price and his bikini-clad girlfriend, Juliana, to double-cross Celli and abscond with the platinum, the robbery is successful and the plane makes its getaway.

All the gang's efforts are for naught, however, when the plane's bomb doors are accidentally opened and the platinum descends into the waiting arms of the police.

Reviews

Renata Adler, *The New York Times,* January 18, 1968

"[It] begins like one of those really bad movies that are unintentionally funny. Then it becomes clear that it intends to be funny and isn't. . . . By the time Edward G. Robinson appears, his wrinkled countenance, flat eyes and generally turtlish appearance make it seem everyone might be on location for *The Wind in the Willows.*"

Archer Winsten, *New York Post,* January 18, 1968

"Godfrey Cambridge and Edward G. Robinson go

With Raquel Welch in **The Biggest Bundle of them All.**

With Adolfo Celi in **Grand Slam.**

through their criminal paces without the distinction that marks their work in other lines."

Whit., *Variety*, January 11, 1968

"Edward G. Robinson contributes one of his usual smooth performances as a professor in crime called in to blueprint the robbery."

AD OGNI COSTO (U.S. title: *Grand Slam*) (Paramount, 1968) 120 M. Color.

Producer, Harry Colombo and George Papi; director, Giuliano Montaldo; screenplay, Mino Roli, Caminito, Marcello Fondato, Antonio De La Loma and Marcello Coscia; assistant director, Mauro Sacripanti, Carlos Luiz Corito and Federico Canudas; music, Ennio Morricone; art director, Alberto Boccianti; camera; Antonio Macasoli; editor, Nino Baragli.

PROF. JAMES ANDERS .... Edward G. Robinson

MARY ANN .... Janet Leigh
MARK MILFORD .... Adolph Celi
ERICH WEISS .... Klaus Kinski
GREGG .... George Rigaud
JEAN-PAUL AUDRY .... Robert Hoffman
AGOSTINO ROSSI .... Riccardo Cucciolla
STETUAKA .... Jussara
MANAGER .... Miguel Del Castillo

Synopsis

Professor James Anders, retiring after 30 years as a teacher in Rio De Janeiro, flies to New York, where he visits an old pal, Mark Milford, who operates a nightclub as a front for his criminal activities. The old teacher, seeking backing for a big heist, has come with a business proposition.

Anders tells Milford that he has often watched the bi-annual delivery of jewels to the Brazilian Diamond Co. from his classroom window and that he has a plan to steal $10 million in diamonds and emeralds after the next delivery. He has detailed plans, and needs just four good men to pull the job.

From Milford's extensive files, the quartet is selected: Erich Weiss, team leader; Gregg, a safe-

With Janet Leigh in Grand Slam.

cracker; Agostino Rossi, an electronics expert; and Jean-Paul Audry whose job it is to seduce Mary Ann, the American secretary to the company's manager, who holds a special magnetic key to the strong-room.

The day before the Carnival, the jewel delivery is made, but the gang discovers that a new security alarm system, Grand Slam 70, has been installed in the strong-room.

The thieves formulate a new master plan and execute the robbery. However, Mary Ann discovers that something is wrong and alerts the police. Before long, inter-gang rivalry and the police have seen to the demise of the quartet, with Milford recovering an empty jewel case for his efforts.

Back in Rome, Mary Ann meets Anders, and is about to turn over to him the real jewel case, all according to his plan, when a purse-snatcher zooms by on a motorcycle and grabs it from her, leaving the duo aghast, and emptyhanded.

Reviews

Howard Thompson, *The New York Times,* February 21, 1968

"Edward G. Robinson, as a retired teacher who engineers the caper, smoothly ambles in early and returns for the fade-out."

Ann Guarino, *Daily News,* February 21, 1968

"Edward G. Robinson, who just finished engineering a major heist in *The Biggest Bundle of Them All,* returns as a real mastermind in *Grand Slam.* . . . Portraying a mild school teacher, [he] retires after thirty years in Rio de Janeiro and plots to rob a diamond company across the way from his former classroom."

UNO SCACCO TUTTO MATTO (U.S. title: *Mad Checkmate*) * (Kinesis Films/Miniter/Tecisa, 1968) 89 M. Color.

Producer, Franco Porro; director, Robert Fiz; screenplay, Fiz, Massimilliano Capriccoli, Ennio De Concini, Jose G. Maesso, Leonardo Martin, Juan Cesarabea; music, Manuel Asins Arbo; set decorator, Rafael Ferri; camera, Antonio Macasoli; editor, Mario Morra.

MacDOWELL . . . . Edward G. Robinson
JEROME . . . . Terry-Thomas
MONIQUE . . . . Maria Grazia Buccella
and: Adolfo Celi, Manuel Zarzo, Jorge Rigaud, Jose Bodalo, Loris Bazzocchi, Rossella Como.

* Never shown theatrically in the United States, but sold to television under the title, *It's Your Move,* in an American-International Television package.

Synopsis

Returning from his bank one day, MacDowell, a retired Englishman living in Palma di Marjorca, is introduced to his butler's niece, Monique, and is astonished by her resemblance to the secretary of the bank's director. From this chance meeting, a grand scheme begins forming in MacDowell's brain.

Six months later, three men arrive from abroad, each resembling an employee of the bank. Through various subterfuges, each of the three and the girl swap places with their look-alike counterparts, and

With Maria Grazia Buccella in Mad Checkmate.

With Jorge Rigaud in Mad Checkmate.

the fairly complex robbery is completed.

Attempting to make their getaways, though, the quartet runs into a series of comical situations. One of the crooks confronts his "wife" or the wife of the man whose role he has assumed, and is dragged off with her to a supermarket. He becomes lost and decides to keep the booty. His crooked cohorts press a frantic search for him up and down the aisles. Outside, he meets some members of a political party who, mistaking him for the man they know, insist that he join them for a drink in a local bar. The misadventures go on, with the briefcase stuffed with the stolen money changing hands innumerable times.

A while later, MacDowell receives a visit from Police Inspector Vogel, who has come with an accusation that there are three men and a girl being held prisoners in the cellar of the MacDowell's villa.

The "prisoners" are secretly returned to the bank before the police have a chance to investigate the cellar, and the next day, the inspector is forced to pacify the four who claimed they had been kidnapped, although the bank's director swears they had been at their respective jobs as usual at the time of the robbery. MacDowell is present at the questioning, standing by impassively, until the safe is opened. Everything is in order. Apparently there was no robbery. The money is there.

Then a noise is heard and a door opens. Out troop four men in white overalls, each quite dirty, each quite recognizable, though, to MacDowell. They complain that they have been locked inside while repairing the central-heating unit. A surprised MacDowell receives profuse apologies from the bank officials and the police, and his butler drives him home to get over his puzzlement and begin planning another grand scheme.

OPERATION ST. PETER'S (Paramount, 1968) 88 M. Color.

Producer, Turi Vasile; director, Lucio Fulci; screenplay; Ennio De Concini, Adriano Baracco, Roberto Gianviti and Fulci; assistant director, Francesco Massaro; art director, Giorgio Giovannini; camera, Erico Menczer.

NAPOLEON	Lando Buzzanca
JOE	Edward G. Robinson
CARDINAL BRAUN	Heinz Ruhmann
CAJELLA	Jean-Claude Brialy
THE BARON	Pinuccio Ardia
THE CAPTAIN	Dante Maggio
AGONIA	Ugo Fancareggi
MARISA	Marie-Christine Barclay
SAMANTHA	Uta Levka
CESIRA	Antonella Delle Por.

Synopsis

Four small-time thieves—Napoleon, the Captain, the Baron, and Agonia—visiting St. Peter's in Rome during Holy Week, when all the statues are covered by heavy cloths, pull a daring heist. They make off with Michelangelo's Pieta. However, although the statue is worth $30 billion, they have no way to unload it.

At this point, they meet Joe Ventura, an American gangster who has come to Italy with his henchmen and his playmate Samantha on "business." He buys the Pieta from Napoleon for $40 and a large bowl of spaghetti.

The Church, afraid of publicizing the fact that the Pieta has been stolen, sends its own detective force on the trail of the missing art masterpiece. The investigation leads them to Joe Ventura, who has taken the Pieta to a coastal town where he plans to put it aboard ship outside the territorial waters, and later sell it back to the Vatican.

The Vatican calls upon the priests of the area,

With Danto Maggio (the captain), Heinz Ruhman (the cardinal) and Lando Buzzanca .(by railing) in **Operation St. Peters.**

With Marie Christine Barclay in Operation St. Peters.

who all converge on the coastal town in a series of crashes and automobile acrobatics. Napoleon, his gang, and his fiancee Marisa have been enlisted in the statue-hunt.

The high-speed chase ends on the docks as the ship carrying the Pieta draws away. But Cardinal Braun, who in his youth won the Indianapolis Speedway race, accelerates his car, which lunges

In Never a Dull Moment.

across the water and hits the ship's deck. Meanwhile, the band of priests are approaching the ship via anything that floats. They clamber aboard, disarm the crew, and push the gangsters overboard.

NEVER A DULL MOMENT (Buena Vista, 1968) 100 M. Color.

Producer, Ron Miller; director, Jerry Paris; based on the novel by John Godey; screenplay, A. J. Carothers; art director, Carroll Clark, John B. Mansbridge; set director, Emile Kuri, Frank R. McKelvy; special effects, Eustace Lycett; assistant director, John Chulay; music, Robert F. Brunner; camera, William Snyder; editor, Marsh Hendry.

JACK ALBANY	Dick Van Dyke
LEO JOSEPH SMOOTH	Edward G. Robinson
SALLY INWOOD	Dorothy Provine
FRANK BOLEY	Henry Silva
MELANIE SMOOTH	Joanna Moore
FLORIAN	Tony Bill
COWBOY SCHAEFFER	Slim Pickens
ACE WILLIAMS	Jack Elam
RINZY TOBRESKI	Ned Glass
BOBBY MACOON	Richard Bakalyan
FRANCIS	Mickey Shaughnessy
FINGERS FELTON	Philip Coolidge
MUSEUM DIRECTOR	James Millhollin
PROP MAN	Johnny Silver
TONY PRESTON	Anthony Caruso
LENNY	Paul Condylis
2nd T.V. ACTOR (Police Capt. Jacoby)	Bob Homel
1st T.V. ACTOR	Dick Winslow
SEXY GIRL	Jackie Russell
SAM	Rex Dominick
POLICE LIEUTENANT	Ken Lynch
MATRON	Eleanor Audley
1st MUSEUM GUARD	John Cliff
POLICE CHIEF GRAYSON	Tyler McVey
POLICE PHOTOGRAPHER	Jerry Paris
2nd MUSEUM GUARD	John Dennis

Synopsis

Jack Albany, a struggling actor, is mistaken by young hood Florian for Ace Williams, the hired killer he was supposed to pick for his boss, one Leo Joseph Smooth. Albany, fearing death if his identity is discovered, goes along with the hood to Smooth's mansion.

At the hideout with Smooth are his pretty art instructor, Sally Inwood, and his gang, Frank Boley, Cowboy, Rinzy, Bobzby Maccoon, Fingers Felton and Francis, the butler. Assembling the group, Smooth outlines his plan to steal a priceless painting from the New York Museum. He wants to hold the painting until his death, after which it will be returned, provided the trustees agree to rename the museum after him—his claim, he figures, to immortality.

With Dorothy Provine in Never

With Dick Van Dyke, Tony Bill and in Never a Dull Moment.

With Dick Van Dyke and Tony Bill in Never a Dull
Moment.

Sally is suspected of knowing too much, so Leo insists she spend the night as his guest. Jack tries to find Sally to explain, in vain, that he is not a professional hood, just an actor.

When the real hired killer shows up, Leo suggests a bare hands contest in the library to determine the real Ace Williams. With the help of Sally, Jack emerges victorious, and Sally now knows he is not a hood.

Sally, who has been left in the care of Francis, the butler, while the gang goes to the Museum to steal the picture, eventually alerts the police and they catch the crooks at the Museum in the midst of a heist. The cops soon round up Smooth and the rest of the gang.

Reviews

Howard Thompson, *The New York Times,* August 15, 1968

"Apparently determined to live up to the title, the Disney organization has settled for volume and slapstick in *Never a Dull Moment,* a brash and extremely broad romp . . . [about] the robbery of an art museum. The idea of the theft itself has possibilities, with the gang masterminded by an old hand, Edward G. Robinson, as an art authority. . . . [He] plays it cool and casual, wisely, and his hoodlums rough it up with Keystone Kops subtlety."

Ann Guarino, *Daily News,* August 15, 1968

"Edward G. Robinson once again gives an effortless interpretation of a top criminal . . . [with] lines like: 'Keep your hands to yourself or I'll take them away from you!' "

MACKENNA'S GOLD (Columbia, 1969) 136 M. Color.

Producer, Carl Foreman and Dimitri Tiomkin; director, J. Lee Thompson; based on the novel by Will Henry; screenplay, Foreman; art director, Geoffrey Drake and Cary Odell; set director, Alfred E. Spencer; assistant director, David Salven; music, Quincy Jones; special effects, Geoffrey Drake, John Mackey, Bob Cuff, Willis Cook and Larry Butler; camera; Joseph MacDonald; second unit camera, Harold Wellman; second unit director, Tom Shaw; stunt coordinator, Buzz Henry; editor, Bill Lenny.

MACKENNA	Gregory Peck
COLORADO	Omar Shariff
SERGEANT TIBBS	Telly Savalas
INGA	Camilla Sparv
SANCHEZ	Keenan Wynn
HESH-KE	Julie Newmar
HACHITA	Ted Cassidy
THE EDITOR	Lee J. Cobb
THE PREACHER	Raymond Massey
THE STOREKEEPER	Burgess Meredith
OLDER ENGLISHMAN	Anthony Quayle
OLD ADAMS	Edward G. Robinson
BEN BAKER	Eli Wallach
PRAIRIE DOG	Eduardo Ciannelli
AVILA	Dick Peabody
BESH	Rudy Diaz
MONKEY	Robert Phillips
PIMA SQUAW	Shelley Morrison
YOUNG ENGLISHMAN	J. Robert Porter
ADAMS'S BOY	John Garfield Jr.
LAGUNA	Pepe Callahan
OLD APACHE WOMAN	Madeleine Taylor Holmes
LIEUTENANT	Duke Hobbie
NARRATOR	Victor Jory

Synopsis

1872. Mackenna, sheriff of Hadleyburg, is bushwacked in the desert by an old Apache chief, Prairie Dog, whom he mortally wounds. The dying Indian, however, entrusts him with a map of the legendary Valley of Gold. Only one white man, the prospector Adams, whose eyes were put out by the Apaches, has ever seen the gold.

Skeptical about the gold's existence, Mackenna has already burned the map when he is captured by Colorado, a ruthless bandit. Since Colorado has Inga, daughter of the town judge, as hostage, Mackenna agrees to lead the bandit gang to the canyon. They are joined by the "men from Hadleyburg," the local newspaper editor, a preacher, a storekeeper, two Englishmen, and old Adams himself, all driven by greed and a desire to share in the fortune. In brushes with the pursuing cavalry and hostile Apaches, nearly everyone is killed.

Mackenna, Colorado and Inga press on with two Apaches, Hesk-ke and Hachita, and are joined by Sergeant Tibbs who calmly eliminates each member of his own cavalry patrol along the trail.

Arriving in the valley, they find that the gold is a reality, but the squaw Hesk-ke, who loves Mackenna, is killed in trying to dispose of her "rival" Inga. Hachita, meanwhile, kills Tibbs and in turn is shot by Colorado. Colorado and Mackenna then fight, but are interrupted by the Apaches, whose horses cause a landslide which obliterates the canyon.

Colorado, Mackenna and Inga escape, empty-handed, they think. Ironically, Mackenna is riding

With John Garfield Jr. in Mackenna's Gold.

In Mackenna's Gold.

Tibbs's horse, oblivious of the fact that the animal's saddle bags are filled with gold. They separate, with Mackenna swearing to hunt Colorado down.

Reviews

Vincent Canby, *The New York Times*, June 19, 1969

"A western of truly stunning absurdity, [it] is the work of J. Lee Thompson, a thriving example of that old Hollywood maxim about how to succeed by failing big. . . . Although it is set in the Old West, it actually has the shape of French farce: various groups of characters pursuing each other in and out of ambushes in the kind of circular action so dear to Feydeau . . . [including] such people as Lee J. Cobb, Eduardo Cianelli, Raymond Massey, Burgess Meredith, Anthony Quayle, Edward G. Robinson and Eli Wallach, each of whom does a sort of stagger-on and then dies."

SONG OF NORWAY (Cinerama, 1970) 142 M. Color.

Producer, Andrew L. and Virginia Stone; director, Andrew L. Stone; suggested by the stage play—book by Milton Lazarus, music and lyrics (based on the works of Edvard Grieg) by Robert Wright and George Forrest, from a play by Homer Curran; screenplay, Stone; choreographer, Lee Theodore; assistant director, John O'Connor; second-unit director, Yakima Canutt; musical supervisor, orchestrator, conductor, Roland Shaw; live animation sequence director, Kinney-Wolf; camera, Davis Boulton; editor, Virginia Stone.

EDVARD GRIEG . . . . Toralv Maurstad

With Florence Henderson in Song of Norway.

In Song of Norway.

NINA GRIEG	Florence Henderson	CAPTAIN HANSEN	Carl Rigg
THERESE BERG	Christina Schollin	MRS. THORESEN	Aline Towne
RIKARD NORDRAAK	Frank Poretta	IRATE WOMAN	Nan Munro
BJÖRNSTERNE BJÖRNSON	Harry Secombe	BERG'S BUTLER	James Hayter
BERG	Robert Morley	HELSTED	Erik Chitty
KROGSTAD	Edward G. Robinson	VIOLINIST	Manoug Parikian
MRS. BJÖRNSON	Elizabeth Larner	COUNCILMAN 1	Richard Vernon
ENGSTRAND	Oscar Homolka	COUNCILMAN 2	Ernest Clark
HENRIK IBSEN	Frederick Jaeger	BJÖRNSON'S SECRETARY	Eli Lindtner
FRANZ LISZT	Henry Gilbert		
HANS CHRISTIAN ANDERSEN	Richard Wordsworth		
GEORGE NORDRAAK	Bernard Archard		
AUNT ALINE	Susan Richards		
HAGERUP	John Barrie		
MRS. HAGERUP	Wenke Foss		
GADE	Ronald Adam		

Synopsis

Edvard Grieg, a young Norwegian composer who has recently graduated from Leipzig Conservatory, is seeking a grant to continue his studies in Rome, and his classmate, Therese Berg, tries to talk her father, a wealthy music patron, into helping Grieg. The girl makes a secret bargain with her father, who has been hoping to arrange a marriage of convenience with another wealthy family. If he will stage a recital for Grieg with Stockholm's most influential critics in attendance, she will never again see the young pianist. The concert is a success, but Grieg is disturbed by Therese's disappearance.

Sometime later, Grieg travels to Copenhagen where he meets Rikard Nordraak, a fellow Norwegian composer, who becomes a close personal friend and influence on his music. Through him, Grieg meets Hans Christian Andersen, who is delighted when Nina Hagerup, Grieg's cousin, sings some songs the composer has written to the famed author's poems. Grieg and Nina soon begin considering themselves more than cousins and decide to marry over her parents' objections. On their wedding day, Grieg receives a note from Therese saying that her own engagement is off and asking to see him again.

Grieg has married Nina, hoping that Nordraak and his cousin, Björnsterne Björnson, the noted playwright, would be able to get Grieg a conducting post at the National Theater at Christiania, but internal politics prevent it. Grieg is then obliged to give piano lessons to support his wife, and even pleas to get local music society help in organizing concerts fall on deaf ears. Therese, who has been following Grieg's lackluster career in the papers, secretly rents the local concert hall and has Björnson tell Grieg that the Town Council has lowered the rent. He does so, remaining uneasy about the situation, and invites the Griegs to spend Christmas with his family. In the conviviality of the celebration, Grieg and Björnson decide to collaborate on a purely Norwegian opera based on the legendary Trolls.

Grieg's long-hoped-for concert is less than well-received, and Therese, who has turned up unexpectedly, tells the Griegs and Björnson that a musician must earn a reputation in Rome or Berlin before the Norwegian people will recognize him.

Nina is shattered by Therese's appearance, especially when the wealthy patroness sends Grieg a magnificent grand piano. Nina had already arranged with Mr. Krogstad, the local piano dealer, to buy a small upright and had sold her only possession, an old family cottage, to pay for it.

A letter arrives from Franz Liszt praising Grieg's music, and Grieg uses it to obtain a grant to go to Rome. The stipend is small, allowing Grieg to go alone, and he sends Nina to live with her mother. Grieg stops first in Berlin, where he finds Nordraak very ill, and promises to return as soon as he sees Liszt. In Italy, Grieg also meets Henrik Ibsen, who asks the composer to score the play,

With Florence Henderson in Song of Norway.

"Peer Gynt," which he [Ibsen] is writing. Despite his friendship to Björnson, Ibsen's greatest rival, Grieg opportunistically accepts.

Therese follows Grieg to Rome and aids him socially, and the composer extends his Rome visit. His initial concerts there are great successes, attended by everyone of importance, including Liszt himself. Among the interested patrons is Krogstad, the piano dealer, who is in Rome on business. He meets Grieg and tells him that Nina never, in fact, went home but stayed on in their bleak house in Christiania, living on the proceeds of the cottage she had originally sold to buy her husband's piano. Grieg also learns that Nordraak has died in Berlin, and, realizing his own selfishness, placing his career above family and friends, he decides to return to Nina and to his artistic mission of composing Norway's national music.

Reviews

Vincent Canby, *The New York Times,* 11/5/70

"*Song of Norway* is no ordinary movie kitsch, but a display to turn Guy Lombardo livid with envy. . . . The cast includes Toralv Maurstad, Frank Poretta and Florence Henderson. Robert Morley,

With Florence Henderson in **Song of Norway.**

Edward G. Robinson and Oscar Homolka appear in nonsinging roles. That they all appear to be a little more foolish than they need be is not only because of the scenario, but also because of [Andrew] Stone's pursuit of realism, in this case, of scenery, which is so overwhelming that the people are reduced to being scenic obstructions."

Rick., *Variety,* 11/4/70

". . . a magnificent motion picture. Unfortunately,

[Andrew] Stone's screenplay imparts a frequently banal, two-dimensional note. . . . Toralv Maurstad as Grieg, Florence Henderson as the cousin he marries, and Frank Poretta as composer Rikard Nordraak, Grieg's closest friend, are primarily required to sing—not bring deep psychological sensitivity to their roles. . . . Edward G. Robinson is kindly and concerned as the kindly concerned old piano dealer."

SHORT FILMS

THE SLIPPERY PEARLS (1932)
A 2-reeler for The Masquers Club

Wallace Beery	Winnie Lightner
Buster Keaton	Wynne Gibson
Edward G. Robinson	Claudia Dell
George E. Stone	Edmund Lowe
Eddie Kane	Victor McLaglen
Laurel and Hardy	El Brendel
Polly Moran	Wheeler and Woolsey
Norma Shearer	Gary Cooper
Hedda Hopper	Charles 'Buddy' Rogers
Joan Crawford	Eugene Pallette
Robert Ames	William Haines
Irene Dunne	Richard Dix
Bebe Daniels	Richard Barthelmess
Ben Lyon	Charles Butterworth
Loretta Young	Louise Fazenda
Douglas Fairbanks Jr.	Lowell Sherman
Maurice Chevalier	Fay Wray
Frank Fay	Jack Oakie
Barbara Stanwyck	Joe E. Brown
Fifi D'Orsay	George 'Gabby' Hayes
Warner Baxter	Mitzi Green

and Members of the Keystone Kops and
Members of Our Gang

VERDENSBEROMTHEDER I KOBENHAVEN (1939)
Produced by Dansk Films in Denmark
with Robert Taylor, Myrna Loy, Edward G. Robinson, Charles Lindbergh, Duke Ellington, Alice Babs Nilsson, Edvard Persson

SCREEN SNAPSHOTS (1942) (Series 22, No. 4)
Produced by Columbia Pictures

Ten minute performance of Russian music with Edward G. Robinson providing humorous introductions.

MOSCOW STRIKES BACK (1942)
Feature-length documentary of the Russian winter counter-offensive of 1941. Narrated by Edward G. Robinson, with English commentary by Albert Maltz and music by Dmitri Tiomkin. Produced by Central Studios, Moscow. Edited by Slavko Vorkapich. Released by Artkino.

THE RED CROSS AT WAR (1943)
Narration spoken by Edward G. Robinson

PROJECTION OF AMERICA (1943)
For the Overseas division of the Office of War Information, Edward G. Robinson talked about this country, about cowboys, about Chicago, etc.

SCREEN SNAPSHOTS (1944) (Series 23, No. 9)
Produced by Columbia Pictures
A one-reel record of cinema history, celebrating the Golden Jubilee of the film industry. Edward G. Robinson appeared along with Fred Astaire, John Barrymore, Carole Lombard, Irene Dunne, Rosalind Russell, Cary Grant, Mary Pickford, Rita Hayworth, Lillian Gish, Lionel Barrymore, Hedy Lamarr, Wallace Beery, Humphrey Bogart, others.

WHERE DO YOU GET OFF? (1948)
One-reel short for United Jewish Appeal with Edward G. Robinson narrating.

SCREEN SNAPSHOTS (1950)
Produced by Columbia Pictures

With David Ben-Gurion during the filming of "Israel."

Edward G. Robinson, Dan Duryea, Dana Andrews and Wanda Hendrix, among others, appear in "Ice Capades Premiere."

THE HEART OF SHOW BUSINESS (1957)
Produced by Columbia Pictures
    40-minute documentary on the history of Variety

Clubs International. Edward G. Robinson was one of the narrators, along with Bing Crosby, Bob Hope, James Stewart, Burt Lancaster and Cecil B. DeMille. Stars who also participated included Harry Belafonte, Victor Borge, Maurice Chevalier, Lena Horne, Art Linkletter, Sophie Tucker, Jimmy Durante, and Edgar Bergen and Charlie McCarthy.

ISRAEL (1959)
Produced and written for Warner Brothers by Leon Uris and directed by Sam Zebba
Edward G. Robinson narrated 29-minute pictorial tour of Israel, combining picturesque sites of Biblical times and the scope of the country's dramatic modern day achievements. Score arranged and conducted by Elmer Bernstein. Filmed in WarnerScope and Technicolor.

OTHER FILMS USING CLIPS OF PREVIOUS EDWARD G. ROBINSON PERFORMANCES

"OKAY FOR SOUND" (1946)
Twenty minute Vitaphone short produced by Gordon Hollingshead to commemorate the anniversary of the pioneer Warner talking motion pictures.
Among clips from past films produced by the company were one from *Little Caesar* and one from *Dr. Ehrlich's Magic Bullet*.

"WHEN THE TALKIES WERE YOUNG" (1956)
Seventeen minute Vitaphone short produced by Robert Youngson.
A clip from *Five-Star Final* was incorporated into it.

"MYRA BRECKENRIDGE" (1970)
Feature-length 20th Century-Fox film produced by Robert Fryer.
Scenes from earlier 20th Century-Fox pictures were utilized, among them, a portion of the Edward G. Robinson episode in *Tales of Manhattan*.

CARTOONS UTILIZING THE ANIMATED CHARACTER LIKENESS OF EDWARD G. ROBINSON

"COOCOONUT GROVE" (1936) Merrie Melodies cartoon directed by I. Freleng
"HOLLWOOD CANINE CANTEEN" (1945) Merrie Melodies cartoon directed by Robert McKimson
"RACKET RABBIT" (1947) Looney Tunes cartoon directed by I. Freleng

HIS DRAMATIC WORK ON RADIO

November 7, 1933—*California Melodies* (CBS)

February 1, 1935—*Hollywood Hotel* (CBS)

January 13, 1936—*Lux Radio Theater* (CBS): "The Boss"

January 30, 1936—*The Standard Brands Hour* (NBC): "The Inner Voice" with Ruth Easton and Len Hollister

May 8, 1936—*Hollywood Hotel* (CBS): "Bullets or Ballots"

January 18, 1937—*Lux Radio Theater* (CBS): "Criminal Code" with Beverly Roberts

March 10, 1937—*Hollywood Showcase* (CBS)

April 29, 1937—*Kate Smith A&P Bandwagon* (CBS): "Thunder in the City"

August 2, 1937—*CBS Shakespeare Theater* (CBS): "Taming of the Shrew" with Frieda Inescourt

October 19, 1937 to July 2, 1942—Starred as Steve Wilson on "Big Town" (CBS)

December 19, 1938—*Lux Radio Theater* (CBS): "Kid Galahad" with Wayne Morris, Andrea Leeds, Joan Bennett

April 17, 1939—*Lux Radio Theater* (CBS): "Bullets or Ballots" with Mary Astor, Humphrey Bogart, Otto Kruger

February 25, 1940—*Gulf Screen Guild Theater* (CBS): "Blind Alley" with Joseph Calleia, Isabel Jewell, Leatrice Joy

November 2, 1941—*Gulf Screen Guild Theater* (CBS): "The Amazing Dr. Clitterhouse" with Humphrey Bogart, Marsha Hunt

March 16, 1942—*Lux Radio Theater* (CBS): "Manpower" with Marlene Dietrich and George Raft

January 4, 1943—*Lockheed's Ceiling Unlimited* (CBS): (substitute narrator for host Orson Welles)

February 8, 1943—*Lux Radio Theater* (CBS): "The Maltese Falcon" with Laird Cregar and Gail Patrick

March 15, 1943—*DuPont Cavalcade of America* (NBC): "A Case for the FBI"

April 18, 1943—*Radio Reader's Digest* (ABC)

April 26, 1943—*Lockheed's Ceiling Unlimited* (CBS): As Steve Wilson in "World of Tomorrow"

June 30, 1943—As narrator and master of ceremonies on program of Motion Picture Committee for Hollywood War Savings Staff (NBC)

July 4, 1943—*U.S. Rubber Hour* (CBS): "Our American Scriptures" (doing readings from the Constitution and from Jefferson's letters)

April 3, 1944—*Lux Radio Theater* (CBS): "Destroyer" with Marguerite Chapman, Dennis O'Keefe

June 5, 1944—*Lady Esther's Screen Guild Theater* (NBC): "The Amazing Dr. Clitterhouse" with Claire Trevor, Lloyd Nolan

October 2, 1944—*DuPont Cavalcade of America* (NBC): "Voice On The Stairs" narrated by Walter Huston

March 1, 1945—*Suspense* (CBS): "My Wife Geraldine"

April 8, 1945—*P. Lorillard Comedy Theater* (NBC): "A Slight Case of Murder"

April 16, 1945—*Lux Radio Theater* (CBS): (guest producer)

April 30, 1945—*DuPont Cavalcade of America* (NBC): "The Philippines Never Surrender"

June 25, 1945—*Lux Radio Theater* (CBS): "The Woman in the Window" with Joan Bennett, Dan Duryea

October 13, 1945—*Lady Esther Screen Guild Players* (CBS): "Flesh and Fantasy" with Dame May Whitty, Vincent Price

March 11, 1946—*DuPont Cavalcade of America* (NBC): "The Man With Hope in His Hands"

March 26, 1946—*Colgate Theater of Romance* (CBS): "The Woman in the Window"

October 17, 1946—*Suspense* (CBS): "The Man Who Thought He Was Edward G. Robinson"

November 18, 1946—*Lady Esther Screen Guild Players* (CBS): "Blind Alley" with Broderick Crawford, Isabel Jewell, Frank Albertson

December 7, 1946—*Proctor and Gamble's This Is Hollywood* (CBS): "The Stranger" with Ruth Hussey

November 25, 1947—*Gulf's We the People* (CBS)

March 14, 1948—*The Eternal Light* (NBC): "The Island in the Wilderness" (narrator)

April 12, 1948—*Camel's Screen Guild Players* (CBS): "The Great Man Votes" with Edmund Gwenn, Frank McHugh

November 11, 1948—*Camel's Screen Guild Players* (NBC): "All My Sons" with Burt Lancaster

January 28, 1949—*Ford Theater* (CBS): "The Woman in the Window" with Linda Darnell, Stephen McNally

February 27, 1949—*NBC Theater* (NBC): "Night Has a Thousand Eyes" with William Demarest

November 28, 1939—*Lux Radio Theater* (CBS): "Key Largo" with Claire Trevor, Edmond O'Brien

December 2, 1949—*Screen Director's Playhouse* (NBC): "All My Sons" with Jeff Chandler

February 3, 1950—*Screen Director's Playhouse* (NBC): "The Sea Wolf" with Paul Frees and Lurene Tuttle

January 25, 1951—*Screen Director's Playhouse* (ABC): "House of Strangers" with Victor Mature, June Havoc

December 7, 1952—*Eternal Light* (NBC): As Chaim Weizmann in "Trial and Error"

October 21, 1953—State Of Israel Bond Program (NBC): "Jerusalem Is Her Name" with Paul Muni (taped broadcast of special Madison Square Garden Show)

December 7, 1953—*Lux Radio Theater* (CBS): "Man on a Tightrope" with Terry Moore

December 20, 1953—*The Eternal Light* (NBC): "Face to Face with Gabriel"

January 24, 1954—*NBC Star Playhouse* (NBC): "A Slight Case of Murder" with Elspeth Eric, Pat Hosley, William Redfield, Wendell Holmes, Larry Haines

As Steve Wilson on CBS radio's Big Town *series.*

With Kate Smith at the Palace Theater, New York.

With Claire Trevor and Gale Gordon on Big Town.

With Claire Trevor in "The Million Dollar Dog Stealing Racket" on the Big Town series.

With Ona Munson on Big Town.

With Ona Munson and ZaSu Pitts on Big Town.

With wife Gladys Robinson and producer William Spier at rehearsal for Suspense.

With Ida Lupino and Robert Young in "Only Yes-terday" on Lux Radio Theatre.

DRAMATIC TELEVISION APPEARANCES

1954 FOR THE DEFENSE 30 M. "The Case of Kenny Jason" (pilot for proposed weekly series)
Director: James Neilson
Producer: Samuel Bischoff
Teleplay: Donn Mullally
cast:
   EDWARD G. ROBINSON (Matthew Considine)
   GLENN VERNON (Kenny Jason)
   ANN DORAN (Mrs. Jason)
   JOHN HOYT (Captain Thomas Hardy)
   ROBERT OSTERLOH (Duke)
   VIC PERRIN (Barney)
   HERBERT HAYES (Judge)
   MORRIS ANKRUM (District Attorney)
   TOM DUGAN (Desk Sergeant)

12/9/54 CLIMAX (CBS): "Epitaph For a Spy" 60 M.
Director: Alan Reisner
Producer: Bretaigne Windust
Teleplay: Donald S. Sanford
Novel: Eric Amber
cast:
   EDWARD G. ROBINSON (Josef Vadassy)
   MELVILLE COOPER
   ROBERT F. SIMON
   IVAN TRESSAULT
   NICHOLAS JOY

1/13/55 FORD THEATER (NBC): ". . . And Son" 30 M.
Story: I. A. R. Wylie

Adapted for television by Peter Packer and Robert Bassing
cast:
   EDWARD G. ROBINSON (John Derwent)
   JOHN BAER (Larry Derwent)
   ERIN O'BRIEN-MOORE (Elsa Derwent)
   WILLIS BOUCHEY (Charlie Crichton
   J. P. O'DONNELL (Receptionist)

12/29/55 FORD THEATER (NBC): "A Set of Values" 30 M.
cast:
   EDWARD G. ROBINSON (Baron Carter)
   ANN DORAN (Sue Carter)
   TOMMY COOK (Jerry Carter)
   PAUL FIX (Franklin)
   JOSEPH DOWNING (Arnie)

9/30/56– THE $64,000 CHALLENGE (CBS)
10/28/56 30 M.
EDWARD G. ROBINSON and VINCENT PRICE vie in the category of art. (Price had previously triumphed over famed jockey Billy Pearson in the same category.)

10/23/58 PLAYHOUSE 90 (CBS): "Shadows Tremble" 90 M.
Director: Herbert Hirshman
Producer: Fred Coe
Teleplay: Ernest Kinoy
cast:
   EDWARD G. ROBINSON (Oscar Bromek)

RAY WALSTON (Patridge)
BEATRICE STRAIGHT
FRANK CONROY
PARKER FENNELLY
ROBERT WEBBER

3/2/59 GOODYEAR THEATER (NBC): "A Good Name" 30 M.
Director: Eliot Silverstein
Producer: Winston O'Keefe
Teleplay: Richard Alan Simmons
cast:
EDWARD G. ROBINSON (Harry Harper)
LEE PHILIPS (Vincent Harper)
PARLEY BAER (Walter Brodsky)
JACQUELINE SCOTT (Ann Harper)
CARLETON G. YOUNG (Gene Morley)
GLENN TAYLOR (Mike Hudson)
OLAN SOULE (Thin Member)

4/2/59 ZANE GREY THEATER (CBS): "Loyalty" 30 M.
cast:
EDWARD G. ROBINSON (Victor Bers)
EDWARD G. ROBINSON JR. (Hunt Bers)
JOHN HACKETT (Lieutenant)
DAN BARTON
GEORGE WALLACE
ROBERT BLAKE

10/24/60 THE RIGHT MAN (CBS) 60 M.
Historical revue of U.S. presidential campaigns
Director: Burt Shevelove
Producer: Fred Freed
Narrator: Garry Moore
EDWARD G. ROBINSON played Theodore Roosevelt

2/17/60 NBC-TV SPECIAL: "The Devil and Daniel Webster" (repeated CBS-TV 4/30/62) 60 M.
Director: Tom Donovan
Teleplay: Phil Reisman Jr.
Story: Stephen Vincent Benet
cast:
EDWARD G. ROBINSON (Daniel Webster)
DAVID WAYNE (Devil)
TIM O'CONNOR (Jabel Stone)

BETTY LOU HOLLAND (Dorcas Stone)
ROYAL BEAL (Justice Hawthorn)
STUART GERMAIN (Stevens)
HOWARD FREEMAN (Pinkham)
and EDGAR BERGEN, host

1/29/61 GENERAL ELECTRIC THEATER (CBS): "The Drop-Out" 30 M.
Director: Richard Irving
Producer: Stanley Rubin
Teleplay: Roger O. Hirson
cast:
EDWARD G. ROBINSON (Bert Alquist)
BILLY GRAY (Jerry Alquist)
CARMEN MATTHEWS (Mrs. Alquist)
RAY MONTGOMERY (Cooper)

10/6/61 THE DETECTIVES (NBC): "The Legend of Jim Riva" 60 M.
Director: Richard Carlson
Producer: Arthur Nadel
Teleplay: John K. Butler and Boyd Correll
Story: Arthur Browne Jr.
cast:
EDWARD G. ROBINSON (Jim Riva)
RUDY SOLARI (Nathan Riva)
BUTCH PATRICK (Bobby)
ROBERT TAYLOR (Captain Matt Holbrook)
TIGE ANDREWS (Lt. Johnny Russo)
MARK GODDARD (Sgt. Chris Ballard)
ADAM WEST (Nelson)

3/18/62 PROJECT TWENTY (NBC): "Cops and Robbers" 60 M.
Director: Don Hyatt
Producer: Don Hyatt
Written by Phil Reisman Jr.
EDWARD G. ROBINSON as the narrator

12/1/63 THE WORLD'S GREATEST SHOWMAN (NBC) 90 M.
Tribute to Cecil B. DeMille
Hosted by EDWARD G. ROBINSON, BETTY HUTTON, CORNEL WILDE and BARBARA STANWYCK

1/9/65 HOLLYWOOD PALACE (ABC) 90 M.

Dramatic reading of patriotic essay, "This Is It"

2/19/65 XEROX SPECIAL (ABC): "Who Has Seen the Wind" 90 M.
Director: George Sidney
Producer: George Sidney
Teleplay: Don Mankiewicz
Story: Tad Mosel
cast:
EDWARD G. ROBINSON (Captain)
STANLEY BAKER (Janos)
MARIA SCHELL (The Mother)
VERONICA CARTWRIGHT (Kiri)
GYPSY ROSE LEE (Proprietress)
LILIA SKALA (Nun)
SIMON OAKLAND (Inspector)
PAUL RICHARDS (Father Ashton)
VICTOR JORY (Peralton)

6/17/67– EYE ON ART (CBS) 30 M.
6/24/67

EDWARD G. ROBINSON as narrator of two of six parts of this series, and tour guide of galleries, museums and art studios in Chicago on first show and Los Angeles on second.

4/17/69 CBS MOVIE WORLD PREMIERE: "U.M.C." 120 M.
Director: Boris Sagal
Producer: A. C. Ward
Teleplay: A. C. Ward
cast:
RICHARD BRADFORD (Dr. Joseph M. Gannon)
EDWARD G. ROBINSON (Dr. Lee Forestman)
JAMES DALEY (Dr. Paul Lochner)
KIM STANLEY (Joanna Hanson)
MAURICE EVANS (Dr. George Barger)
KEVIN McCARTHY (Coswell)
J. D. CANNON (Jarris)
WILLIAM WINDOM (Hanson)
DON QUINE (Martin)
SHELLEY FABARES (Mike)
JAMES SHIGETA (Chief Resident)
WILLIAM MARSHALL (Dr. Tawn)

ALFRED RYDER (Dr. Corlane)
ROBERT EMHARDT (Judge)

10/13/70 THE ABC MOVIE OF THE WEEK: "The Old Man Who Cried Wolf" 90 M.
Director: Walter Grauman
Producer: Walter Grauman
Teleplay: Luther Davis
Story: Arnold Horwitt
Executive Producer: Aaron Spelling
Assistant to the Executive Producer: Edward G. Robinson Jr.
cast:
EDWARD G. ROBINSON (Emile Pulska)
MARTIN BALSAM (Stanley Pulska)
DIANE BAKER (Peggy Pulska)
PERCY RODRIGUES (Frank Jones)
RUTH ROMAN (Lois)
EDWARD ASNER (Dr. Morheim)
MARTIN E. BROOKS (Hudson Ewing)
PAUL PICERNI (Detective Green)
SAM JAFFE (Abe Stillman)
ROBERT YURO (Detective Seroly)
BILL ELLIOTT (Carl)
JAMES A. WATSON (Leon)
NAOMI STEVENS (Mrs. Raspili)
VIRGINIA CHRISTINE (Miss Cummings)
J. C. FLIPPEN (Pawnbroker)

10/23/70 BRACKEN'S WORLD (NBC): "The Mary Tree" 60 M.
Director: Paul Henreid
Producer: Stanley Rubin
Teleplay: Jerry Ziegman
cast:
EDWARD G. ROBINSON (Elstyn Draper)
DIANA HYLAND (Mary Draper)
LESLIE NIELSEN (John Bracken)
PETER HASKELL (Kevin Grant)
ELIZABETH ALLEN (Laura Dean)
EDWARD G. ROBINSON JR. (Bill Lawrence)
CLAUDIA BRYAR (Housekeeper)
TIM HERBERT (Connie Rose)
JEFF DONNELL (Joan Elliot)

10/23/70 THIS IS TOM JONES (ABC) 60 M.
          Dramatic reading of "I Will Not Go
          Back" and Kipling's poem "The Be-
          trothed"

5/4/71   HOLLYWOOD TELEVISION THE-
          ATRE (Public Broadcasting Ser-
          vice) 150 M.
          John Dos Passos's "U.S.A."
          Director: George Schaefer
          EDWARD G. ROBINSON delivered

the prologue and epilogue.

12/15/71 ROD SERLING'S NIGHT GAL-
          LERY (NBC): "The Messiah on
          Mott Street" (One segment of multi-
          part weekly series)
          Director: Don Taylor
          Producer: Jack Laird
          Teleplay: Rod Serling
          EDWARD G. ROBINSON was an im-
          poverished old man who refused to
          die until the coming of the Messiah.

*With Ann Doran and Glenn Vernon in "For the De-
fense."*

*With Beatrice Straight on "Shadows Tremble," an
episode of* Playhouse 90.

With emcee Ralph Storey and Vincent Price in **The $64,000 Challenge.**

On the set of "Heritage," an episode of Zane Grey Theatre.

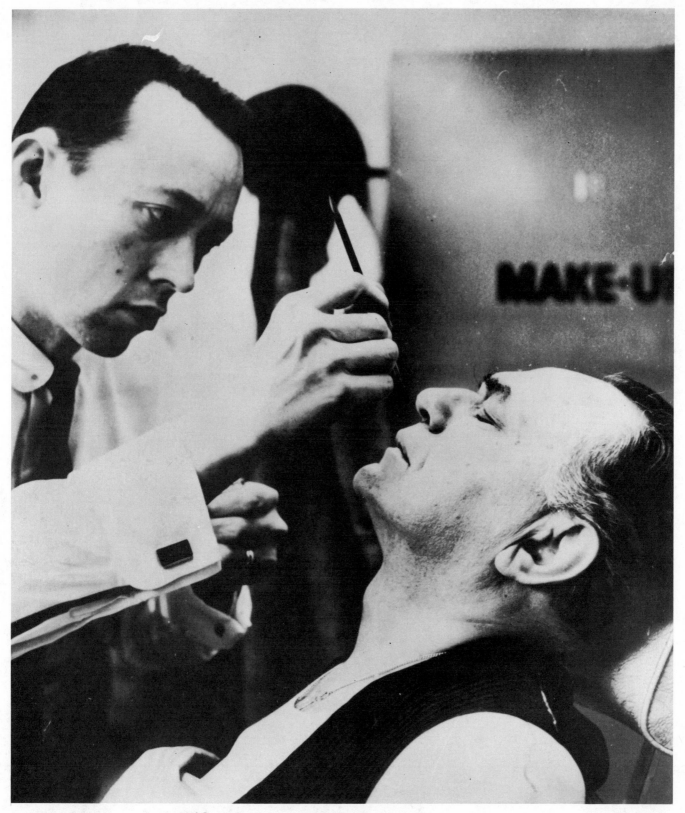

With makeup man Dick Smith, preparing for "The Devil and Daniel Webster."

With Billy Gray in "The Drop-Out," an episode of
General Electric Theatre.

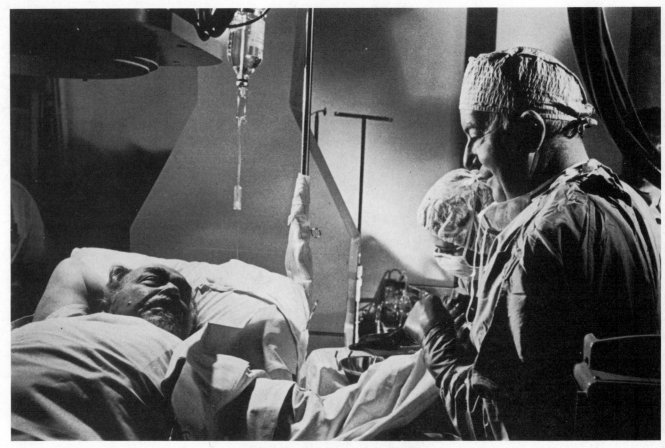

With Maurice Evans in UMC.

In CBS-TV's UMC, *the pilot film for the* Medical Center *series*.

With Sam Jaffe in "The Man Who Cried Wolf," on
ABC's *Movie of the Week.*

In "The Mary Tree," an episode of NBC's Bracken's World.